Praise for **"Unchained"**

"Dominique has a brave approach, exposing some holy cows, that many refuse to address, from the media to the pulpit. She's not afraid to address matters that have become silent issues in our homes and churches. What makes Unchained such a brilliant read, is that Dominique has a hold on the trends of our modern day, she addresses them and exposes the dangers of many of them. Unchained is a truthful, thought provoking, and vulnerable read. Dominique says it clearly, 'There are some mistakes we don't have to make.' Her notion that, 'The unchaining of your heart is so much more than a destination to arrive at, it is a process…' really sets the journey that this book will take you on. I recommend you read this book and allow God to deal with those unspoken issues that you may have been fighting secretly.

– **Dr. Stafford Petersen, Moderator of the Full Gospel Church of God in South Africa**

"Unchained is thought provoking and unapologetic in its intent to provide direction and healing. For the past ten years, as Dominique's senior pastoral couple, my wife and I have had the distinct privilege of having a front row seat to the unfolding developments leading to the writing of this book. Dominique does not shy away from addressing the burning issues around love, dating, intimacy, and relationships according to biblical standards. It is our prayer that God will use Unchained to touch countless lives."

– **Ps JC & Eleanor Francis, Bethel Tabernacle FGC**

"Unchained is an answer to the prayers and cries of this generation: for healthy, functional relationships. Dominique addresses God's heart for relationships and community in a way that I have never experienced before. She touches on real issues pertaining to our humanity that echoes God's grace for His children, and she does not fail to share the truth of God's word and the standard of sanctification He has called us to. I highly recommend this book, no matter where you find yourself in life.

– **Kelly Jacobs, Counsellor (HPCSA: PRC 0031860) and Owner of Therapy with Kelly**

"Broken people do better when they listen to God and allow God to lead them to those who will journey with them from their place of misery. I have concluded that Unchained will play a very important role in helping people deal with brokenness and equipping those tasked by God to lead people to healing and wholeness.

– **Ps Mark Harris, Senior Pastor, Blessed Hope FGC**

"This book is brilliant! It is enjoyable and entertaining yet filled with so much revelation knowledge, I found myself wanting more. The Word of God was used so effectively to shed light and reveal the naked truth about love, lust, sexuality, and relationships. I love that Dominique chose to unashamedly share her story in ink. When you read *Unchained*, you will realize that the stale and phony tactics of the enemy will fail miserably. Your trauma will become your powerful testimony when you pursue a true and authentic relationship with Jesus."

– **Dr. Rechelle Jacobs, Lecturer UWC, CEO & Founder of Master Mind Foundation**

"Unchained is a heartfelt theology that speaks directly to the soul and addresses the deep-rooted issues that can prevent individuals from living a fulfilled and wholesome life. You will experience a profound resonance with this book that will leave you feeling empowered to live your life in complete alignment with God's divine purpose. This book is seriously a game-changer and I cannot recommend it enough!

– **Rev Claudene Sebolai, BTH, BA Hons, MA (UWC), Managing Editor of the Christian Lifestyle Magazine**

"Unchained is not an ordinary book, it is authentic and speaks to the heart of all generations. While reading Unchained, introspection takes place as the book deals with real life situations. Our young people need to know what they are up against. In this book a spade is a spade, and the reader is allowed to see things for what it is. This book is what we need.

– Ps Jennifer Van Der Ross, Chaplain - South African Navy

"What an emotive and relevant read...! Unchained is a raw depiction of the sad and at times refreshing realities the broken find themselves in. I appreciated Dominique's honesty and transparency. I believe Unchained will become a toolkit for the modern day Christian, young and old as it brings you to a point of reflection into some of your past experiences, more so relationships. The truth that the book carries will liberate many generations. It is undoubtedly living up to its name UNCHAINED! May it free many in Jesus Name!"

– Michelle Benjamin, Presiding Magistrate, Child Justice Court, Pastor at Tehilla Ministries Extreme Oasis

UNCHAINED.

DOMINIQUE ADONIS

UNCHAINED.
HOW TO NEVER HAVE ANOTHER DYSFUNCTIONAL RELATIONSHIP

UNCHAINED.
How to never have another dysfunctional relationship!

First Edition 2023
ISBN: 978-1-7764321-5-8
Copyright © Dominique Adonis

Published by: Inspired Publishing
PO Box 82058 | Southdale | 2135 Johannesburg, South Africa
Email: info@inspiredpublishing.co.za
www.inspiredpublishing.co.za

© All rights are reserved. Apart from any fair dealing for the purpose of research, criticism or review as permitted under the Copyright Act, no part of this publication may be reproduced, stored in a retrieval system or transmitted, in any form or by any means, electronic, mechanical, photocopying, recording, or otherwise, without the prior written permission of the copyright holder.

To my first born, Tiffany Skyler Adonis.

"And who knows but that you have come to your royal position for a time such as this." **- Esther 4:14**

Your name means "Revelation of God."
Even as young as you are you live up to your name daily, teaching and revealing to me God's heart towards me and our family. I am confident that God's plan for you will prevail and that He will empower you to walk in His purpose for your life.

Because of Jesus, I broke chains so that you don't have to. Only in Jesus you'll be able to continue to walk in the freedom He secured for you. Choose Jesus always.

Your father and I love you fiercely with unchained hearts.

CONTENT

Acknowledgements 7
Foreword 9

The Big Picture 11

Part One 21
Awakened 22
Betrayed With A Kiss 50
The Heart Of The Matter 70

Part Two 93
The Chase 94
Boy Meets Girl 116
Sexuality By Design 137

Part Three 161
Love, Lust & Stilletto's 162
Broken 213
Soulties 268

Part Four 285
Healed And Whole 286
Unashamed 321
Unapologetic 331
Unchained 345

References 370

Acknowledgements

To the love of my life, my husband, dearest friend, lover, confidant and king, Ricardo. Thank you for being so patient and supportive during the process of living and writing Unchained. Thank you for sitting up into the watches of the night and for praying me through the most gruelling of chapters.

To our children Tiffany and Rocco. You bring us tremendous joy but also serious perspective of the times and world we live in. Your heart for God and childlike wonder inspire and command our souls to continue to walk in the freedom Jesus Christ died to give us.

To my parents, Michael and Gloria Swartz. You have stood the test of time; your lives and love are a testament to the goodness of God and the power of broken chains. You are my greatest supporters, cheerleaders and prayer warriors.

To the youth leadership of Bethel Tabernacle FGC, GK Crew Youth. You saw the vision of Unchain My Heart and subsequently, Unchained, before anyone else did and didn't hesitate to run towards it. You helped me work through and interrogate the difficult and controversial themes expressed in this work.

To Regina Harris, Melanie Lewin, Moira Stemmet, Homelia Esau, Margaret Adonis, Tanya Van Niekerk, Katy Muller, Rene Fortuin and Michelle Minaar, my intercessors. You have gone above and beyond the call of duty in prayer, intercession, prophetic utterance and encouragement on this journey of writing.

To Nicole Schierhout, my accountability partner. When I wanted to give up, you made sure I knew you were watching. Despite your own pain and trauma, you helped keep my eye on the prize.

To Eloise Scoble, you are an Editor of note. Thank you for your sharp eye, keen mind and surrendered heart in the editing of this work.

To Darren and Arlene August and the Inspired Publishing team. Darren, I am convinced that you're an "author whisperer". I could not have asked for a better Publisher. Thank you for living your message and making sure I went from blank page to published author.

Most importantly, my heart, love and gratitude to my Lord and Saviour, Jesus Christ. Even if I had a thousand tongues and had a thousand years to express my thanks for all You've done for me, it would not be enough. I don't have to write another book, but I'll do it again in a heartbeat… only if You say so. You have broken every chain and I am forever grateful.

Foreword

In 1961, world renowned recording artist Ray Charles released a song entitled "Unchain My Heart", written by Bobby Sharp. The song achieved great success on the charts in the United States, and down through the years, as other artists have recorded the song, it continues to resonate with music lovers all over the world. That may not seem like a big deal to most, but as a lover of music, I've always wondered what it is about a particular song that makes it so popular with so many? For lots of people, they will say, "it's the music" or "it's the beat". For many others it could simply be because of the artist who recorded it... they are diehard fans and will listen to anything they release. But I would venture to say, that most songs truly resonate with people because of the lyrics... the words used in the song to convey a particular message.

In this particular case, the songwriter seemed to tap into the idea of being held captive by a lover who truly didn't love him. One lyric reads, "I'm under your spell like a man in a trance, but I know darn well that I don't stand a chance. So, unchain my heart... please set me free". He's begging to be released from a power that he believes he has no control over. He's pleading with a lover to release him... to set him free! This songwriter used words put to music to express his feelings of captivity in such a way that millions of people around the world resonated with him, and to this day, they sing that same cry for freedom with every artist that covers the song.

To my knowledge, Dominique Adonis is not a songwriter, nor does she play any instruments or considers herself a singer. However, Dominique has been given an extremely unique ability to use words to convey the cries of a generation longing for a heart... UNCHAINED! This beautiful, powerful, spirit-filled woman of God has heard the cry of her own heart and the cries of the broken around her, and has responded to the leading of the Holy Spirit of God to deliver a message of FREEDOM to those held captive to the lies that have held so many people in relational bondage for generations. Holding nothing back, Dominique suits up, FULL ARMOR, and goes to WAR against the spiritual darkness and the lies that this generation is adopting, and lays before the reader the truth, as only she can.

So, for anyone who has felt chained by physical and spiritual abuse, neglect, abandonment, and rejection… this book is for you. If you or a loved one has come to believe that God's way of engaging in relationships isn't relevant for this generation, yet you can't shake this longing on the inside for something more… this book is for you. Our enemy, the prince of darkness, wants nothing more than to keep this generation spiritually and relationally bound, because he knows that if they take a step toward the freedom they have already been given access to in Jesus Christ, there will unleash a host of warriors ready to advance the Kingdom of God! God has anointed Dominique Adonis with a Rhema word for THIS generation, and I have the utmost faith and confidence that all who read and apply the truths presented here will step boldly into a new life… UNCHAINED!

– April Christina; *Pastor and Director of Care at Buckhead Church in Atlanta, GA, and the co-founder of D&A Ministries, LLC and Farmer Music LLC*

chapter one
The Big Picture

When one door closes, another opens, but we so often look upon the closed door that we do not see the one that has opened for us.
~ **Alexander Graham Bell**

I should have given up on writing this book, I'm so glad I didn't. What you're about to read was worth every tear, every prayer, every sacrifice and every "get-up-one-more-time" moment I had to endure. One of the major setbacks was losing my initial manuscript. It took so much to just get started and then to have it disappear into thin air, was devastating. Well, it didn't exactly *disappear*. It's probably in a folder or in some cloud somewhere, but when it does eventually resurface, we'll exchange memes, eat some pizza, and hopefully be able to find some humour in my trauma. The best way for me to accurately describe what I was feeling at this loss, comes in the form of just one loaded expression - Eish!

If you are not from South Africa, then allow me to introduce you to this term, which is used to express anything from pain, to disbelief, confusion, surprise, shock, exasperation, and even regret and resignation. With all the emotions I was experiencing I asked myself, "how do I do it all over again?" And then in the thick of my doubts and disappointment, while separating washing and changing nappies, the statement came to me... not *how*, but *why*. When in moments of difficulty or adversity it is not your *how* but your *why* that will get you back on course, back in line, and back up one more time. When your *why* takes up enough place in your heart, your head will find your *how*.

I had to find my *why*! I had to dig deep and ask, "why get up and start again?" The answer to that question was so loud that it kept me up at night. It kept me on my knees, trusting and writing. This was my answer - *"Before any word of this manuscript or the previous one was ever put to paper it was already in my heart"*- and my heart would not allow me to give up. Friedrich Nietzsche so eloquently stated, "He who has a *why* to live for can bear almost any *how*." In my heart was a vision to see the hearts of people - young and old - restored, healed and set free from their chains and wounds. I have a vision to see people free to love and build godly and healthy relationships.

And vision, dear reader, is a powerful thing. Vision is more than sight; it is the ability to see beyond the here and now. It is the power to see what could be, the ability to see what God sees. Being able to see what God sees is no pie-in-the-sky-when-you-die philosophy, rather it is the ability to see accurately. Sight without vision is a wretched way to live. It's like being an eagle in a chicken coop. God created you to be powerful, intelligent and beautiful - filled with great potential. But often times, we live with our heads so bowed down, and focused on the dirt, and not the sky, that we don't know that we can fly. So… we don't. I was not going to be *that* eagle. God had given me a vision and I was going to move towards it, with or without a manuscript.

HAVE YOU SEEN HER?
It was in the year 2013, when I came face to face with a broken heart. For the first time it was not my own, but it was like a mirror to my own soul. This broken heart belonged to a young lady, who, for the sake of this story, we will call "Melissa". Melissa fell madly in love with a boy - we'll call him Byron. As the story goes, Byron didn't feel the same way about Melissa, but that didn't stop him from saying things he should not have said and seducing her into doing things she should not have done. Feeling used, Melissa soon discovered that Byron was not who he had portrayed himself to be. Melissa began to

see a pattern that, Byron, like most of the men in her life, made promises he had no intention of keeping. Byron had promised to marry her, but she later discovered that she was just one of the many girls he referred to as "wifey". Eventually, he left her, abandoning and rejecting her, just like her father did.

Fast forward though pregnancy tests, tears, drugs, bitterness and failed suicide attempts. This is where I come in. As I sat there, face to face with this young lady, who was but a shadow of the girl she used to be, everything I had been trained to say in those situations seemed like a foreign language to her. They struck no chords and evoked no real emotion in Melissa. That night, I went to bed angry, confused and deeply disturbed. I woke up in the early hours of the morning and cried out to God, petitioning for her heart. I needed to know why she was so unresponsive to the truth of God's Word and why she seemed untouched and unmoved by His Holy Spirit. Then it dawned on me, that her heart was on lockdown; it was chained.

The sad reality was that Melissa's story is not an isolated or unique story. To a certain degree, Melissa's story is a reflection of our own hearts in chains, especially when we have been hurt and heartbroken. God started opening my eyes and ears to the dangers of how we do relationships in this generation, and through much prayer, this now became my burden for young people and their hearts, and in this a new vision was born. Everywhere I turned God challenged me to face my own brokenness, and to be the voice I so desperately needed when I was navigating the murky and often turbulent waters of relationships.

I CAN SEE CLEARLY NOW

I was willing to be the voice for the vision but like with every vision, I needed a team. There is an African proverb that goes, *"If you want to go fast, go alone. If you want to go far, go together"* and I wanted to go far. It was with this in mind that I started communicating, mobilizing, and strategizing and very soon the vision I had, became a series - the Unchain My Heart (UCMH) 4 Part Relationship Series. This series has grown into a conference of sorts, that sees the hearts of young people healed and restored. It is wired to be a platform to equip young people with the necessary tools and wisdom to successfully navigate through, and thrive in, one of the key areas of their lives - relationships. It is also aimed at igniting passion and purpose in the most vital relationship of all - their relationship with Christ! Over the years, we've had some hot topics, which have led to awesome encounters and countless testimonies of how God healed and restored broken hearts and lives. We had been blessed with dynamic speakers who handled the subject matter like expert builders and taught with such clarity and grace. They were authentic, vulnerable, and instrumental in revealing the will and ways of God when it comes to relationships and what they should consists of.

In 2020 I had the daunting task of being the one and only UCMH speaker and needless to say, I was terrified. This was also the same year that the world came to a screeching halt, with the onset of Covid-19 and the subsequent national lock down. At this point, we were already two sessions into UCMH, in what should have been our greatest series yet. The lockdown to close the door on all our plans. I couldn't see past it! I was shattered.

In exasperation and desperation, I asked, "What about the vision Lord? What about the hearts of young people?" I reasoned that plans were made, programmes were drawn up, guest artists were secured, and youth groups were looking to us for direction. We prayed, fasted, and went into warfare, but *"Corona"* was going nowhere, and the lock down remained. She dug her heels into the ground and arrogantly gave us the middle finger. It was then that God reminded me about how, in our promotional material, I kept on mentioning the word "lockdown" when referring to hearts. It was like the Lord was whispering, *"Trust me. No one can unchain a heart like I can; no one can liberate a heart on lockdown like I can. Watch me."* And there was Peace, the silent assurance of God's presence and a hopeful expectation of His grace.

In light of this, we sent out an official communication stating that UCMH would be on hold until further notice.

MAN IN THE MIRROR

Then came the knock on the door. Enter a young man we'll call *"Mason"*. Mason sat at our family room table and shed tear after tear recalling how the Holy Spirit was working in his heart. He recalled dreams God had given him, and confirmations he had received at the UCMH conference. My jaw dropped. My husband and I could not hold back the flood of tears we had stored up over the years for Mason.

You see, Mason used to belong to our youth group, and he proved himself to be entitled, rebellious and reckless with the hearts of others. By his own confession, he lived his life for himself and didn't care who he hurt. He would intentionally form relationships with "good" girls and turn their lives upside down with his lies, seduction, and *"player"* mentality. Mason would win their hearts and then trample it in the dust, and then matter-of-factly, just move on. He was the epitome of the kind of guy your mother warns you about.

That evening Mason confessed and asked our forgiveness for every heart he broke. He asked our forgiveness for the many times we warned him, and tried to help him, and he refused our help. Time and confidentiality do not allow me to share the harrowing details of the pain he caused others, but I will say that I sat there in awe of God. Not only did he feel the need to ask our forgiveness, but he made appointments with every girl he ever hurt to ask their forgiveness and that of their parents. The only response that came to mind is "Sjoe!" This is another colloquialism used in my beloved country, to express surprise, or admiration (among other exclamations). It's the kind of word you use when you have no words. Mason didn't know how he would be received but knew he needed to be obedient to God and meeting with us that day was the first step.

In that moment, it was like God was tapping me on the shoulder and reminding me, *"You see? I'm bigger than UCMH or any platform that you can construct. I am the Creator and Re-creator of the heart, as well as its Healer. I am the One who breaks chains and bondages, and lifts hearts on lockdown. Thank you for seeing the vision I gave you for the hearts of young people, but I AM bigger."*

Instinctively I knew that God leveraged a pandemic to expose what was in my heart. I wanted God's vision done *my* way. I repented.

I've observed that this is often how God works in scripture, and in my life. He will use the brokenness of the world, of our lives and our circumstances, to expose the self-will and self-reliance in our hearts - not for His sake, but for ours. In hindsight, seeing the vision for UCMH was the easy part. What God wanted me to see, was that He was bigger than the vision. He wanted me to see how I was limiting outcomes by envisioning UCMH happening my way.

God already knew what was in my heart, He needed me to see it and respond. He did it with Abraham using his son (Genesis.22: 1-2), with Moses using a murder (Ex. 2: 14) and with the Israelites using a desert (Deut. 8: 2) and He did it with me and a global crisis. Our hearts matter to God, He sees what's in it and He will test it. *"A crucible is for silver and a smelter for gold, but the Lord is a tester of hearts"* (Prov.17: 3-4).

This is the take home. The Blesser is always greater than the blessing; the Promise Maker is always greater than the promise. Much like the Creator is always greater than the creation, you get the picture. God's ways are higher and so much better than our ways. I made the mistake of wanting God's vision done my way. God wanted me to see that His vision done His way gets Him all the glory. When we come to understand *this* we will finally see past any closed door and see the door that's open.

EYES TO SEE
Seeing God clearly - that is, seeing God for Who He truly is - is of utmost importance whether it be for a vision or in our pain, because it means that we will be in better position to trust His heart when we cannot see His hand. This is especially true in those times and seasons when things don't work out the way we prayed or planned for; those times when God feels distant or when we wonder if He's listening if He even cares. The person who understands that God is always

greater will know that God is still in control no matter what they're going through.

The crux of the matter is that although programs are good, and reaching young people is good, and UCMH is a powerful tool, it can never ever substitute the power of God in the hearts and lives of people.

God, being the good Father that He is, pulled me close, put my ear to His heart and whispered, *"Watch me pivot UCMH and catapult your reach farther than you ever could otherwise. Watch Me work all things together for your good and My glory."*

Right there in that moment, with tears streaming down my face, I sensed God releasing me to take UCMH online. I enlisted the help of the planning team, and we got the approval of our church leadership. In this way we were able to impact thousands instead of the hundreds we would have had reached, had we gathered in our little auditorium. Look at God! The enemy thought he could shut up and lock down the body of Christ, yet he didn't count on God maximizing a global pandemic to get the gospel into spaces and places that might not have reached previously! He didn't count on UCMH going online and the writing of this book! He didn't count on God working on my heart first!

The book you have in your hand is part of a vision given to me by God Himself, and I believe that He will use this resource to take you on a journey to healing, and restoration, and help you confront and break every chain meant to keep your heart in bondage. This book in and of itself, cannot heal, restore, or liberate, only God can do that, and if you allow Him to, He can and will use it not as a substitute but as a reference point, a marker that states that someone has been where you are, and has come out on the other side, healed and stronger!

The truth of the matter is that we were all created within the context of, and *for* relationships. In Genesis. 1:26 we see that God is intrinsically relational, and because we are made in the image of a relational God, we are intrinsically relational ourselves. We are in relationship with our Creator and with our fellow creatures. We are made for good, thriving relationships with God Himself and also with other people, but somewhere along the line things got a bit messed up. How we do relationships in this generation has caused us to inflict pain on ourselves and others and to move away from the relationship that means more and gives meaning to it all - our relationship with Jesus Christ, and that initial relationship with God. My hope is that you would use this book as a tool to navigate your past, anchor your present and set sail to your future. As you continue to read this book, do so alongside your bible, and under the guidance of the Holy Spirit.

You may ask: why be healed? Why be restored? Why be free? Well, so that you, like the eagle can looked up and see yourself the way God sees you and can be and do all that God has called you to. Ultimately, to love God and love people, by His design and for His glory.
I want to clarify that not all chains on our hearts are caused by someone breaking up with us or breaking our hearts. There are chains caused by childhood trauma, rejection, abandonment, abuse, unforgiveness, bitterness, crisis, dysfunction, faulty thinking, bad habits, weakness, and sin; the list goes on. Regardless of what has imprisoned your heart, the principles shared in this book are reference points for you to search through, study and apply to your own heart and life.

THE TRUTH IS...
I have to be honest with you, there will be days when you will feel like giving up on your heart, healing and freedom. When that happens, you will have to dig deep to remind yourself of your *why*. Remember, your *why* will lead you to your *how*. The question you will have to ask yourself is, will you still trust God when you can't feel Him? When you can't find His hand, will you press in for His heart? Make sure your answer is yes, then, like the champion that you are, get back up again.

Some days wounds will be reopened, and you might find yourself in a dark place, just know that your heart is being tested, not because God doesn't know what's in it, but because He needs you to know and to make the change. He needs you to crown Him as Lord, greater than your pain, greater than the chains and greater than any vision you could have for your life. Don't get stuck at what seems like a closed door, lift your gaze higher and look for the door He's opening. The unchaining of your heart is so much more than a destination, it is a process, sometimes slow and grueling. Other times it may be immediate and miraculous, whatever it looks like at any given moment remember to *trust* Him.

"Trust God from the bottom of your heart; don't try to figure out everything on your own. Listen for God's voice in everything you do, everywhere you go; He's the One who will keep you on track."
- Proverbs 3: 5 THE MESSAGE

To trust God in this text means to *rely on*, have *confidence* and *be secure* in Him. The thing about trust is that its required most when you're tested most. Anybody can trust God when He's showing up and *"flexing"*, when you feel loved, and your needs are being met. However, trust is only truly trust when you can't see what He's doing, or when you're scared out of your mind and cannot foresee the process or the outcome. Fundamentally, it is trusting in the character of God, in the absence of the details, knowing that whatever happens, Gods heart for you will not fail you.

My friend, Father God, has the capacity to take you deeper, higher and farther than you ever dreamt possible. Let's take this moment to pray together as we embark on your journey toward healing and restoration.

Our Father, we honour and glorify Your Name. It is the cry of our hearts to know You more and to have Your Kingdom come and Your will be done in and through our lives. Lord, we confess that sometimes we lose sight of You. Father, help us see what You see for our lives in spite of our pain. It's true that often we struggle with pain, trauma and disappointment. Holy Spirit come and convict, teach and open the eyes of our hearts to know the length and width, height and depth of God's love, and to know Christ's love that surpasses knowledge, so that we may be filled with all the fullness of God. Lord, we need Your healing and restoration to mark our lives and to transform our God-given relationships. Lord, forgive us where we have brought hurt, trauma and toxicity to the hearts and lives of others, forgive us for where we crossed the line from victim to perpetrator. Forgive us we pray. Father, we ask that You open every prison door and break every chain. Lord, we pray that You would use this book to echo Your Word, bring clarity and minister to those dark, messy and often chaotic areas of our lives. Holy Spirit, empower us to practically apply the principles highlighted in this book so that we can live life unchained, in Jesus Name we pray. Amen.

PART ONE

chapter two
Awakened

As you awaken you will come to understand that the journey to love isn't about finding the one - - it is about becoming the one.
~ **Creig Crippen**

It would happen often. I would forget to breathe. I would find myself gasping for air. No, I didn't have asthma or a tight chest. Instead, it was my occasional check-in at heart break hotel, where tears stung, words cut, and memories would open wounds. What I experienced was similar to "stress cardiomyopathy" - the medical term for what we call a broken heart, or in more severe cases, "broken heart syndrome".

Have you ever had your heart broken to the point that it literally aches, that you actually experience physical pain? Have you ever grabbed your chest, like I did in the middle of the night and prayed that God would take the pain away?

Have you ever looked at Psalm 118: 17-18 and read in broken whispers, *"I will not die but live, and will proclaim what the Lord has done. The Lord has chastened me severely, but he has not given me over to death."*

Or maybe you looked to something or someone else to numb the pain or take it away? Maybe you just lied to yourself and said it's ok?

Did you also feel like dying? Little did I know that *my* broken heart would take me on a journey to face my past and correct wrong thinking patterns I had about myself and others, and this crazy thing called love.

My story begins the same as many others. I thought he was *the one*. He was supposed to be. He pursued me persistently; he seemed to understand me in ways no-one else did, and in this all-consuming, obsessive love, he promised to marry me. I thought that I had finally found everything I had been wanting and that my deepest needs would be met. I thought that he completed me. The problem was that I thought this about every guy I "fell in love" with since I was 12 years old, and Beyoncé and her hit song "Irreplaceable" didn't help matters much either. Almost every girl knew this anthem well and we sang it at the top of our lungs. In my mind, every relationship I entered had the potential of permanence but was susceptible to being discarded with, without the attachment. I was young and naïve. I thought I could move from one relationship to the next and be unaffected by it.

Being in youth ministry for the past 20 years I've had many young people ask me why moving from one relationship to the next was a problem. In fact, "it could be a good thing" was the follow through. Some have reasoned that through "trial and error" they would then be more equipped to "know what they're looking for". As one young man bluntly put it, "we must test drive before we buy" sadly, exposing the chains of entitlement culture around the hearts and minds of young people. Women are not cars.
A common mindset in advocating dating is so that we can learn how to relate to the opposite sex. The truth is that you don't have to be in a romantic relationship with someone to learn how to relate them. In fact, I now know and understand that you don't have to be in a relationship with everyone you're attracted to.

My problem was, I was moving from one relationship to the next in a heartbeat. I was looking for love in all the wrong places and in hindsight, I was looking for love at the wrong time! Solomon in his wisdom charges the young women of Jerusalem, not once, not twice, but three times (Song of Songs 2:7, 3:5, 8:4), *"Do not arouse or awaken love until it so desires."* And the reason for this is simple. When we enter romantic relationships too young, we run the risk of being chained emotionally, psychologically, physically and spiritually.

A large part of my life was spent in these chains. And today I spend my time counseling young people whose romantic love was awakened too early. There is a time and a season for every aspect of our lives (Eccl.3:1-8). The key is understanding the season you find yourself in. An Afrikaans proverb captures this truth vividly, "*Vroeg ryp, vroeg vrot."* Directly translated, this phrase says, "Early to ripen, early to rot" This phrase can be interpreted as, "rushing something can destroy it". In most instances this phrase is used to refer to young men or women, rushing prematurely into doing "mature/adult" things, without being mature enough to handle the consequences of those things. Doing so, can destroy them, and alter their perception of those things. Essentially taking something that is good, and designed by God, and polluting and defiling it by premature use.

The dangerous reality about how we do relationships in this generation is that we are being groomed by what I call the "divorce culture". We want the perks of marriage without the commitment of vows, so we end up doing relationships like married people and when we break up it looks and feels like a divorce. When we eventually get married, it feels like we've been here before and it's easy to walk away when the other person no longer meets our needs or we "fall out of love".

For me personally, going from one relationship to the next was not my biggest problem, it was only a symptom of something much deeper. What we must realize today is that one of the many reasons young people in this generation are dysfunctional in how they conduct relationships, is often due to a myriad of underlying issues, that form the basis and foundation on which they build their current relations.

AWAKENED TOO SOON
Dictionary.com describes the word *awaken* "as the act of awaking from sleep, also seen as the revival of interest or attention." Words such as

"recognition" and "realization" can also be used to flesh out what it means to awaken. A definition that underscores this chapter is that awaken means *to come into awareness of something*. In his article for Forbes Magazine, on the Power of awareness for Leaders, Business Blogger, David O'Hara states: *"Awareness is a powerful tool that can help us transform our lives in profound ways. By taking the time to be aware of yourself, your surroundings and the practices you engage in daily, you open yourself up to positive growth and change in your company and life."*

While O'Hara's statement rings true in most instances, especially business, there is another element of awareness that can be detrimental. We mentioned this a little earlier, when we touched on maturity. i.e.: being mature enough to handle the newfound information.

When awareness enters too soon the results could be devastating.

Awareness, unfortunately, doesn't ask our permission, or wait until we are ready. I see it in my children, whether it's them becoming aware of time, danger or some new fascination, they can never again return to that state of ignorance, and often innocence they had before the awareness. This is what scares me. To become aware of certain "pleasures" before we are able to set boundaries or maturely deal with them, can be very dangerous. Things such as being introduced to the delirious effects of alcohol, or the euphoria of sex, even the high that a sugar rush can give you, can be extremely detrimental outside the parameters of appropriate guidelines.

We have an enemy who understands the power of being awakened too soon. In fact, the enemy has no intention of waiting until you're old enough to deal with trauma, pain or dysfunction that comes with premature revelation. The enemy's mandate is to kill, steal and destroy (John 10:10) and this mandate does not discriminate - not even vulnerable, innocent children are safe (Ex.1:15-16; Jer.7:30-31; Matt.2:16-18).

Biblically, you will see how the enemy blatantly comes after the children, seeking to end their very lives. In this day and age, if the enemy's attempt at killing them fails, he attacks them young, he exposes them young, and he awakens them young. He leaves them with scars and traumas that they inevitably take with them into the rest of their lives. Knowing that without healing and restoration broken children become broken adults who create broken families, making up broken communities perpetuating brokenness for generations. We have come to know this as "generational curses", or generational trauma.

Generational trauma occurs when parents unintentionally pass their trauma down to their children, and this can affect multiple generations over the course of hundreds of years.

"A lot of people don't tend to understand that intergenerational/generational trauma, unless those patterns are changed, the patterns tend to continue. They don't just go away on their own," says Susan Beaulieu, an assistant extension professor in family development at the University of Minnesota. *"If we don't deal with them, they actually end up compounding over time."*

So to compound brokenness, the enemy attacks them young, and perpetuates that cycle to their offspring, and their offspring and so on etc. That's why the enemy attacked when *you* were a child, and his end game was and will always be your heart in chains.

As a child I always remember feeling "left out". I didn't have the language then, but I now know that as young as 5 years old I battled strong feelings of rejection. Looking back, the dominant thought that would always cross my mind was that there must be something wrong with me. A memory that will forever be etched in my mind is that of my younger brother. He was about 3 years old at the time, walking hand in hand with both my parents - daddy on his right and mommy on the left. It was a picture-perfect moment. At first, I thought it was so beautiful, but as I slowed down, I noticed that no one turned around to see where I was. I walked a little slower and still there was no sign of concern, no turning of heads, no-one calling my name. I walked slower still and heard a voice saying that my family didn't want me and that they'd be better off without me. This voice seemed to come from inside my head. And I believed every word. As I mentioned earlier, all this happened when I was about 5 years old. An age that I was barely self-aware but was made aware of feelings of rejection-whether real or perceived.

As I got older those feelings of rejection didn't get any better. In an effort to not feel left out, to not feel rejected, I created my own little world. I would make up stories about how close my dad and I were, I would tell lies to make my friends laugh and admire the "awesome relationship" my dad and I supposedly had. I became very good at living in this make-believe world that got me the attention and admiration I was seeking. I would justify my lying by convincing myself that all I really wanted was just to be accepted.

I didn't understand where these strong feelings of rejection came from, nor could I pinpoint the exact cause for them.

Until one day, years later, it all just made sense. I was 23 years old when my father and I got into a heated argument. My father had battled with alcoholism for as long as I could remember, and this day in his intoxicated state, he said words that set me up for my *AHA moment. A moment which Kyle Idleman describes as, *"the God moment that changes everything."* (*Awakening. Honesty. Action)

During this incident, I finally gathered the courage to defend myself, and my mother as well, when my father revealed a shocking truth to me. He said that when my mother found out she was pregnant with me, she didn't want me. He described how she tried to get rid of me and how he had to get her off the railway line because she wanted to take her own life and ultimately mine. I have never had an out of body experience but I'm sure that what I felt in that moment came very close. After hearing those words, I heard nothing else. His lips continued moving, but my ears drowned out the sound as my heart went into lock down.

Right here is an example of generational trauma. Allow me - without minimizing the effect of this devastating revelation - to give you some context: My mother, being raised, and having served in the church all her young life, found herself pregnant at the age of 19 years old. While premarital pregnancy is a common trend today, in 1982 it was not, and it brought shame on your entire household. Couple that with the guilt she must have felt at her current reality, and this will give you some insight into her state of mind at that moment, as she stood on that railway line. So let me just say that before my father and mother ever conceived me, they were both pregnant with their own brand of trauma, that was handed down to them from their own parents, dating back as far as, and possibly further than their grandparents.

My father was conceived when his mother was 15 years old. My mother was conceived when her mother was 45 years old. Unwanted for different reasons. But it didn't start there; both their mothers - my paternal and maternal grandmothers - were unwanted in some way, shape or form. In the months before the passing of my paternal great-grandmother she allowed me to see her broken heart and shared with me how she was given up for adoption because her skin was darker than that of her siblings. Rejection ran in my bloodline, and on both sides.

If rejection and I were in a boxing match, there would be no way I could win the fight, because you see, while I was being knit together in my mother's womb, I was already 4 generations deep into rejection. Even at 5 years old, rejection floated around me like a butterfly, but it stung like a bee.

My father's intention with his statement was only meant to stop me from defending my mother, but it awakened me to the rejection that has marked me from the womb. This was my predisposition. From as young as 5-years-old, the enemy used every opportunity to further reinforce what I believed to be my truth - that there was something wrong with me and as a result I was unwanted and rejected.

I have come to find that this is how the enemy works. He attacks while we are young, he awakens our young hearts and minds to pain and trauma, using even the most innocent of occurrences as an opportunity to chain our hearts.

As a child every "no" I heard, every scolding I received, every tinge of sadness, the enemy used as an opportunity to magnify rejection and reinforce his lies.

Now please note this attack on innocence is not always as blatant and painful as we think, often it's very subtle, almost entertaining. You'd think the enemy's blood thirsty nature should be accompanied by horns, a tail, and a pitchfork as we've been led to believe, but sometimes the enemy presents himself as an angel of light (2Cor.11:14). Let's take a sober look at more of the enemy's strategies of attack on the young.

SLEEPING BEAUTY SLEEPS NO MORE

It's adorable, seeing the eyes of little children light up as the television pours out brilliant colours, sing-along songs and catchy, sometimes cheeky phrases! They giggle with sheer delight.

Growing up, I, like most little girls dreamt of being a Disney princess and most little boys saw themselves as the hero. It slowly but surely consumed all our time, attention, and affections. Present but emotionally absent fathers started trading family time for news and sport. Tired and burnt-out mothers allowed cartoons and sitcoms to raise their children. Misdirected teens turned to inappropriate viewing and entertainment to create a world in which their perceived needs could be met.

Author and contributor to the book, "Worldliness", Craig Cabaniss, expounds greatly on the effect of all forms of media on the mind of the Christian and hones in on its influences on our children and how it has shaped society. *"There are few things that have influenced this generation and its worldview like the 'almighty' television."* Ken Meyers weighs in on this by saying that *"television is not only the dominant medium of popular culture but also the single most significant shared reality in our entire society."*

Media is the omnipresent backdrop of life. Think about it, silence is often loud because we're always listening, reading or watching something. Regardless of where you find yourself, you're in what Dan Andrianco calls the *"mediasphere."*

I don't have a problem with the fact that media is always communicating. I do have a problem with *what* it's communicating. See, our thinking is influenced by what we watch, advertising budgets can attest to this. We must not underestimate the power of media. And as Christians, we must not deceive ourselves into thinking we have immunity against its power.

Cabaniss goes on further to say that *"...the packaging and delivery of the world's offerings have advanced technologically, but their substance has remained as primitive as a talking serpent."*

And he is not wrong. Media has the power to awaken and deceive young hearts. And although not all media is inherently bad, I must agree with Cabaniss' statement, that *"We must evaluate the content of media messages and the consequences of their influence..."* because (and I paraphrase) *"all forms of media, to some degree, contain values of a fallen world."*

And as Christians we must recognize that the pull of the world and the desires of the flesh have not changed, *"For everything in the world – the lust of the flesh, the lust of the eyes, and the pride of life – comes not from the Father but from the world"* (1John 2:16). We cannot afford to mindlessly watch and take in media's version of truth. We must actively evaluate our media intake. It is vital that we discern our viewing because we run the risk of drifting from our love for God to love for the world.

And it's not enough for us to avoid the obvious traps such as pornography and the occult, we must acknowledge that even as Christians we are prone to self-deception and that what we watch matters, even our Netflix and chill sessions.

I am not trying to demonize media I am merely highlighting the fact that if adults are tempted by the influx of media information and images, how much more children? Children do not yet possess the discernment required to filter truth from lies, or differentiate between the patterns of the world, and the enemy is having a field day with their innocence and naive minds. Detecting and avoiding the deception of media is a battle, it is warfare, and our children are not trained to fight it. Not to labour the point, but I want to reiterate that something as simple as leaving our kids sitting in front of the television, or with any device that has connection to the internet or radio etc., has the ability to prematurely awaken our kids to things that they should not be exposed to.

BE CAREFUL LITTLE ONES

I remember "giving my heart" to the Lord every Sunday in Sunday School. It wasn't until my teen years, that I understood what this meant in the life of a believer. Now I realize the importance of the foundational teachings I received in that Sunday school class. I especially loved the songs. There was one song in particular that became the theme song for my walk of sanctification with the Holy Spirit. The song was called *"O be careful little eyes"*. This song was so simple but oh so powerful! It is a song with a repetitive melody and repetitive lyrics, with only the focus on action changing with each stanza.

> *"O be careful little eyes what you see*
> *O be careful little eyes what you see*
> *For the Father up above*
> *Is looking down in love*
> *So, be careful little eyes what you see"*

It taught me to be careful about what I saw, what I heard, what I said, what I did, whom I trusted, where I went and what I allowed in my heart and mind for the sole purpose of accountability. It pointed me to the reality that my Heavenly Father watches me with love; that He is involved, daily, with every aspect of my life.

As I matured, I began to understand more and more, the power of practicing God's presence. We walk differently when we know that we have an audience with God. As a young minister I would visit the homes of our church members and cringe at how they would esteem me but totally disregard God; how they would put me on a pedestal by hiding cigarettes, alcohol, turning down the vulgar music and basically hiding their Monday to Saturday lifestyles. It broke my heart that they were more interested in what I thought of them than of what God thought.

I appreciated their respect but not at the expense of reverence for God. Whether we try to hide things from our pastors or God Himself the reality is that our lives are affected by what we allow in, through what I like to call our gates - those things that guard entrance into our lives i.e. our eyes, ears, mouths, hands, feet, minds, and hearts. Whatever is going to enter our lives must come via one of these gates.

While we can probably explore a few things that will enter through these gates I would like to focus on one that has the potential to enter without your permission. Atomic in nature it also forms part of what we unpacked earlier with regards to media. It comes in undetected and before you know it your mood, mindset and heart has been altered, and, in the worst-case scenario - chained!

This is the medium of music.

Years ago, I taught on the power of music and those who harness its power to deceive and bring bondage. I was attacked by the spiritual elite and accused of being a conspiracy theorist. As predicted, what I warned young believers about then, is now revealing itself to be detrimental to our spiritual wellbeing.

Pastor, songwriter, worship leader, and author, Bob Kauflin, says it best: *"Music is neither a demon to be feared nor a god to be idolized. It's simply a part of God's creation intended to serve his glory and our good."*

But it does beg the question: what makes music so powerful?

Let's see if we can answer that.

1. Music was God's idea and from what we can see He enjoys it a lot (1 Sam. 13:14; 1Chron. 16:5-7).
2. Music affects us deeply; its physiological effects cannot be denied.
3. Music is a carrier - ultimately it can carry godliness or godlessness.

Let's pause here for a moment.

Music can carry at least three elements, namely content, context and culture, and like a pied piper it's the content of music that often leads us down the path of no return. It is quite possible to sing anointed songs in a worship service and not mean a word because your heart has been enslaved to lyrics that glorify sexual immorality, profanity, rage, and rebellion. Our playlists can confirm our guilt.

I had a youth leader who understood the lull and pull of music on our generation, allowing us to flirt with the world and sabotage our relationship with God. Because of this grave danger, he forbade us to listen to secular music while in leadership. I thought this to be a bit drastic, but I decided to obey. I noticed a change in my heart posture towards God and the things of God. I found myself starting to cringe at some of the things I heard on the radio and in music videos. The longer I obeyed, the more clearly, I could hear the Holy Spirit when He directed or impressed something on me. I realized that my youth leader was on to something.

Now let's be clear. Hearing a secular song on the radio or while shopping can't make you entertain wild thoughts like Rihanna suggests or cause you to like kissing a girl like Katty Perry, nor can it lead you down the path of obscene speech and profanity like Eminem, Doja Cat, Nicki Minaj, Cardi B and the music elite. Listen, we can't blame Beyonce every time we feel like falling in love and engage in risky sexual behaviour.

However, if we intentionally listen to worldly music consistently and long enough it can position us to drift from our love for God to love for this world.

Understand that there's nothing harmless about love songs for those who are single, and if you listen to some of the love songs today, I doubt it can be helpful to those who are married either. This is due to the content's potential to alter one's emotional state by turning on the power of suggestion and desensitizing the heart to vices that kill spiritual passion.

Now, this may probably sound like a stretch, but I've been called a conspiracy theorist before so I'm going to say it anyway. The music this generation listens to has spell-like qualities. It's like sorcery if you ask me.

Musician & Author Vivek Sahney, hit the nail on the head, when he said, *"Music throws us into a state of ecstatic bewitch!"* I would forgive you for thinking that I'm one of "those people" who sees the devil in everything, but I want to draw your attention to a song that we all know and have probably danced to countless times - Whitney Houston's, "I'm every woman". The video for the song features cameo appearances by Houston's mother Cissy Houston as well as by Chaka Khan, Valerie Simpson, Martha Wash and labelmate TLC. The idea was for it, was to feature phenomenal woman who were taking up space in that era. With this in mind, Whitney approached her good friend CeCe Winans to be part of the video, to which CeCe declined.

CeCe explained that when she was asked, she had to make a decision. Winans stated *"...she was my dear sister and friend, and I remember she was about to do one of her big videos; it was 'I'm every woman'. It's a great video right...when you think about how it was written; it's a great song right, but the lyrics don't line up with the Word of God...She said 'CeCe I want you to be in this video, but I know you're not gonna be in it', I said 'you 're absolutely right, 'cause it started off with I could cast a spell, - I'm not singing that!'* But notice how that message was all wrapped up in a beat; y'all get so hooked onto these beats and its [like] demonic! God says, you're either for Me or against Me, you're with Me or you're not. The biggest *deception is [that] the devil makes you think it's in-between. Show me a scripture that says there's an in-between. There is no in-between!"*

Could the power of music's content be put in plain sight in this song and many others like it? Just a question, a mere thought. Can we blame music? Fundamentally, I don't think so. Each of us must take responsibility for our own actions whether we've been influenced or affected by the content of the music we listen to or not. I think walking into bondage with our eyes open is just as dangerous as being ignorant of our chains.

It is very important for Christians to be intentional and cognizant of the kind of music they indulge in. Me, obeying my youth pastor in cutting off all secular music, was proof that not all music is beneficial, and some music can act as a barrier between you and your connection to God and the Holy Spirit. I am not saying that as a Christian you *must* cut off all secular music in order to connect with Christ, but I would like to remind you of what Paul says in 1 Corinthians 10:23. He says, *"All things are lawful [that is, morally legitimate, permissible], but not all things are beneficial or advantageous. All things are lawful, but not all things are constructive [to character] and edifying [to spiritual life]."*

I would like to just give you some information that will help in your music choices, because we know that we cannot consume all forms of music.

Femi Osunnuyi, lead pastor of City Church, in Lagos, Nigeria, has given us great insight, that I would love to share with you. He states *"...we must make a distinction between non-Christian music and un-Christian music. With non-Christian music, we are talking about music that conveys messages that the Bible will not oppose, and some ways the Bible even teaches. So, songs like Louis Armstrong's 'What a Beautiful World', Onyeka Onwenu's 'One Love', classical jazz, classical music, songs about injustice, songs about love... all of those things we can, and surely even, listen to. And then there is un-Christian music. Its music that conveys messages that are in direct opposition to ethics and things that the Bible teaches. We need to reject those types of music."*

In light of this, if media and more specifically music, has an effect on adults who should take responsibility for our own lives, what about children who have the vices of their little hearts awakened too early by lyrics that promote the degrading of women, sensuality, fornication and the latest addition, the forceful push of gender ideology?

I clearly remember my dad seeing my early awakening to messages and information embedded in the music I was listening to. Back in those days I was getting my fair share of worldly music videos highlighting and glorifying our fallen nature and broken world. One time he instructed me to turn off the MTV because it was *"having a bad influence on me."* I was so mad at him, and I used the same excuse young people use today. I argued that it was not about the lyrics, but about the beat. What I now know that I wish I understood back then is that the beat carries its own content, and *that* content wants our hearts.

I did a little survey a while back in our youth group, and I want to share my observations with you. I'm going to give you the music reality among some of the young believers I ministered to on a weekly basis at our local church. Firstly, I wasn't surprised that one of the things they all had in common was music, they listen to all genre's not just gospel.

What blew my mind was that although their *media* intake on their phones was between 8 - 10 hours per day on average; their *music* intake could not be quantified. Music seemed to be ever-present; it played even while they were sleeping. I also observed that the top common challenges that they had in their walk with God was their lack of spiritual fervor. They experienced little to no desire to read or study God's word and needed some kind of external motivation to engage in spiritual disciplines that could build their faith. Some of them even experienced spiritual apathy from time to time.

There's no doubt that they loved God and wanted to be in His presence, even though they often couldn't sense Him or understand His Word. Their inability to do so, caused a lot of frustration for them, but still, they made no connection between that and the music they listened to. I realized that this was true of *my* spiritual reality before I made the decision to cut out worldly music from my media regimen as a young leader. When I looked at their spiritual reality, I knew that they probably experienced what I did; what I allowed in through my gates brought chains to my heart and stunted my process of sanctification as a young believer.

What's more, it informed my thoughts and feelings toward myself, my world and those in my world. The content of the music I listened to as a child and a young adult downplayed my value as a human, woman, and child of God. I settled for the knock-off of femininity made popular in many songs. The content in these songs reinforced the narrative that I was what I felt and that feelings were truth. Lies.

Thank God for a discerning and courageous youth leader who wasn't afraid to call out music for what it was in my life, a carrier of content contrary to the truth of God's word. It soon became apparent that there was so much untruth I needed to unlearn and how I did that was through the putting off of everything that hindered - including worldly music - and the putting on of Christ and all that pertains to my new identity, new nature and new life in Him.

Music set the values, tone, and objective for all the romantic relationships I found myself in and it reinforced my drift from a fervent and passionate relationship with God. We are setting up our children for failure if we allow worldly content to be downloaded into their precious hearts, by the music we allow them to listen to, or fail to stop them listening to. We are no better than a handler trafficking a child to a life of bondage and slavery if we do not protect their gates against the harmful content in music today.

A bit heavy handed with the imagery? No, not at all. Children are too vulnerable to stand at their own gates; they need us to defend their innocent hearts. We must do it *for* them and *train* them until they're strong enough to do it for themselves.

IN PLAIN SIGHT

It is said that sometimes the best hiding place is the one that is "in plain sight". I want to submit to you that the sexual awakening of a generation, abruptly and too soon has been in the works for decades. What media communicates today was set in motion years ago. Like a steam locomotive, it has been building momentum over distance and time, and the enemy's ultimate agenda is now in full throttle.

For years, Disney, the beloved kids' choice in animated features, has long been suspected of hiding subliminal sexual messages in its animated films, and has been feeding subversive pornographic images and content to its viewers. From rogue penises on VHS covers, priests with visible erections, shots of naked women, and even the word "sex" floating in the breeze during The Lion King. Former Disney animator, Tom Sito pretty much confirmed that the company has been cleaning up "old jokes", during an interview with the *Huffington Post*. He said, *"You know in pre-video and pre-VHS and VCR and stuff, people used to put little inside jokes in films..." "... [cartoonists] will do that as a joke"*.

Those were the days when this kind of profanity was hidden, and covert, but more recently, in November 2022, Balenciaga, a Spanish luxury fashion house based in Paris France, broke the internet with fashion campaigns and images that sparked a public outcry. It is alleged that Balenciaga executives were present during shoots, oversaw props and signed off on imagery that sexualized children, and featuring children holding teddy bears in bondage harnesses and costumes. One ad highlighted a Supreme Court case on child pornography. Needless to say, Balenciaga got "cancelled".

People were enraged and rightly so. A little too late if you ask me. Mediums such as Tik Tok have become more overt in grooming children, yes, but, as I previously stated, Disney has been doing it for decades. I say we overthrow Hollywood. It's time that we take a stand and boldly and uncompromisingly declare, just like Jesus did in Matthew 12:30 that *"anyone who isn't with me opposes me, and anyone who isn't working with me is actually working against me."* We can no longer compromise with an enemy that is coming at us and our children in full force. As Christian warriors, we may come in peace but that doesn't mean we're not ready for war. The enemy is not hiding anymore, and we shouldn't either!

Now like never before we must have eyes to see and ears to hear what God is doing and saying to His Bride, the Church - the Ecclesia; the called-out ones. When we have discerning hearts yielded to the searching power of the Holy Spirit, we will be able to see what's being hidden in plain sight.

We can then act immediately when we spiritually discern the power of darkness at work even when something seems ordinary or innocent. This is your call to radical awareness of your media intake and that of those you must give an account for, your children, those you lead and those you disciple. The enemy's agenda is not hidden in a safe somewhere unknown: its right in front of us.

THE RUDE AWAKENING

I got a call from one of our church members, who had a niece who needed counsel. I agreed to see her, but soon realized that I was not fully equipped to deal with what she was going through. What she was about to share with me, would test the mettle of my theological training and really stretch my ability to sit, hold space and counsel with the hurt and broken. To say that what I encountered in our time together triggered me, is an understatement!

(For the sake of anonymity, let's call this young lady "Jade") Session after session, Jade, would share with me the harrowing details of grooming and sexual molestation at the hands of an uncle. As with most victims of abuse, her predator was someone known to her. This person was privy to her living space, her safe spaces. He frequented her family home. She had to endure sharing meals and celebrations with him, and he even shared the responsibility of caring for her. Until one day his care and affection crossed the line, and he went from one who was to be a protector, to perpetrator.

As a child, Jade was forced to engage in sexual acts that no child should even be made aware of, all for his sadistic, perverse pleasure. He had no shame, and his audacity extended to him molesting her in close proximity to her family. Unfortunately, as is the case with most victims of sexual abuse, this would not be her only encounter with a sexual predator. Jade trembled as she stammered through the harrowing details of what she endured. Her struggle to reconcile her trauma to her faith, was evident as she spoke. To add insult to injury when she did summon the courage to disclose the betrayal, she was not protected or defended, but rather questioned and interrogated. In the ultimate act of betrayal and injustice, she was forced back into the arms of her perpetrator as she was encouraged to rather, *"Forgive and forget."*

How do you forgive what you can't forget? Forgiveness is vital for healing, yes, and we will unpack that later in this book. In counselling, we use the word "trigger" to refer to the intense emotional distress you may feel suddenly when you're faced with something that reminds you of a past traumatic experience. This is exactly what was happening to me.

As we progressed with sessions, I started remembering smells, and sounds and places. Thoughts and emotions that I encountered during my own experiences of molestation, at the hands of people I knew *and* people I didn't know suddenly came to mind. My own history is riddled with stories of abuse. I experienced molestation by males *and* females; I was molested by other children - some my age and others a bit older than I was. I was molested by neighbours, by two family friend's daughters who were supposed to take care of me – both of whom, were from my home church, by children at daycare, and by teenage girls down the street.

At some point our need for self-preservation kicks in, and I remember reaching a stage where I became smart about the sexual exploitation. I remember one instance, where I felt the grave need to ask a teenage boy to stop his fondling of me, by telling him that I heard my mom calling me. This was not true, but I knew I needed to get away from him, because what he was doing had started to hurt me and knowing what I know now, he was—probably preparing my body for penetration. By some miracle, my mom really did start calling my name. He had no choice but to let me go, and to let me go quickly. We were behind a house that was close to my house. He made me promise not to tell. Just as a side note - secrets and silence is what perpetuates most vices, and this act of depravity is no different.

One day I spoke up. I told my mom about my grandmother's friend who had been touching me inappropriately. It may have been his first time touching me, but it wasn't my first time being fondled, kissed, or touched, and it was most certainly not his first-time preying on the innocent.

My earliest memory of molestation is around 5 years old, but this specific incident happened when I was about 9 years old. He was an old man, a drunkard, and a pedophile. My mother told my father who dealt with the matter swiftly and heavy handedly. In that moment I felt protected, but that was short lived, because there were others, and I just didn't know how to disclose them.

I feel the need to make this disclaimer right here: my parents have always loved each other, and their children, very deeply. They weren't perfect, but they loved us fiercely and have always made provision for, nurtured, and protected us, to the best of their ability. The nature of predators is that they will find a way to get to your child. Please do understand that this was happening to me in the 1980's. In that era there were no "obvious signs" or even covert signs that your child was being abused. It was a time where people trusted that their brother, or their father, or their uncle, or their neighbor, would protect and not hurt their children. This especially true during apartheid, when parents of colour had to leave their kids with those they trusted to ensure that there was food on the table.

At a time when "it takes a village" was a trusted motto. If a child "acted out" or withdrew, they were not questioned, and their "feelings" were not examined. There were no classes on "good touch, bad touch" and that generation had no idea what it is for a child to show "dissociative behavior". All in all, there were no signs. None.

There were no helps, no "googling" on the internet on why your child was acting the way he/she was. So, when we say our parents didn't know, they really didn't know and they had no frame of reference to even suspect it. Today, there are tools and guides and helps, and social media is rife with what to look for. Parents are more attuned with their kids' feelings and behavior, and children's rights are at the center of the search to find, expose and lock away predators and groomers.

So, if you are finding it difficult to forgive your parents for "not knowing" what was happening to you, understand that they probably really had no clue, but it does not mean that they loved you any less. Yes, there are parents out there, who did know, and parents and family members who not only allowed it, but justified it, and for that atrocity, I offer my sincerest apologies to you, and I hope that with this book, I can help you on your journey through healing to wholeness.

I do cringe at how many times I've had to counsel a victim of molestation, not only through the initial trauma of coming to terms with having been abused, but because of family meetings that were designed to justify the actions of the perpetrator. In too many communities the stigma is placed on the victim, and the desire to avoid "shame on the family" is so overwhelming, that all most parents did was to call "family meeting" instead of reporting the crime to the police. I can't count how many times I had to counsel a young person who was sent to live somewhere else while the perpetrator enjoyed the freedom of their family home.

The sad reality is that a child experiencing sexual molestation, thinks that they are the problem. As a child, I didn't know that the burden of the blame lies with the perpetrator. I thought there was something wrong with me. I blamed myself and, for the most part, I was shamed into silence. In my counseling with Jade, I was confronted with my own rude awakening. The first confrontation I had with the reality of my own molestation was when I was around 22 years of age.

What I didn't know was that our brains are wired to save and store trauma until we have the emotional capacity to deal with it. The brain will literally block a memory to get through a traumatic event. Many counselors and therapists will confirm that sexual trauma is not always evident in children, especially at face value. Children who have experienced sexual trauma may still play and behave as normally as though nothing has happened. In these cases, their brain is keeping them from being crushed under the weight of the emotional turmoil.

Medical Doctor, psychiatrist and clinical assistant professor with the Texas A&M College of Medicine, Dr Darlene McLaughlin, explains how your mind may help you get through a traumatic event. According to McLaughlin, if the brain registers an overwhelming trauma, then it can essentially block that memory in a process called dissociation—or detachment from reality. "*The brain will attempt to protect itself,*" she added.

"Dissociation causes a lack of connection in a person's thoughts, memory and/or sense of identity and it's extremely common to experience a case of mild dissociation. For example, if you've recently gotten "lost" in a book or daydreamed at work, then you've experienced a common form of mild dissociation" - Quoted taken from "Psychiatrist explains how the brain blocks memory to help get through traumatic event" as published in News Medical. In more layman's terms, it basically means the mental process of disconnecting from one's thoughts, feelings, or memories.

But, getting back to my first confrontation with regards to the reality of my own experience with abuse, all I remember was, that I suddenly saw the faces of those who molested me; I came face to face with my own vulnerability in those encounters; the questions, and the frustration at not understanding my trauma was staring me in the face. All of this happened because of one my father's explosive episodes. My parents thought I was just having an emotional outburst in response to the current event, but every one of those horrific memories suddenly came flooding back to me. That was the first encounter.

The second, was triggered not only by Jade retelling of the events that had befallen her, but by the mental, emotional, relational, and sexual brokenness that had occurred after that. It was then that I was introduced to a more severe and chronic form of dissociation, that was occurring in Jade's life. Because of the sexual trauma Jade's had been subject to, and her inability to cope with it mentally, she was introduced to all sorts of medication and interventions. These were to manage schizophrenia, bi-polar and manic-depressive episodes. And even though she loves God, this is her life, and it is hard.

What has made this even harder was that, despite her courage in pressing charges against her perpetrator, he has denied any guilt or wrongdoing, and has attempted to use her mental illness as grounds to have the charges against him either dropped or minimized. To add salt to that very bitter wound, Jade also had the daunting and even impossible burden of trying to prove to those closest to her, that she was indeed, as a child, molested by the uncle that was supposed to protect her.

All the waves of trauma after trauma left Jade open, bleeding and vulnerable. She was already broken emotionally, her will was severely diminished and so the devil came for her spirit. Jade distinctly remembers the moment that the idea of lesbianism entered her life - it entered with a thought. Because she was so fragmented and raw, longing for a healing type of love, she allowed herself to wonder what the touch, affection and the love of a woman would feel like. She wanted to know what that would be like, so in an attempt at wholeness, Jade has chosen to seek the acceptance and love she yearns for in the LGBTQIA+ Community.

My confession is that my own sexual brokenness manifested in a silent battle with same sex attraction and loud entanglements with "bad boys". I became a serial girlfriend - I sought out toxic and dysfunctional relationships with the sole purpose of being anyone's girlfriend.

My battle with same sex attraction was silent because it wasn't something I really understood. My saving grace was the still small voice inside of me that would not allow me to explore this as an option. I already struggled with rejection and the thought of not being fully accepted into the faith community with this struggle would have crushed me. Thankfully I belonged to a community of mature believers who weren't afraid to dissect the difficult issues. I had a group of older women who might not have been able to verbalize my struggle, but they sensed it all the same. They embraced me and spoke life into my trauma and confusion.

The male mentors in my life were God-fearing and honourable. These men, by their example and exemplary relationships with their own wives and daughters, taught me what healthy attention looks like; they taught me to differentiate between appropriate an inappropriate touch, and the value of godly interactions between men and women.

The female mentors in my life exercised compassion and grace and taught me what a healthy, sisterly relationship looks like between women who honour God. They modeled godly relationships between the sexes. Pastor Bert Pretorius, the Senior Pastor of 3C Church in Pretoria once said something that rings true in what I call our awakening era. He said: *"Women, children and the vulnerable are only safe with men and women who love and fear the Lord."*

The fact that I was able to get so triggered, demanded that I rehashed the very foundations of my healing. I was reminded that I found my healing and restoration from sexual trauma in godly relationships based on the word of God and the empowerment of the Holy Spirit. I learnt the essence of womanhood from godly women and the standard for masculinity from godly men and what that should look like. My biggest desire for Jade, is to be to her what others have been to me.

Every young person who has been awakened too soon needs mature believers who will courageously and unapologetically speak to sexual trauma and brokenness. And not just speak to the fragmented pieces, and the suffering places, but to replace the anarchy within, with healing and wholeness. The kind of courage I'm talking about doesn't end with words but is sustained by *being* the standard we call the broken to; being who God has called us to be, created in His image and true to our calling. This is an army of people who are not perfect but have surrendered their lives to being perfected by the sanctifying work of the Holy Spirit.

Unfortunately, even in the spaces we try to make safe for the hurting, we have found a contingent of leaders who no longer fear God, who call themselves spiritual leaders but who prey on people instead of praying for people. These "wolves in sheep's clothing" pounce on any opportunity to exploit God's people.

It is true that one's true character is most transparent when placed in a position of power, and when greedy, unwise, and power-hungry men, place themselves over the vulnerable sheep that God has commanded to be loved, exploitation is the result. You see this when a leader is aware of sexual brokenness and sexual sin in the life of a gifted or resourceful believer but does not do the hard work of discipleship and accountability. The giftings and resources outweigh the need for spiritual intervention in the life of the believer. I've also seen leaders unable to correct sexually immoral believers because the leaders are guilty themselves. And their exploitation is not restricted to sexuality but is pervasive in nature and touches on every element of our humanity and spirituality. Unfortunately, there are some church communities that can't wait to exercise the letter of the law without doing the due diligence of reaching, teaching, and discipling the broken. On the flip side there are spiritual leaders who are not willing to minister to the sexually broken but would rather stand in judgement and condemnation. Both these types of leaders make ministry difficult for the rest of us who understand the assignment!

My intervention with Jade reignited in me the desire to see the chains of sexual trauma and sexual brokenness, broken off the hearts of those awakened too soon. I want to see those with sexual brokenness healed and restored in faith-filled communities that create safe spaces where believers struggling with sexual brokenness can disclose it without the fear of rejection or condemnation; where they can tell their story and know that they are heard and will find the support and healing they need; where grace is extended through sexual discipleship - the understanding of God's design and purpose for sexual identity and sexuality and uncovering the truth behind gender ideology and sexual immorality.

Then there is an awakening, which is unlike any other. This awakening happens at just the right time and enables you to walk fully awake and alert to God, to the entirety of life, with yourself and with those connected to you. It's the kind of awakening that empowers you to be present and powerful. This is your spiritual awakening.

Biblically, a spiritual awakening is not a waking from spiritual sleep but a resurrection from spiritual death. All people are born in sin and are spiritually dead. Ephesians 2:1 states that, before we knew Christ, we were dead in transgressions and sins. We cannot experience, understand, or relate to a holy and perfect God in our unregenerate state, nor can we enter His kingdom. Our need for spiritual awakening is profound:

"The god of this age has blinded the minds of unbelievers, so that they cannot see the light of the gospel that displays the glory of Christ."
- 2 Corinthians 4:4

The true spiritual awakening occurs not by some physical, mental, or emotional process but by the power of the Holy Spirit. One who is awakened by the Holy Spirit is recreated into a completely new person (2Cor.5:17; Tit.3:5; 1Pet.1:3). That new creation is characterized by a new heart that wants to please and obey God and live for Him (2Cor.5:9). He has been awakened to a new reality, one that centers on the Saviour who redeemed him, the Spirit who awakened him, and the kingdom of God to which he now belongs. This is the true spiritual awakening.

When we're awakened to pain and trauma, we run the risk of becoming disconnected and disengaged, and very often we blame God, or we run from Him. We then need this kind of awakening to reconnect us to God and to be empowered by His Holy Spirit. This kind of awakening has always been initiated by God Himself, as per

Luke 10:19 *"For the Son of Man came to seek and save (restore) those who are lost"* but He has also made provision for us to reach out to Him - Jeremiah 29:12-14(a) *"Then you will call upon Me and come and pray to Me, and I will listen to you. You will seek Me and find Me when you search for Me with all your heart. I will be found by you, declares the LORD, and I will restore you from captivity..."*

Yes, there's a call from Heaven to wake up to God, His goodness, His plan and His purposes. While the enemy tries to awaken us to a dark and wicked agenda, God wakens us to His glory. And God's grace and glory is not without effect (1Cor.15:10).

When we awaken to God we can rise up from every awakening that tried to bring us down, we can shine despite any awakening that tried to dim our light. When we awaken to God, He not only works in us but through us.

> *"Rise up in splendor and be radiant, for your light has dawned, and Yahweh's glory now streams from you! Look carefully! Darkness blankets the earth, and thick gloom covers the nations, but Yahweh arises upon you and the brightness of his glory appears over you!"*
> **- Isaiah 60:1-2 TPT**

Never could I have imagined that the premature and gruesome awakening I had encountered could be redeemed by and used of God, not only in my life but also in the lives of others; that God would do a work in me that could be transferred through me for the awakening of others to the love, grace, power, and glory of God.

The truth is that being awakened on so many fronts has left this generation in darkness and chains. We were too young to defend or stand up for ourselves. But now that we're here, now that we've been awakened to the light of The One, who laid His life down for us, Jesus Christ our Lord, we know our light has come and our chains have been broken. We must now walk in that reality.

"Take no part in and have no fellowship with the fruitless deeds and enterprises of darkness, but instead [let your lives be so in contrast as to] expose and reprove and convict them. For it is a shame even to speak of or mention the things that [such people] practice in secret. But when anything is exposed and reproved by the light, it is made visible and clear; and where everything is visible and clear there is light. There He says, 'Awake, O Sleeper, and arise from the dead, and Christ shall shine (make day dawn) upon you and give you light."
- **Ephesians 5: 11-14**

In my new-found spiritual awakening, I realized that I no longer had an obsessive desire to find love and acceptance in dysfunctional relationships. I no longer desired to be just "anyone's girlfriend", instead I profoundly was awakened to the fact that the journey to love isn't about finding the one, but it's about *becoming* the one.

chapter three
Betrayed With A Kiss

"No matter how loyal you are, you will still have some traitors. Betrayal is a part of real life. Jesus was a loyal friend and leader, but He had Judas."
~Dag Heward Mills

Betrayal is *not* for the faint hearted. Betrayal has the potential to obliterate a heart, rendering it unable to trust or love again. The thing that makes betrayal so potent and dangerous, is that it always comes from someone we love and trust. The severity of the betrayal is usually determined by the closeness of the relationship.

Jesus was betrayed with a kiss. Given the culture, it was not uncommon for a student who had great respect for his teacher to offer a kiss as a healthy expression of respect and honour. Judas chose the symbol of honour to deal the deathly blow of betrayal.

I think it would be safe to say that we have all, at some point in our lives, been betrayed by someone, or have betrayed someone. If you've ever been in a relationship and had your trust violated or violated the trust of the other person, you're probably familiar with betrayal, and in the context of romantic relationships, it's not far off to say that it was quite possibly *"betrayal with a kiss."*

For the purposes of what I am about to reveal to you, it is pertinent to note that a kiss can be symbolic of honour and respect, but can also be representative of intimacy, sensuality or even lust.

In this chapter we're going to touch on what we cognitively know but fail to walk out experientially and as a result find ourselves confused, ashamed and chained. I want us to critically review what we view as culturally acceptable, even celebrated and see it for what it truly is, betrayal. We know that we're living in a sexually charged culture, which at best pushes the boundaries God has set out for us in relationships, and at worst, it completely violates His standards for relationships, romantic and otherwise. What's scary is that for many of us, even though we know this we still conduct our relationships according to cultural trends, values, and beliefs. For instance, I've observed that generally believers would rather follow the relationship advise of an influencer or celebrity than to go to God's Word and seek His heart for our hearts and relationships. I used to be *that* believer. I've learnt that it's vital that we think critically, especially about cultures influence on how we conduct relationships!

This is why Paul warns and I know you'll appreciate The Message Translation on this, *"Don't become so well adjusted to your culture that you fit into it without thinking."* - **Romans 12: 1-3.**

We've become so used to relational dysfunction and toxicity that we become suspicious of anyone who conducts relationships God's way. I had a conversation with a university student, and what she shared with me was just the tip of the iceberg of how this generation views romantic relationships. She confessed that when it comes to relationships, there's a saying among her peers that goes, *"you don't have someone, you just have a turn."* This statement got my jaw to drop, but what broke my heart was realizing that this thinking has been planted by culture and is taking root in the minds and hearts of young followers of Christ.

When we do a God-thing, cultures way, it will always leave us disillusioned.

Are relationships a God-thing? Yes! As established in an earlier chapter, God is relational. God created us *in* relationship *for* relationship. God does not make this a secret. Thinking back on my own life, this spiritual reality was right there in God's Word. I just didn't take the time to study it, had I done so I would have been able to correctly handle and apply it (2Tim. 2:15).

God has a will, and He has a way of fulfilling His will, and when we do God's will God's way, we will have the healthy, godly, and blessed relationships He desires us to have. One of the side effects of not doing relationships Gods way, and trying to push our own agenda, and trying to get God on board with our plans, is that we become more susceptible to betraying one another. This is what the Apostle Paul had to say on this matter:

> *"It is God's will that you should be sanctified: that you should avoid sexual immorality; that each of you should learn to control your own body, in a way that is holy and honourable, not in passionate lust like the pagans, who do not know God; and that in this matter no one should wrong or take advantage of a brother or sister."*
> **– 1 Thessalonians 4: 3-6a**

Some translations use the phrase, *"that no one should take advantage of and defraud his brother in this matter."*

When we engage in relationships according to the culture and our own selfish desires, we cheat others out of the honour and respect due to them. What's worse is that we cheat ourselves as well. Based on the words of Apostle Paul, we are led to examine the difference between fraud (deceit) and betrayal: while fraud is any act of deception carried out for the purpose of unfair, undeserved and/or unlawful gain, betrayal on the other hand is the *"act of delivering someone into the hands of an enemy by treachery or fraud (deceit), in violation of trust."* – Rajen Patel.

By this definition, the two definitions go hand in hand. We betray by means of deceit and fraudulent behavior, actions, and intentions. When we do relationships our own way, we defraud one another and by implication we betray ourselves and others into the hands and chains of the enemy. You might say, Dominique these are strong allegations!? Well, dear reader, how we conduct relationships, especially as born-again believers, is an indictment against ourselves.

When we have given ourselves over into this sexually charged culture, we begin to filter life through the captivity of our chains, becoming more broken with every failed relationship. The prevalent culture of our day has so exalted sex that all of life is lived toward that end. They have taken it outside the bounds of marriage, where it has lost its sanctity, and is now a "free-for-all". Romantic relationships have become just about foreplay and climaxes. We have failed to put sex in its proper place, and as a result our relationships are broken and dangerous.

Jason Perry makes a statement that speaks into this. He states, *"Think of a person whom you consider to have beautiful eyes. Now imagine one of those eyes is the size of the person's head. Is that still a pretty picture? Obviously not! This, however, is the picture of what sex has become in our society. That which is beautiful by design has lost its appeal because it has grown entirely out of proportion to the rest of our lives - larger than what was ever intended."*

The problem is that sex has become the end goal of relationships. The benefits and blessings of sex, solely meant for marriage, have been cheaply given away in pseudo, makeshift relationships. These entanglements, "situation-ships" and hook ups, are devoid of commitment, and bereft of any form of responsibility or accountability.

CONFUSED MUCH

In 1997 Joshua Harris, a 21-year-old, unmarried Christian wrote a book entitled, *"I kissed dating goodbye."* Harris' book sold over a million copies and totally revolutionized the evangelical-Christian dating scene, and its impact was felt throughout the world. I remember how some of my friends would argue against these "far-reaching" ideas, and how some almost "lost their Jesus" about some of the radical and counter cultural teachings on dating and purity expressed in his book.

The premise of the book was to encourage young people to dismiss casual dating in favour of intentional relationships, and to embark on those relationships only with someone they could picture themselves marrying them in the near future. Joshua remembers praying, *"God let me write a book that will change the world."* Well, churches, families and thousands of single men and women embraced his book so much so that the teachings in his book reshaped how many young people viewed purity and sex. Fast forward 20 years later, Joshua Harris retracted his book and has apologized.

Wait! What? Joshua Harris released a statement admitting that he no longer believes in much of what his book taught. He stated that a major part of his advice was *"wrong, unbiblical, and caused damage"*. It dawned on me that he didn't just wake up one morning and decide that what he believed and spent his life advocating was erroneous, or blasphemous. He went as far as to admit that it *"contributed to a culture of exclusion and bigotry"* in relation to the LGBT community, and the condemnation of gay marriages. Harris admitted to an initial push back to "I Kissed Dating Goodbye" but he was encouraged to stand strong. However, after 20 years, his resolve crumbled as more and more Christians came forward sharing how they've been harmed by his teachings and the purity culture he perpetuated. Many said it made them feel ashamed and guilty about attraction and desire.

With all this controversy surrounding this book, I couldn't help but ask myself: *"did we even read the same book?"* Harris' apology, and later the retraction of his book with a documentary in-between was set off by a single tweet.

Elizabeth Esther
@elizabethesther

Replying to @HarrisJosh

@HarrisJosh honestly, your book was used against me like a weapon. But now, I just feel compassion for the kid you were when you wrote it.

5:36 AM · May 11, 2016 · Twitter for iPhone

Elizabeth Esther was not alone. The documentary, "I Survived I Kissed Dating Goodbye" chronicles similar stories of how "purity culture" and the teachings by Harris hurt and traumatized young people. The common thread of these accounts was that the "unbiblical" teachings expressed by Harris caused the fear of sex, even in marriage, crippled their ability to develop relationships with the opposite sex and for some of them, left them depressed and alone. One can't help but feel for those sharing their stories of pain and disappointment. This was Harris' public apology:

"In trying to warn people of the potential pitfalls of dating, it instilled fear for some — fear of making mistakes or having their heart broken. The book also gave some the impression that a certain methodology of relationships would deliver a happy ever-after ending — a great marriage, a great sex life — even though this is not promised by scripture. To those who read my book and were misdirected or unhelpfully influenced by it, I am sincerely sorry. I never intended to hurt you. I know this apology doesn't change anything for you and it's coming too late, but I want you to hear that I regret any way that my ideas restricted you, hurt you, or gave you a less-than-biblical view of yourself, your sexuality, your relationships, and God."

I read the book and my question is, can we with a clear conscience blame Harris for pointing us back to purity? Can we blame him for inspiring us to look to God's word for the standard God holds us to when it comes to our conduct in dating and relationships? Harris certainly cannot be held responsible for the evangelical church at the time, using his book as a "weapon" against young people to try and control their sexual urges and lives.

The outcry I witnessed in this documentary is as old as the Garden - we have our pitchforks ready to blame a young man for our inability to rightly divide the word of God and scourging him for speaking the unpopular truth of the word of God (2Tim.2:15).

If we must blame, let's blame celebrity culture! Accepting everything public figures say without thinking. Let's blame our own laziness to search God's word for ourselves. "I Kissed Dating Goodbye" was a reference point, inspired and referenced by Holy Scripture. If there was any point that one felt "guilted" or "shamed" that was an opportunity to seek the whole counsel of God. That was the place to differentiate between the conviction of the Holy Spirit, and self-condemnation. In joining the debate on "purity culture", we missed an opportunity to be like the Bereans, who were open minded and critical thinkers.

"And the people of Berea were more open-minded than those in Thessalonica, and they listened eagerly to Paul's message. They searched the Scriptures day after day to see if Paul and Silas were teaching the truth. - **Acts 17:11**

Some argue that Harris was too young to have written on the subject matter. I disagree. Understand this dear reader, *"Maturity in Christ is not measured by years. Maturity in Christ is measured by your obedience to the Word of God"* – Oswald Chambers. What I will say is that, without the Holy Spirit, scripture can become lethal (2Cor.3:16 - *The letter kills, the Spirit gives life*). It is when we are led by the Holy Spirit that we can understand God's heart on any subject matter. He empowers us to correctly handle the word of truth and apply it to our lives, even in romance and purity. In my opinion Harris only scratched the surface on God's heart for our hearts. We should always do our homework. We should always search the heart of God. Harris has since renounced his faith and no longer considers himself a Christian. My heart is broken. I sincerely pray for him and his family.

INTIMACY

It was Chicago based teacher and artistic director, Martin De Maat who first coined the phrase *"intimacy is... into-me-you-see"*. Some of our deepest desires are to know and be known, to love and be loved, to have purpose and be significant. We long for intimacy, to be seen for who we truly are and yet loved unconditionally. This sets us free to pursue our purpose and be significant without the fear of rejection or disappointment. But intimacy has a time and a season in which it blooms. If the conditions are conducive and both parties are intentional, intimacy will not only bloom, but flourish.

PsycheCentral.com defines intimacy *"as a positive, give-and-take cycle involving each person in the relationship. Each person helps foster the conditions — like warmth, confidentiality, and understanding — that allow them to be vulnerable and authentic with each other, increasing the closeness of the relationship..."*

Our challenge is not whether we date or not, our challenge is being intimate with people we're not sure will be committed to us or even be around for the long haul. People fiercely attacked Joshua Harris for being "unbiblical" in his attempt to point out the pitfalls of dating, and yet the concept of dating is not found anywhere in the bible. If we were to use the bible literally as a blueprint for romantic relationships, then suffice to say, we would all be headed toward arranged marriages.

Dating is not the enemy here, but pre-mature intimacy is; being "known" physically, emotionally, spiritually, and psychologically, before our time. Unfortunately, this era's model for relationships lends itself to pre-mature intimacy. Contrary to popular belief, intimacy is not just a physical thing. We think that just because we haven't slept with someone, we are safe from pre-mature intimacy. Here's the truth: you can know me intimately without laying a hand on my body.

We can take this a step further - where we enter into "illegitimate intimacy", this is when we're intimate with someone other than our spouse, without having to sleep with them. Ever heard of a "work wife" or a "work husband"? Wikipedia defines a work spouse as *"a special, platonic friendship with a work colleague characterized by a close emotional bond, high levels of disclosure and support, and mutual trust, honesty, loyalty, and respect."*

This is a person who hasn't necessarily slept with your spouse but knows them in a certain way, overstepping some very serious boundaries. This kind of intimacy can be classified as an "emotional affair". Notice I didn't say attraction; please understand attraction is not intimacy. Intimacy is knowing someone beyond what you see. Intimacy is not just physical, there are different kinds of intimacies.

Emotional Intimacy is most common. For emotional intimacy to take place there must be a level of trust and a feeling of safety present to share fears, hopes, disappointments and often difficult and complicated feelings and experiences. Moreover, having a sense that the other person understands - and accepts without judgment - your unseen and often dark side. In recent years, social media has been a catalyst in this area, making it easier for people to bare it all. I have been a witness to a 5-year virtual relationship a young person had with someone they had never met but chatted with online. It was the weirdest thing for me to see. She would check in and out every morning and evening, spend quality time, laugh, share, and even have phone sex. An intimate emotional bond was created because this young person felt safe and understood.

Intellectual Intimacy is my personal favourite. It is the freedom and comfort one experiences in sharing your perspective and point of view on matters. Each person feels free to share their independent thoughts, even though opposing, and has no pressure whatsoever to agree with the other person. A genuine respect and value for your opinion is expressed creating stimulating conversation. It's the connection you have with someone who cares about your thoughts, ideas and respects your thought processes and vice versa.

Experiential Intimacy refers to shared experiences which leads to inside jokes and is often expressed in rehashing private memories. It's also a proven fact that shared trauma experiences can intensify a connection. Often a girl and boy will bond over their love for rock climbing, or their interest in a certain activity and that commonality becomes the basis of their connection. They could easily become "best friends". But I dare you to find me any young lady who says it's ok for her boyfriend to have a girl best friend other than her. That's the power of experiential intimacy.

Spiritual Intimacy is built through shared spiritual moments with your significant other. Such as prayer, worship, bible study and is reinforced through common beliefs on spirituality and faith. Spiritual intimacy is expressed best in a marital relationship - I view it as the bonding agent of intimacies. I have seen, what many not-so-mature believers have mistaken for spiritual intimacy, cloud their judgement and wreak so much havoc. These young people sincerely believe that because they share word, engage in bible study and share spiritual responsibility that they are immune to the temptation of physical intimacy. They believe that that because they have "built their relationship" on spiritual intimacy that it *must* work, but they negate the fact that you cannot make your choices and desire for a relationship without the leading of the Holy Spirit and expect God to just fall in line with your plans. This kind of intimacy, unfortunately stains and taints their shared spiritual experience. When the romantic relationship fails, their spirituality and walk with God is gravely affected. When these relationships end, we have young people who are disillusioned with Christianity and their walk with God.

When we enter intimacy on any level prematurely, we run the risk of baring ourselves to someone who might not necessarily have the capacity to love and commit to who we truly are. This is high treason, the crime of betrayal by overthrowing the times and seasons as set out by God for our lives and relationships.

When we engage in pre-mature intimacy, we're not only betraying each other but we are betraying ourselves. There's a part of you reserved to be made known, handled, and loved only in marriage, pre-mature intimacy hands that part of you over to the enemy.

I believe there are beautiful lessons to be found in the animal kingdom.

Let's look at the majestic eagle. Eagles mate for life, but it is the female who selects the mate. Even though she makes the selection, mating will not commence until the male eagle has been tested. She does not test his ability to mate with her, - so she's not looking at "compatibility"- but his ability to be *her* mate. She's looking for certain characteristics, one of which is commitment. The female eagle will pick a stick, then drop it and watch to see if the male eagle will be able to catch it and she does this several times. Each time the male eagle catches her stick, she will find a larger stick, fly higher and drop it and watch. Should he fail to catch a stick, she'll fly away from him as a signal that he is not the male she wants to mate with.

This test can go on for hours, with the height increasing until the female eagle is assured that the male eagle has mastered the art of catching the twig, which shows tenacity and commitment. Then and only then, will she allow him to mate with her.

Lesson #1 - *Test before you trust.* Only until he passes the initial test can he move onto the other tests. Neither his flying skills nor speed qualifies him. What moves him along to the next test is his ability, resilience, and tenacity in catching the stick, no matter how many times it is dropped. What is your initial qualifying factor? A person's attractiveness does not make a good indicator for choosing a suitable partner. What "test" do they need to pass, that will allow them to move onto the next level?

Lessons #2 - *Never settle.* Each time the male eagle passes a test, the female eagle moves onto the next test. Should he fail the test, she stops testing, and starts the process all over again - with a other male. Just because someone is good *to* you doesn't mean they are good *for* you. Just because everyone else is in a relationship doesn't mean you have to be. Just because you're attracted to someone doesn't mean you have to be in a romantic relationship with that person. Did they pass the test? Don't mark down your test to match their inability to pass it. The female eagle will not lower her standard to fit the male eagle. As clichéd as it might sound, it *is* better to marry late than to marry wrong. Having criteria set out *before* you start looking for a partner gives you the opportunity to evaluate what you want. Understand, that what you are asking for, is not "too much". You are worth every single effort to win you. The female eagle doesn't settle, and neither should you!

Lesson #3 - *Intimacy is secured by commitment.* We've grown used to giving intimacy before commitment and as a result we've left intimacy at the mercy of regret. Commitment is what creates the sacred space for intimacy, to be all that it was created to be - raw, vulnerable, beautiful - an uncovering of ones' true self, without the fear of judgment or condemnation; without the fear of abandonment or rejection; a commitment to stay and love regardless. The greater the degree of commitment, the deeper the level of intimacy, and the height of that form of commitment, is a Vow.

THE B-WORD

If only I had a penny for every time I heard someone drop the word "boundary" without actually understanding its power and purpose in their own lives first, before it pertains to other people. I believe that boundaries are powerful and serve a purpose in our lives and relationships, I just find that instead of it being a symbol of honour and respect it becomes a list of do's and don'ts, sometimes even used as an excuse and a weapon.

Dr. Henry Cloud, acclaimed leadership expert, clinical psychologist, and New York Times bestselling author, has made major inroads in unpacking the concept of boundaries in personal growth, leadership, business and relationships. From his books on boundaries, we understand that a boundary is a structure that determines what will exist and what will not.

I concur boundaries are important, very important and almost every sermon, talk and series I've listened to on relationships included some teaching, encouragement, or challenge to establish boundaries. However, I discovered what makes sense cognitively doesn't always translate well experientially. Something almost always got lost in translation. The reality is that we have a natural tendency to try and push boundaries.

There is nothing wrong with boundaries, the problem is our inability to adhere to them. Our flesh is always going to try to see how close we can get to a boundary without crossing it or we'll try to see how far we can push a boundary before it breaks. The closer we come to a boundary the further we will want to go. You're going to want to peek and see, touch and feel, and experience what's on the other side of the boundary. It's a law of nature. I see this law at work in my flesh; I see it in my children.

My daughter will not suggest to me that she would like to hand her device in 30mins before the time we usually switch off devices in our home. No, my baby girl, bone of my bone and flesh of my flesh will get as close to device-down-time as possible and what I've noticed is that she even will go over her device time if I allow her to. A typical example of pushing boundaries to their limits, is watching people on the road. You see it that all the time, people who drive aggressively, they don't let anyone in, they drive on the shoulder, they literally sit inches away from your rear end bumper, acting in ways that we all know are not acceptable. Is it illegal for them to push so aggressively in traffic? No. Are they breaking any laws but honking their horn to get to where they want to be any faster? No. Did they almost bump into you? Yes, quite possibly, but *almost* is not a chargeable offense. They are doing just enough to hit the barrier of the boundary of driving etiquette, but not enough to be penalized and brought to task.

I hate to be the one to break it to you but even as we mature, even when we accept Christ as Lord, even though we're anointed with a special call from God we all run the risk of falling for the temptation to get as close to the line as possible. Sadly, I've counseled many who have crossed a line and it showed, in the form of an unexpected or unwanted pregnancy, and even when it didn't show physically, their hearts could not escape the chains.

This is why we have boundaries, because they're important… boundaries protect what's valuable and keep out what's undesirable, but boundaries are not sustainable without *non-negotiables*. The boundary is the *what*, but the non-negotiable is the *why*. Unless you establish the *why* to a boundary you will find that soon the boundary will become *non applicable*. This is the reason most romantic relationships start off right but end up so wrong, because the boundaries were not supported by non-negotiables.

A non-negotiable is something that is not open for discussion. A non-negotiable says that there will be no but's, if's or and's. And that no correspondence will be entered into.

Negotiation? Not even an option. If you want a solid foundation for your boundary to stand on, consider what your non-negotiables will be. Non-negotiables will give your boundaries more power in your life and relationship. When you understand your *why* you will have capacity for your *what*. But Dominique, aren't relationships about compromise?
Oh, for sure, but here's what I had to learn the hard way - as a child of God there are some things that you simply cannot compromise on. The reason I always found myself in toxic, dysfunctional relationships was because I didn't have non-negotiables; everything was open for discussion, manipulation, and compromise. So, boundaries were set up but crumbled at the first sign of opposition, seduction, or melodrama.

When I came to understand the power and value of non-negotiables my relationships - both romantic and otherwise - changed dramatically. I started to treat my boundaries with reverence and honour and so did others, because strictly speaking, a non-negotiable is a deal breaker. It is the deciding factor as to whether someone moves forward with you in a relationship or if it's time to cut them off. If someone tries to push your boundary knowing your non-negotiable, you have an enemy in your camp and not an ally. When someone recognizes your non-negotiables and takes intentional steps to respect your boundaries you've gained a true friend. Watch how they steward your non-negotiables; it says a lot.

A non-negotiable is not something you decide to establish when you're already in a relationship. No, non-negotiables are foundational truths, beliefs, and values you establish *before* you enter any kind of relationship. This might sound like a platitude, but if you don't know what you're standing for, you'll fall for anything. This is why being single is such a necessary part of your development and growth as a person because it's in the season of singleness that you discover and establish your non-negotiables.

I'm living proof that it's never too late to establish boundaries. I was well into my 20's when I discovered and established my non-negotiables. It started with prayer, careful consideration of what I believed to be true about God, my relationship with Him and others. I also interrogated my values and what I would like to see, not just in the relationship but in myself. I established a few non-negotiables but here are my top 5.

- God
- Sanctification
- Priorities
- Vision
- Work Ethic

I came to a point in my walk with God where if Jesus was not a founding member of a relationship, then unfortunately there was no relationship. I would not open myself to negotiation on this matter. I did not have the time or energy for missionary dating - that is dating with the hopes of converting the "bad boy" because you "see potential.".

There's a difference between going to church and *being* a part of the Church and this is where sanctification comes in. A lot of young men know the "lingo" and are fluent in "Christianese" but fail to live up to what they say.

Listen, non-negotiables will even change the kind of person you attract, it will upgrade you. I believe that men should not be afraid to have non-negotiables too. And because they're wired differently to what women are. Their non-negotiables will look different but are equally important. Non-negotiables have nothing to do with her outward appearance but everything to do with her character and heart.

Sanctification was important to me because of the call God had placed on my life to serve Him for the rest of my life, through ministry. Being in relationship with someone who did not value sanctification would only hinder the work of the ministry in my life. For example, because sanctification was a non-negotiable one of my boundaries was substance abuse. I was not willing to be in a relationship with someone who was a smoker or who drank alcohol. That would just be a trigger for me and keep me from focusing on what I believe God was calling me to do. Non-negotiables change the relationship landscape completely.

YOU ARE THE PRIZE

So, what happens when boundaries are crossed? Well, I've found that in many cases people just settle, especially women. The number one issue single mother's face when it comes to dating, is the reluctance of men, to respect the boundary on physicality. For single moms themselves, this "boundary" may also seem irrelevant because it's quite evident that abstinence was not a hard line before.

This is generally the mentality even in "Christian" relationships. This just breaks my heart. But I'm not surprised.

I've heard well-meaning pastors and leaders attach one's intrinsic value to whether you're a virgin or not. While this teaching is not entirely wrong, it's not entirely right either. And I need to be careful here because I don't want to downplay the absolute beauty of purity and virginity, it is special. Allow me to say that it should be honoured, not worshipped. Purity and virginity are not the same, there's a difference, which we will unpack as we go further along.

While I agree with a lot of what Jason L. Perry writes in his book, "How Far Can You go?", there's a questionable statement in his book, that left me somewhat dumbstruck:

> *"The more you're handled, the more you've been devalued. As a virgin, you are of greater value because you are in the original condition. That alone increases your value because it is increasingly rare to find a young person with that quality. To those who are looking for someone special, there is no better gift than being able to present them a life and body that has been kept in its original condition."*

I cannot help but cringe. While I understand and can appreciate the statement, it has the potential to become a weapon when used to devalue women based on their past, their mistakes or life before Christ. Our problem is that we use virginity and purity interchangeably. We assume that just because someone is a virgin, they're automatically pure. This is not always the case, and on the flip side we deduce that just because someone is not a virgin that they are not pure.

Here's my thought process. If my intrinsic value is attached to my virginity, then I'm not worth much. I've had 3 pregnancies; 2 babies and I've been pretty much "handled" in the past 12 years of marriage. There are simply too many dynamics to consider when making a blanket statement like, "the more you're handled, the more you're devalued." We run the risk of misrepresenting God's heart when we ascribe value by comparison. What we must not miss is that when we say that a virgin has more value there is a sexually broken generation that hears, "because you're not a virgin, you have less value."

We might not have said it, but that's what they've heard, and that's why they settle for anyone showing a little interest and that's why they stay in toxic and dysfunctional relationships with people who do the bare minimum. They conclude that because what they have, or what they have left, is not valuable, what's the point in even trying to preserve it.

What concerns me is that I've heard this narrative among self-proclaiming "high value" men, discussing what "high value women" are and should be, and the fundamental issue with this narrative is that men attach a women's worth not to who she is or what she brings to the table but what she brings to his bed. I believe that this narrative does not speak to God's whole counsel on our intrinsic value.

When I was growing up, I witnessed speakers, predominantly males, speak about purity, send a rose around the room and have each person smell it and break off a petal. By the time the rose got through the room it was in a state of despair, undesirable. And most times this analogy was gender specific; it was an object lesson for girls. Notice that when we speak of virgins, we generally are referring to girls, not boys.

I've observed that because an *incomplete teaching* we sit with a spectrum of "handled women" who have come to know Christ, who still believe that their value is dependent on their virginity or lack thereof. And here's the psychology of value perception - you will not respect, protect, or cherish what you deem as not valuable. This is true for themselves and for those who estimate their value. Women are not cattle.

This incomplete teaching has been used as a pass for virgins to get as close to penetration as possible and still "maintain" their "value" or "purity", perpetuating the misconception that they're of more value that those who are not virgins - a spiritual pride of sorts. And so, because virginity - not purity - is the prize, anything goes: - pornography, masturbation, oral sex, you name it, as long as there's no penetration.

Two extremes. Both harmful. Chains accompany both. Virginity is God-ordained, it is honourable and beautiful. It is how we should all enter marriage. I repeat virginity is God-ordained. We must be careful not to worship the created thing over and above the Creator. We must not elevate ourselves or others to God-like status or debase ourselves or one another because of an incomplete teaching.

Here's an analogy that drove me to searching God's word and heart for *"handled people"* like myself. I witnessed a speaker taking a R200 note which represented everyone in the room, we agreed that it had value, we agreed that we knew what its value was. We then watched how the speaker dropped it to the floor, stepped on it, picked it up again, dropped it to the floor again and stepped on it several times. Every time the speaker did something to the R200 we were asked if it still had the same value. The speaker then got serious about trying to diminish its value, he crumbled it up, jumped on it some more and then threw it in the bin. The speaker threw some more rubbish in the bin and asked again, "Is the R200 still worth R200, or did it lose its value?" By now we were all about ready to run to the stage to retrieve the crumbled and handled R200. But the speaker only chose one person. Then the proverbial penny dropped. There wasn't a dry eye in the room. We all knew that Jesus was the only one who can find us where we are and remove from us the sin that debased us, trampled us, and made a mess of the glory, beauty, and splendor we were created for. In that room we all realized we were image bearers, but unless Jesus lifted us, we would never realize our true worth. The speaker went on to explain that this analogy could never truly reflect our worth. I certainly thought that *this* analogy was better than the ravished rose. He explained that the value of the R200 was subject to other dynamics such as the economy, and what if that crashed? Could we then say that before we come to know Jesus, we're like a R200 in a crashed economy? But that wouldn't be completely correct either would it? And what about the value of the R200 in other economies? What about its value increasing or decreasing because of an exchange rate? We *could* say that living outside of the will of God for our lives and relationships effects our value and worth, but that also wouldn't be completely correct. The speaker then said something that I will never forget and ultimately became a game changer when it came to navigating dating and relationships. He said*: "The Cross is the only thing that accurately reflects our value and worth. What we bring to the table in any setting, but more specifically relationships, is what God thinks of us."* Dear Reader, you are the prize, and your value was determined by the blood of Jesus, and His blood in invaluable, making you priceless. When I perceived my infinite value, I started thinking, speaking and doing things differently. My non-negotiables, boundaries and expectations got an upgrade.

Here's what sealed it for me. The speaker warned us that there will be times that the enemy, or even our very own souls would minister to us and say that we're not worthy. Instead of the R200 analogy lift up the finished work of the cross and declare that you are made worthy regardless of what you feel or what others think of you!

"So I, the prisoner for the Lord, appeal to you to live a life worthy of the calling to which you have been called [that is, to live a life that exhibits godly character, moral courage, personal integrity, and mature behavior – a life that expresses gratitude to God for your salvation]."
- Ephesians 4:1 AMP

And so, I say to you, you've been *made* worthy by the precious blood of Jesus, now go and *be* worthy. You are the prize and don't you forget it.

chapter four
The Heart of The Matter

"Out of all the things that belong to God there is one thing that God will not take ownership of until it is freely given...that one thing is your heart."
~ Dominique Adonis

As children of God, we are taught to guard our hearts above all things. Why? Because everything we do flows from it (Prov 4:23). If our hearts are bitter, unforgiving, and selfish, everything we do will be contaminated with bitterness, unforgiveness and self. This literally means that the condition of our hearts influences everything we do, for good or bad, it could qualify or disqualify the most honourable of actions. A simple everyday example of this is as parents, we have the honour and privilege of raising the children God has entrusted to us, but even with all our best intentions, any bitterness that we still may harbor in our hearts toward anyone for any reason, that bitterness not only has influence on your children but access to their own hearts. Believe me, what is in your heart is transferable; anxiety is transferable; fear is transferable, embedded trauma responses are transferable. It flows into everything you do. And I do mean everything. Even though you love your child and raise them to the best of your ability, your child is affected by what's in your heart.

I have always found it quite ironic that we have insurance and take protective measures for everything else, accept what is truly important in our lives. Nothing gets put in place to guard, protect and watch over our hearts, and yet "all issues of life "flow from there.

Yet the instruction is clear, *we* are to guard our *own* hearts. We ought to guard our hearts, not *harden* it. Not hide, suppress, or ignore it, but guard it. We must protect that part of us that holds our motivations, feelings, hopes, dreams, and that filters and affects all of life. Our heart is central to the quality of our lives and our capacity to live it well. And in the same way our pursuit of purity should be at the heart of living an unchained life. It is purity and not good intentions that plays a pivotal role in us walking in healthy relationship with God and others. Purity may be the last thing one thinks of when one enters a romantic relationship, but purity lies at the heart of the matter for all relationships.

THE TRUTH ABOUT PURITY

The first thing we need to do is properly define what purity is. We've already defined what purity is *not* - purity is *not* defined by the fact that one's physical virginity is still intact. Before we delve deeper into this subject, I would like to state that purity, in all its forms, has been under attack over the last while. All the controversy, and the subsequent fallout we unpacked with regards to Joshua Harris' book "I kissed Dating Goodbye" is proof thereof. There's a train of thought that has gone as far as equating purity and the exercise thereof to legalism. Purity has been reduced to a set of legalistic rules and placed neatly in a box filled with distorted truths and shame induced pseudo-Christian doctrine known as "purity culture". The very mention of these words invokes the feeling that there must be something wrong with purity, or the way that Christians have spoken about it or defined it.

Purity Culture is a sub-culture of evangelical Christianity and swept like a wave across the church globally in what was believed to be the Church's response to the onslaught of HIV/Aids, Sexually Transmitted diseases, unwanted pregnancies, and the push for abortion that came with it. This sub-culture began in the 1990's and was seen as an attempt to ground sexuality in biblical ethics.

Joe Carter, in his article *The FAQs: What You Should Know About Purity Culture"* states that, *"'Purity culture' is the term often used for the evangelical movement that attempts to promote a biblical view of purity (1Thess.4:3-8) by discouraging dating and promoting virginity before marriage, often through the use of tools such as purity pledges, symbols such as purity rings, and events such as purity balls."*

Without giving my age away too much, I'm sure that there are some of my readers who will remember the "True Love Waits" movement. This was a narrative that was being pumped into schools and youth groups, across South Africa, and not by "radical Christian groups". In the late 2000's a dozen government departments, aid organizations and religious leaders signed an agreement with True Love Waits International to promote abstinence in schools within South Africa. The movement had already garnered much success across the United States, so they brought this model here. Within three months, over 4,500 South African students, in one province alone, made TLW commitments, stating that they commit to *"my God, myself, my family, my country, my friends, my future spouse and my future children to remain sexually pure until the day I give myself only to my marriage partner in a faithful marriage relationship."*

This is how South Arica came on board. It was an attempt to bring people back to God's design for sex and sexuality, and this is where, "I Kissed Dating Good-bye" by Joshua Harris gained traction. The stage was set to skyrocket his teachings on dating and sexuality, but we saw how that ended. It seems like we have an entire generation traumatized by the teachings of the purity culture. Natalie Collins, a critic of the purity culture zeros down the teachings of the purity culture to the following:

- Women are responsible for men's sexual sin.
- Women's bodies are something to be ashamed of
- Women shouldn't have sexual desires.
- Your virginity is the only thing of worth about you.
- Women don't enjoy sex as much as men.
- If women have sex before marriage, everything will go wrong.
- There's no difference between sexual abuse and sex before marriage.

And as you can see according to her critique and many others like hers, women bear the brunt of the teachings of purity culture, placing the weight of purity squarely on the shoulders of the woman. There seems to be a sense of guilt, shame, fear, misogyny, and hopelessness associated with purity culture. While the teachings found in purity culture started with the bible, it was not filtered through the Word and Character of the God of the bible. It was filtered through the emotions, beliefs systems, convictions, and condemnations of ordinary people; fallible, imperfect, and broken people. It could be said that purity culture and its teachings do not contain the *whole* counsel of God's word. It contains only one half-truth, and the other half human interventions, speculation, and condemnation. This is very dangerous, because as Benjamin Franklin so eloquently stated: *"A half-truth is often a great lie"*, and more recently quoted as *"a half truth is whole lie."* Anurag Shourie, Author of "Half A Shadow" explains why this is dangerous. He states:

> *"A half-truth is even more dangerous than a lie [because] a lie you can detect at some stage, but half a truth is sure to mislead you for long."*

Could it be that we have made the purity culture out to be something that it's not? The purity movement taught a God who gave us moral rules to follow but underemphasized His redemptive nature. It gave law but no grace for those who already broke that law, and no hope for those whose purity was taken from them by no fault of their own. It was a set of rules that claimed, if followed correctly and consistently, would bring us closer to God and ultimately bring us our happily ever after. When the desired outcome was not produced, and many found themselves in failed relationships and marriages, despite having practiced abstinence, they were left feeling disillusioned, lied to, and deceived by the God of that quoted text.

And therein lies our problem. Purity is not just a mere culture, it's more than a set of values we idolize and strive to attain. Abstinence alone doesn't equal purity. When we reduce purity to a man-made culture we must not be surprised at the shame and pain in its wake. Not so long ago I came across a Facebook post reducing purity to a culture, a mere value system. To see purity for what it truly is, you will have to see it from God's perspective. Purity is more than a culture, it's a standard, a non-negotiable, set out by God Himself. It's an ancient boundary line that cannot be moved. And if we think of it as nothing more than abstaining from sex, we miss the mark altogether and invite sexual ignorance and trauma to have its way with us. When we see purity God's way, it will create within us a desire to be pure and a surrender to the power purity wields over us. Let's break it down. Purity and holiness are twins, same DNA different personalities. If likened to a tree, it would be separate branches stemming from the same root. So, allow me to use them interchangeably.

To be pure means to be uncontaminated, undefiled, and clean. To be holy means to be set apart, separate, transcendent, and totally other. To be pure and holy means to be uncontaminated in who God has called us to be and to be set apart in what God has called us to do. These two words have the same Greek root word and demands that we understand their nature. Baseline... their nature is rooted in God Himself. My, my, my... Purity is not just something we do or don't do, it's more than a culture, it's who we are, and unless we are pure, we can have no part in God and what He's called us to.

> *"But just as He who called you is holy, so be holy in all you do; for it is written: "Be holy, because I am holy." –* **1 Peter 1:15-16**

Being holy is not always something we can get our minds around but watch what the writer of Hebrews points out.

> *"Make every effort to live and peace with everyone and to be holy; without holiness no one will see the Lord." -* **Hebrews 12:14**

God is very serious about purity.

> *"Dear Friends, now we are children of God, and what we will be has not yet been made known. But we know that when Christ appears, we shall be like Him, for we shall see Him as He is. All who have this hope in Him purify themselves, just as He is pure." –* **1 John 3:2-3**

You ever play-fight with a sibling or friend? And things start to get serious, and you realize you're not play-fighting anymore, all of a sudden, you're gasping for air, and you have the taste of blood in your mouth. Well with these scriptures there's a realization that we're not playing with purity, the fight is real. What the "purity culture" got right was establishing that purity is a God-thing. He initiated it, not us. He put it in place, not us. God demands it, the problem is we don't understand it, and we have failed to see it from God's perspective. So where does that leave you and me? The very thought of purity and holiness sets the bar very high for any relationship, and moreover a romantic relationship. How do we navigate dating, courting or the means you've chosen for finding a partner with purity being at the heart of the matter?

SET UP FOR FAILURE
The truth of the matter is that we have set ourselves up for failure by divorcing God's perspective of purity from God's heart towards us. We've reduced purity to a mere set of rules to be followed, a list of do's and don'ts and if you tried to *be* pure in the context of romantic relationships, you've probably come to the following conclusions

- It's hard.
- It's painful.
- It's unrealistic.
- It's undesirable.
- It's not for you
- It's impossible.

Think of the many times you tried to remain pure, to have your thoughts sets on holy things, or to not laugh at a dirty joke, or watch a morally compromising TV show or movie. Think of the times you were casually listening to music and suddenly realized that the lyrics were sexual and deviant, or violent and degrading, or how about the innocent kissing of your girlfriend/boyfriend, that lead to heavy petting and even sex. The condemnation that we feel when we fail is often so overwhelming, that we just stop trying altogether; we stop praying or stop going to church, stop reading our bible. If you mustered the courage to go to church, you stood there feeling numb or unworthy, feeling like God was touching everyone but you, that somehow the pastor was preaching directly to you because God had told him or her what an impure and unholy person you were the night before.

Here's the truth: Purity is impossible. True purity as set out by God *is impossible* to attain. It's impossible to attain *on your own*.

In truth, there are many young people who *are* saving themselves for marriage, or waiting on "the one", who somehow think that this garners some sort of righteousness on their part. They may not be sexually active, but overlook inclinations toward lust, or soft or hard porn, and think that because masturbation is not overtly mentioned in the bible, it should be "okay". Or, as we elaborated on earlier, with virginity vs. purity, there are those who stop just short of penetration. This may safeguard virginity, but not purity. There are many who have remained virgins but find themselves disillusioned when they get married. They finally have sex but don't enjoy it. They feel "dirty" or "used" and even sinful because they have associated purity with abstinence. Alternatively, there are those who might be fully aware of their inability to live up to the standard of purity that God demands, and so they've internalized their failure and have just given up the fight for purity, just going through the motions of church but are dying inside. They are the people whom Paul describes (2Tim.3:5) as *"having a form of godliness but denying the power thereof."*

It's a travesty. How do we go about dealing with it? We've outlined the fact that purity is a God-thing, that He initiated it and goes as far as to demand it but are now uncovering that we are unable to attain it on our own. This is a very frustrating conundrum to deal with. Misunderstanding purity robbed and chained me, as it has countless others. There's one scripture you might be familiar with.

> *"We know that the law is spiritual: but I am unspiritual, sold as a slave to sin. I do not understand what I do. For what I want to do I do not do, but what I hate I do."* **- Romans 7:14-15**

Paul gives us insight into his battle and struggle against that which contaminates and compromises our purity and holiness. This is the struggle of every believer trying to do the good they should in their own strength but who find themselves doing what they should not. Paul defines this as *"a law at work in us"*: that although we want to do good, evil is right there with us (verse 21) and in our natural unspiritual selves, we succumb to it.

Because of this struggle, Paul describes himself as *wretched* – A very strong word which means to have *extreme misery* or *unhappiness*. His inability to live up to the standard of God in his life caused him misery. Despite our best intentions we still do what we know we should not. In a state of depression and desperation Paul cries out by asking in verse 24, *"Who will rescue me from this body of death?"* And though he answers himself in the very next sentence, we must not think that revelation comes so soon. The Gaither vocal band sings a song called "Sometimes it takes a mountain."

These are the chorus lyrics:

'Sometimes it takes a mountain
Sometimes a troubled sea
Sometimes it takes a desert
To get a hold of me'

In Layman's terms; sometimes it takes a heartbreak, sometimes it takes loneliness, rejection, pain, sometimes it takes failure, for God to get through to us. Sometimes it takes the realization that you can't attain purity on your own to come to the place that God wants you to be. Whatever it takes, may we come to Paul's conclusion.

"Thanks be to God, who delivers me through Jesus Christ our Lord!
- Romans 7:25

This right here is the heart of God, our Father, towards us. Will God give us a standard and not give us the ability to attain it? No. God is not like Pharaoh who brought bondage with unrealistic standards and expectations (Ex.5:6-14). God is a good Father, who has a good plan and it's all for our good! So, here's the glorious liberation. God's standard for purity and holiness is impossible in our own strength; it can only be attained and lived out through Christ's finished work on the Cross and the Power of the Holy Spirit. God will not ask us to be and do something without giving us the power to do it. So, here's what you must know about purity.

Purity is a standard. In this day and age of compromise where everyone has "their own truth", our great and awesome God has been reduced to a "friend with benefits" deity. We've lost our sense of awe and wonder for the God who created us in His image. Now, we have made Him into whatever we desire Him to be - much like a genie in a bottle who will give us what we want if we rub Him the right way. If we pray, attend church, give generously, and read our bible. If we tick all those boxes that, without a contrite heart, is nothing more than lip service. Subconsciously we believe that if we "perform" and hold our end of the bargain - even without sincerity or true seeking the heart of the Father - then He's obligated to hold His. Our familiarity with God, really does breed contempt.

Songs like "I am a friend of God" by Israel Houghton, has further reinforced this familiarity with God. We sing it as "feel good" song and have placed ourselves entitled to that title simply by virtue of being in church and the raising of our hands but dismally failing to search out or to understand why it was that Abraham was called a "friend of God". Abraham showed his love for God through his faith accompanied by obedience. His obedience and faith were marked by his willingness to sacrifice his only son, to a God that merely just asked him to. Based on this, can we really call ourselves a "friend of God"? But still, we have the audacity to project our distorted view of friend onto God and downsize Him to what we can handle, a God we can control. As much as He is loving, kind, patient, and compassionate, He is also a consuming fire (Heb.12:29). Addison Bevere makes a statement fitting to our dilemma, *"A low view of God has always been humanity's undoing."*

I think many of us are more accurately described as an acquaintance of God, than a friend. Is God not compassionate, gracious, merciful, slow to anger and abounding in love? Of course, He is! But He's more than that as well. God's very nature allows Him to be both merciful and mighty, kind and just; Jesus is both the Lion and the Lamb. Despite this worlds propensity to downplay the magnitude of our great God we must never lose sight of the fact that God is Holy, and He has set His standard that we are to be no less (Lev.20:26). From the garden to the cross, God has not minced His words or made his requirements for purity a secret. Purity is God's standard, not ours. It's His measuring stick; it weighs our actions and every inclination of our hearts. And this is what we've been saying, right? It is a high standard. Unattainable. Throughout the Old Testament, God's chosen people tried, but failed, and failed, and failed again. Sometimes it takes failure to help us see that we can't achieve God's standard of purity on our own. He could have just told them from the beginning, but I get the suspicion that they wouldn't have believed Him. Year in and year out, they made the same sacrifices for sin, shedding the blood of a spotless lamb so that they could be pure and holy, and acceptable to a Holy God (Heb.10:1).

Purity is a disposition. Despite their best efforts, God's chosen people, could not maintain God's standard for purity. So, God the Son enters humanity by means of a virgin birth, to do what we could never do. He lives, dies, and is resurrected from death. He ascends to heaven and through all that, offers eternal life to every person who confesses Him as Lord, and believes in His name. In His bodily departure from us, we are then introduced to the third person of the Godhead - the Holy Spirit. When it comes to purity, we make the fundamental error of overlooking and undermining His death. Here's why we should never rush past the death of Jesus Christ; why His death should not only be acknowledged once a year, on a good Friday, but every single day of our lives. It's for life, the duration of our lives, and the quality of our lives.

Because the death of Jesus Christ was not only atonement, and the securing of our forgiveness, but it was substitutionary - Jesus took our place.

That means that a Holy God required a Holy people, but no law, rule, purification ritual or animal sacrifice could impart holiness and specifically purity. People could do holy and pure things, but they could not be pure indefinitely, they would always mess it up and disqualify themselves from meeting God's standard. So, God the Son, dies a substitutionary death, shedding His blood once and for all so that we could not only meet God's standard, but in Christ, you and I would be holy, pure, without spot, wrinkle, or blemish. Jesus not only died the death you and I should have died but gave us the disposition of purity and holiness that you and I could never attain.

I once counseled a girl struggling terribly with acceptance, identity, and purity. I walked her through how God sees her, because of the finished work of Jesus. I opened my bible and read to her what the Word of God says

"Once you were alienated from God and were enemies in your minds because of your evil behaviour. But now He has reconciled you by Christ's physical body through death to present you holy in his sight, without blemish and free from accusation." **- Colossians 1: 21-22**

This broken young lady suddenly found herself so overwhelmed with emotion; she could not believe that God would see her as holy. It was the weirdest thing to her. The Message translation says it best:

"You yourselves are a case study of what he does. At one time you all had your backs turned to God, thinking rebellious thoughts of him, giving him trouble every chance you got. But now, by giving himself completely at the Cross, actually dying for you, Christ brought you over to God's side and put your lives together, whole and holy in his presence."

In Christ, being pure is what is imparted to you because of what Jesus did for you. You couldn't earn it, you don't deserve it, and you're not entitled to it. It's yours because Jesus died for you, and this dear friend is a game changer in the fight for purity. The finished work of the cross makes the fight for purity a fixed fight.

Purity is a choice. Let's talk about the power of choice. Fundamentally, we always have a choice. Not making a choice is also a choice. While it is true that there are times when we haven't chosen pain, trauma, or a fight, we do choose our responses to them. What I've learnt in my unchained journey is that power is not intrinsic to the choice, the power of choice lies in the ability to choose. It is your ability to choose that is powerful regardless of what your choice might be. We have the power to choose. And choose we must. What's key to understand, is that purity is not only a standard and a disposition, it is also a choice; it's a choice that we have the power to make because of our disposition. Allow me to break it down for you: "Pure" is something we *are* because of Christ and "purity" is something we *experience* with every choice made by the power of the Holy Spirit. While the standard and disposition of purity is on God, the choice for purity is on us. We choose. I tried and failed at purity because I never understood that purity isn't just something that must be done, it's something that's already been done, and because of what's been done I can choose purity daily.

As a young Christian I always found the analogy of the white dog vs the black dog very helpful as I tried to navigate relationships and the standard of purity as set out by God. The analogy is as follows; it says that the dog you feed the most wins the fight. So, if you feed the white dog more, purity wins, and if you feed the black dog more impurity wins. But this analogy only helped me to a certain point. While it was helpful in that it inspired me to feed my spirit and starve my flesh, it wasn't completely accurate, the thought process of this analogy nullifies the finished work of Jesus on the Cross. Because of what Christ did on the Cross, the fight for purity is a fixed fight, the outcome has been determined. All we need to do is choose purity and walk in it. Our disposition has been wired to win every time. Feeding the white dog helps but it's our disposition of purity that ends the struggle for purity. We battle against impurity from a place of victory, therefore no matter how weak, tempted, or impure we feel, when we choose what Christ has already done, we walk in purity! When this revelation enters our hearts, Christ's last words on the Cross of Calvary - *"It is finished"* - hits different.

Purity is a standard, a state of being and a walk we choose daily and when we walk in what's already been done for us it becomes a lifestyle. Will we fail in choosing purity? Definitely! It is when we understand what purity is and what purity is not that our failure to choose purity will be accidental and not intentional. There may be a fine line, but the difference is huge.

Purity is a lifestyle. I wish I knew this sooner; I would have saved myself a lot of time, tears, and embarrassment. It's not just about not having sex or not watching porn or not touching yourself, but about how you live, from your thoughts to emotions, motivations, to your conduct; it's as much about what you don't do as it is about what you do. The standard, disposition and choice for purity touches every aspect of your life.

> *"For God did not call us to be impure, but to live a holy life."*
> **– 1 Thessalonians 4:12**

The more you choose it because of God's standard and your disposition in Christ, and not out of fear or ignorance, the more you will live it, the more it will become a lifestyle. A lifestyle takes intentionality, consistency, and time. Until I got the revelation that in Christ, I'm pure, my walk of purity occurred in jumps and starts. A Scripture that sealed this revelation in my heart is Hebrews 10:14.

> *"For by one sacrifice He has made perfect forever those who are being made holy."*

Two things are happening here, because of Christ's finished work on the Cross.

- You have *been* made perfect or holy as the context indicates.
- You are *being* made holy.

Purity has a dual reality, it's a finished work and it's an ongoing process. I was 21 years old when I finally understood what Christ meant in John 8:31-32 when He said, *"If you hold to my teaching, you are really my disciples. Then you will know the truth, and the truth will set you free."* What a liberating truth; that because of what Jesus did for me, I am pure, and that purity is possible by the power of His Holy Spirit!

THE QUESTION IS HOW?

And now we're here, where the revelation demands application. What does purity really look like, not only in the heart, but also in the life of a believer? I can tell you what it does *not* look like.

- It is not a legalistic set of rules.
- It's not a list of do's and don'ts
- It's not a book like Unchained or "I kissed Dating Goodbye" used against you to instill fear or anxiety around relationships or your God-given sexuality.
- And it's definitely not locking yourself up in your room.

I remember opening my window and readying my heart for my time of prayer before seeing my very first saved boyfriend. Up until this point, I was moving from one relationship to the next with young men who had no intention of honouring or protecting my purity. While I was very active in church and participated in youth ministry, I was still strongly attracted to the kind of young men your mother would warn you against - and not all of them were out in the club or on the street corners, some of them were in the church, sitting in the pews. Even under the anointed preaching of the word they would be premeditating their move on you, and I must confess that I was doing the same thing. I didn't know what it was then, but I know now I wanted to so badly to be their hero, their saviour. I call it the "Jesus Syndrome".

The Jesus Syndrome is when you want to save someone by sacrificing yourself to get them from "being bad" to "being good"; to bring about the change you think they need, so you sacrifice your identity, your calling, your family, your future, your relationship with God and your purity. You follow the delusion that physical intimacy with you will be the push they need to receive Jesus Christ as Lord and Saviour. And then you pray for their salvation for no other reason than to justify the mess you created by premature intimacy. Yes, that was me.

I remember praying for a certain boyfriend to be saved and sure enough he accepted Jesus Christ as Lord and Saviour, and in my prayer time the Holy Spirit convicted me of the Jesus Syndrome. As I felt my heart shatter, I instinctively knew that I had to break up with him. I knew that for God to do what only He could do in that young man's life, I needed to get out of the way. And so, I did.

A couple of relationships later I finally had a saved boyfriend and found myself in what was supposed to be a pure and sanctified relationship. Despite my best intentions it turned out to be the same script, different cast. Let me tell you, if it looks like Egypt and it smells like Egypt, you better believe its Egypt - different Pharaoh but the same chains. I was trying to conduct this relationship in the same way I did all the others.

The question was how would I live out what I already was? How would I keep myself and our relationship pure? How was I going to live up to what Christ had already attained for me? To the 21-year-old me, the answer was simple but radical at the same time.

> *"How can those who are young, keep their way pure? By living according to Your word."* - **Psalm 119:9**

Don't be misled into thinking that only the young have a struggle with keeping their way pure. This scripture is as much for older persons as it is for the young person - whether you're married, divorced, single or dating, this scripture is for you. It's fundamental to understand that regardless of your life station, there is no substitute for the application of God's word to lead and guide you into living a pure life. What is key, is to correctly apply God's word. Remember this same word of God can harm or kill if not understood and used correctly.

The reason we have so many casualties in the area of purity in relationships is because we've been given a diet of misinformation on the word, the will and the ways of God. It is the will of God that we be sanctified (1Thess.4:3-5), and we will find His will in His word. You will not know His will if you're not in His Word. The problem with this generation is that we've taken the "take-what-you-need" approach. There is no longer "The Truth", but there's *your truth* and *my truth*. We believe and adhere to what *feels* right and comfortable and have discarded what we feel is "not for us". Unfortunately, the word of God is not a buffet where we pick and choose and make things "optional". We've allowed it to become another suggestion on how-to, instead of our go-to.

The word of God informs us on the will of God, the Spirit of God informs on the ways of God. When you know the will of God but are not led by the Spirit of God, you can miss the ways of God. Allow me to explain and then give you an example.

So, God calls Abraham and promises to make him a great nation. - you can read the magnitude of God's promise in Genesis 12 - 15. As you read that portion of scripture, you will notice that it's not cryptic, vague, or hidden. God candidly tells Abraham what the end game is. What we don't really know is how, because Abraham is not as young as he used to be and Sarah, his wife, is way past childbearing age. Abraham laments that since God has still not provided him an heir, one of the servants in his household would inherit all he had (Gen.15:3). Based on the law of the time if Abraham died at that very moment, with no heir coming from his own loins, all that he owned would be passed on to one of his servants, but God assures him, that His promise will be fulfilled through a son that will come from his own body (Gen 15: 4).

It is later Sarah who suggests "another way" to "spur on the promise", when she advises that Abraham fulfill the will of God through her servant Hagar (Gen 16:2). You must know that by this time it had already been 10 years since God made the promise to Sarah and Abraham, and Sarah began to fear that they would miss the window of opportunity for Abraham's seed to still be able to take root. In her urgency and fear, she puts forth Hagar. Her plan may well have not been Gods design, but it was a normal custom in the culture of their day, that if a wife could not bear a child herself, she could assign the role to a servant who would become another wife to the husband. If the servant became pregnant, the child would still belong to the first wife, as the servant was her property. This was the only other obvious solution that Sarah could come up with. Abraham does as his wife proposed and what seems to be the right way at first - because Hagar conceives - turns out to be everything but the right way. God then needs to step in again, this time in person through three angels who visit with Abraham and Sarah (Gen.18:1-15), and they reveal that the way of God's will is through Abraham and Sarah. When we go about God's will our own way, we usually end up with Ishmael results. Ishmael represents the natural way (Gal.4:28-29), and we know that in our natural selves we are self-reliant and self-centered, prone to break things. And likewise going about purity our own way, results in Ishmael relationships. Ishmael relationships are brought about by self-effort, self-reliance and doing things our way. It seems to be the human way to insist on our own way even though our best efforts often result in brokenness.

> *"My people have committed two sins: they have forsaken me, the spring of living water, and have dug their own cisterns, broken cisterns that cannot hold water."* - **Jeremiah 2:13**

Doing things our own way does provide immediate gratification, and does feel good in the moment, and may even sometimes have immediate results, but lacks the capacity to hold what's good for us. Purity is God's will, and it works best done God's way.

I was pleasantly surprised to learn that God's way wasn't at all what I thought it would be. For a long time, I had a one-dimensional understanding of purity. Only when I studied God's word for myself and showed myself approved, correctly handling the word of truth, did purity come from a place of rest and trust in God and in His ability to empower me - one choice at a time. Instead of trying to suppress feelings, desires, and attractions I started thanking God for them. Instead of trying not to think impure thoughts, I started thinking of what was lovely, pure, and holy (Phil. 4:8).

I realized that the more you try to *not* do something, the more likely you are to end up doing it, so focus on what you can do and watch the enemy's plan come to nothing. I started taking ownership of my heart, purity and sexuality as prescribed in God's word. The more I focused on Jesus the more purity became a lifestyle.

"Keep your eyes on Jesus, who both began and finished this race we're in. Study how He did it. Because He never lost of where He was headed - that exhilarating finish in and with God - He could put up
with anything along the way; cross, shame, whatever."
– Hebrews 12: 3-4 The Message

The application of this scripture doesn't seem realistically possible, because, well, we are not Jesus. But the good news child of God, is that as He is, so are we in this world. (1Jn.4:17). You *are* like Him. His purity is your purity; His power is your power; His love story is your love story. Jesus' love story is that of the Church, His bride. We have so much to learn from Christ's love story. The bottom line is that purity is a mission possible, in singleness, marriage and in any and every relationship you form a part of.

A PURE HEART
David is affectionately described as a "man after God's own heart", despite having an adulterous affair and trying to cover it up by schemes and murder (2 Sam.11-12).

"After removing Saul, he made David their king. God testified concerning him: 'I have found David son of Jesse, a man after my own heart; he will do everything I want him to do."
- Acts 13:22 NIV

God makes this statement about David knowing full well that he would fail God - and this is key - the potential to fail is always with us, while in this body, and on this side of eternity. Do we then give up the fight for purity? No. It's a fixed fight remember - we may take a few hits, a few knocks and punches to the head and gut, but we keep going. What truly matters is that our hearts are committed to the

Lord and His process of sanctification - which is a purifying process the heart of every true believer goes through. And we must note that David's heart was not only committed to God, but it was repentant before Him. After David was confronted with his sin, he was truly contrite about his repentance.

> *"Create in me a pure heart, O God, and renew a steadfast spirit within me."* **- Psalm 51:10**

In Christ, God gave us a pure heart and by the power of His Holy Spirit it undergoes the lifelong process of sanctification. That is why this prayer never gets old. For as long as you and I live in Christ our hearts are pure positionally, and because of the sanctification of the Holy Spirit we will walk out purity experientially - but this remains our choice.

There are 3 habits we must develop if we choose to live with a pure heart.

Awareness

When it comes to having a pure heart, we need to tap into the power of awareness. Awareness is the state of being conscious of something. For many years I thought that sin-consciousness would give me the ability to walk in purity. I was wrong. While it made me aware of impurity, it only made me more prone to the impure. Our most basic instinct is to touch what we're told not to, to go where we know we should not, and to do what we know is harmful. It's human nature to gravitate towards what we focus on. So, if trying not to sin is the focus, guess what the outcome will be? When our focus is Christ-consciousness things change drastically. The more aware you are of Christ, the more aware you are of your need for Him. Isaiah is the Old Testament example of this. In Isaiah 6:1-5 he sees a vision of the Lord, high and lifted up, he sees angels all around Him and they called to one another, *"Holy, holy, holy is the Lord Almighty; the whole earth is filled with his glory."*

Notice that Isaiah's awareness of God and His holiness pointed out Isaiah's need for him. When we see God for who He truly is we will always see ourselves for who we truly are and more importantly our need for Him.

"Woe to me! I cried. I am ruined! For I am a man of unclean lips, and I live among a people of unclean lips, and my eyes have seen the King, the Lord Almighty." **- Isaiah 6: 5 NIV**

Isaiah needed God's intervention, but it started with awareness. Likewise, when we are in Christ and we become mindful of whom God is, what Christ has done for us and is busy doing in and through us we exercise Christ-consciousness. When we fix your eyes, thoughts, and heart on Jesus we begin the difficult but rewarding process of having a pure heart in relationships.

Accountability

I've learnt that while your walk with God is personal, it's not private. It impacts and affects all areas of your life and all the people in your life. Your walk with God is very public. And this is the same for relationships. While I strongly advise discretion when it comes to your life and your relationships, I do encourage transparency and accountability to godly authority and friendships.

I've counseled with young believers in steady relationships who thought that they did not have to give an account of their relationship because it was a private and personal matter, between themselves and God. They didn't want these voices – albeit their spiritual oversight - in the private workings of their romance. The more I tried to show them that accountability would build their relationship with God and with one another the more they insisted on privacy. Their secrecy was their undoing and left a trail of tears and embarrassment in the wake of their compromise and subsequent break up. Every King David needs a Nathan, and by that, I mean that every believer needs someone who will call then to accountability for a pure heart.

As their youth leader at the time, I had to release them from accountability. It was sad but necessary. If your leader or spiritual oversight can't hold you accountable, they can't cover you.

There are several reasons people refuse accountability, but the two most common reasons that I have found, is that they have either not fully surrendered to the Lordship of Christ in certain areas of their lives (Prov.18:1) and want to remain in that state or number two, they care too much about what people will think or say about them. They ultimately fear getting judged, hurt, or betrayed. It is not uncommon to be skeptical of accountability, however there is no excuse for not having accountability in our lives (James 5:16). Accountability gives godly voices in your life the permission to speak into your life and to ask the difficult questions. Those who hold us accountable have the freedom to inform us of what they see ahead, if we continue on the path we're on. Accountability also demands our humility.

Years ago, I mentored a young lady who had the habit of making sure that people knew she was accountable to me but still seemed to do her own thing, informing me of poor decisions after the fact. She would justify her actions to others with, *"but I told Pastor Dominique."* It became evident to me that she wasn't looking for accountability or my covering; she was looking for an excuse and a cover up. Accountability is not an information session where you update your leader or friend of what you have already decided to do. True accountability exposes blind spots, engages in courageous conversations and is not afraid to call for correction. A pure heart depends on it.

Acceptance

We underestimate the power of acceptance - the acceptance of what Christ did so that you and I can be pure positionally and ultimately walk out purity as a way of life. We strive and struggle because we think we don't deserve or are unworthy of such a great gift - and as you know, gifts can either be accepted or rejected. For years I thought that I had to suffer and prove myself to be worthy of purity and holiness.

The truth is, that *we are* unworthy and undeserving, we are, as Louie Giglio describes in his series – History - *"the traitor race"*. There was nothing in us to qualify us for the privilege and honour of being pure. We did nothing to deserve the beauty, joy and freedom found in

Christ taking our place and accrediting us. We played no part in it; all we can do is accept it. In our acceptance lies our victory.

- Accept that Christ died in your place.
- Accept that you did nothing to deserve it.
- Accept that because of Jesus you are pure.
- Accept that because of Jesus you are blameless.
- Accept that God has set the standard for purity.
- Accept that apart from Christ you cannot attain God's standard for purity.
- Accept that apart from the Holy Spirit you will not be able to walk in it.
- Accept that Christ-conscious living is how we approach purity.
- Accept that accountability is part of the purity package.

We must accept that we can rely and depend on the Holy Spirit to empower us to choose purity, one choice at a time. Purity becomes our lifestyle when our disposition becomes our manifestation, when our position of purity becomes evident in our thoughts, words, actions, and lives. This does not happen overnight! It is a process of awareness, accountability and acceptance that keeps you going and growing in the right direction. I know firsthand the frustration that comes with unlearning impurity. I remember how I would condemn myself for impure thoughts, because when you are born again, it's your spirit that is born again not your body, not your mind. This is why we must discipline the flesh and renew the mind. What I didn't know back then was that not all thoughts were my own, some were sent by the enemy. I also did not know that I could take captive every thought and bring it to the obedience of Christ. I thought that I was powerless and couldn't help my thoughts, that if they were bad, it meant that I was bad. What this usually does is start a cycle of performance driven actions and condemnation in the life of the believer, which is devoid of truth. God will not work in any place devoid of truth.

I also thought that feelings of attraction and desire for intimacy and companionship were wrong and therefore disqualified me from purity. One of the main objectives of this book is to point you to the Truth, so that you will know it, and that it will set you free.

PART TWO

chapter five
The Chase

"With the catching end the pleasures of the chase."
~ **Abraham Lincoln**

The chase is real. It owned me. I was addicted to the thrill of it all; I was in love with the feeling of love. I wanted the can't-catch-my-breath moments, the break-up-to-make-up dramas and everything in between. And with every chase I needed a higher high. The harder it was to get, the greater the return on investment. I wanted intensity so badly that I was willing to risk my character and reputation. They said good girls don't chase - so I went rogue, and I chased. I chased and caught him. He was the strong and silent type and the textbook case for what happens when the hunted becomes the hunter. There's this understanding that men are hunters and women are not and that by divine design we have assigned gender roles. Now it's not to say that there aren't exceptions but in essence we were created to function optimally fulfilling our roles according to our gender - not our assigned chores by the standard of societal norms, but God-given roles. I'm not talking about who does the cleaning, or cooks or makes the tea, but which roles we fulfill in answering God's call on our lives.

In my rogue experience, I became so blinded by the chase that I missed every single red flag. I had red flags of my own, yes, but when you become so focused on what you want it's easy to overlook all warning or danger signs. The reality was that we were entangled in an unhealthy attachment.

When we chase, we stop at nothing to catch the object of our affection, and in many cases, we are too blind to see that they're either running away or allowing themselves to be caught. Why is this important? Because reciprocity and connection are key in entering a romantic relationship. What we need to be considering is the art of pursuing not chasing. A pursuit is undertaken when there is a shared interest in a potential relationship, whereas chasing is one sided. Best-selling author, speaker and relationship coach, Stephan Labossiere does a talk on the 7 reasons a woman should not chase a man.

#1
How you start is how you will finish.

The premise behind this, is that once a woman has presented herself, made her intentions known to her love interest - and he's not tried to pursue her that she should note that her taking the initiative and driving the connection could possibly be counterproductive. If her desire is to be with a man who is not afraid to take the lead in all areas of his life and more specifically their relationship, then she should rethink being the initiator. Her "making things happen" could result in establishing a relationship dynamic that she cannot sustain. The result is that she will always be the one putting in the effort and having to take the lead. If she can sustain that, then and only then, should she chase.

#2
Men have a hard time rejecting women.

Generally, men have a hard time being the one to reject a woman; they don't want to be the villain in a love story. Stephan uses the example of a woman who extended a marriage proposal to her boyfriend, now there are many things to consider with this example, but it comes down to showing that generally men do not want to break a woman's heart. So, even though the man was not in love with his girlfriend he accepted her proposal to avoid rejecting and ultimately hurting her. It is interesting to note that this man confessed to Stephan that the only reason he married his wife was because he couldn't say "no". I too have had discussions with young men who had no intention of marriage but didn't want to break off the relationship because they didn't want to be the cause of pain for their girlfriends.

#3
Women tend to overlook red flags.

The thought here is that it is easy to become so caught up with one's love interest that nothing else matters, not even red flags. It is possible to become blinded by your own pursuit. But it doesn't end there; Stephan asserts that women who do see the red flags have the tendency to rationalize them. Women are known to make excuses for the deficiencies in their love interests' character. They fail to discern between reality and potential, and he uses a great quote to substantiate his thoughts on this, "women marry hoping that they can change their man, men marry with the hope that their women won't change."

#4
It's difficult for a woman to walk away from an unhealthy attachment because of how much she's invested.

Women who find themselves in unhealthy attachments will continue to try and sustain the relationship despite them being hurt or disadvantaged by the relationship. They do this because they value the resources, time, sacrifices and effort that went into the relationship. They are not willing to cut their losses but rather sacrifice themselves for the sake of return on investment. They'll stay in the toxic relationship believing that their sacrifice will result in a changed man. In essence, they will want to complete what they started.

#5
She might lose touch with her feminine energy.

Stephan points out that femininity has an energy associated with it, and masculinity the same. When a woman slides into a dominant energy, she will push a masculine man away. While it might be inviting at first, a masculine man will lose interest if she continues to drive efforts and is unwilling to allow him to lead.

#6

It's easy to get caught up in what she wants and totally overlook what she needs.

Not only do women often overlook what they need in the moment but what they need in the long run; needs, such as connection, character and the qualities that will build a strong and healthy relationship. When one is caught up in the moment you fail to see if you have what you need for the relationship to go the distance. This is why it's important to take a step back and see if there's alignment between what you want and what you need in the moment and going forward. Emotionality can hinder this process.

#7

There's a big possibility that the uninterested man will just drag her along.

Again, men typically struggle to reject women's advances, especially women who have one or two things going for them, such as resources or chemistry, or both. If he doesn't take the lead after the woman has done her part in showing interest, it means he is not interested. And yes, there are exceptions to this, but generally speaking, a man will not easily reject a woman he's not interested in and her continuing to chase him will cause her to be dragged along and used for what she can give him until someone else comes along.

Men and women are wired differently, and then we also need to take into consideration, our differences as individuals. Gender roles are not an indictment but rather an affirmation of our uniqueness, not only as men and women but as sons and daughters made in the image of God. Do we have roles as men and women? Yes, I believe we do but when we say that women can't lead or take initiative, we discredit the times that God has allowed or lead women to present themselves or to initiate a relationship (Ruth 3:7-14).

There's a difference between a woman in control and a controlling woman, just like there's a difference between how a woman pursues and how a man does. Our challenge is not who should or should not pursue but *how* we are designed to pursue. A woman presents herself; a man declares himself.

As women we make the mistake of trying to pursue a man - the *way* a man would. And men I believe, make a mistake when they pursue a woman the way the culture dictates they should. The key to understanding how to pursue regardless of our gender, is our pursuit of God.

It is in seeking God that we find Him and ultimately find ourselves. When we discover who He is, we discover ourselves, and our wants and needs get put into divine perspective. The pursuit of God trains and prepares us for pursuit of love. It builds our internal fortitude and capacity to not only *find* or to be *found* by the proverbial one, but to *be* the one. Many people have asked me if everyone has soul mate? And, what if they don't find "the one"? I've seen young people freak out at the thought that they could possibly miss the one God has set aside for them.

I will go into more depth answering the question on soulmates, but for now, what I will say is, if I knew then what I know now, I would have done a whole lot differently. I would have waited to be pursued and not rush into the chase.

OBSESSED

When it comes to love and relationships, ours is the generation that has fallen down the rabbit hole of obsession. And don't get me wrong, love and romantic relationships are good things but they're not the only things. There's more to life than falling in love. There's so much more to you than how attractive you are or who you're attracted to. Believe it or not there's more to marriage than sex. Trust me. But we don't see that in a dopamine chasing, euphoria driven culture. And the church is not exempt from the disease called obsession.

Obsession isn't just a catchy song on a TikTok trend. We underestimate the stranglehold it has on our hearts and minds. Obsession is defined as *"a persistent disturbing preoccupation with an often-unreasonable idea or feeling."* (Merriam-Webster, online Dictionary.) We're obsessed with love - or rather our understanding of love - so much so, that we miss out on life right now. We have become so obsessed with romantic love and as a result we've become obsessed with dating, or more correctly, our poor understanding of it.

What we don't get is that obsession has the potential to impact your overall sense of wellbeing and immobilize you completely. When you are obsessed, you become so caught up with emotions, desires, and thoughts that nothing else matters and everything suffers.

I was obsessed with love and wanting to be loved, to such a great degree, that everything of value suffered in my life – from friendships and family bonds to my personal growth and vision for my life – nothing was safe from the pervasive influence of obsession. I started cutting myself off from godly voices in my life. My relationship with my parents suffered. Allow me to explain something to you; our parents are not perfect and they're not always right but believe me when I say that parents can usually see a mess a mile off - and my dad saw the mess. But, because I was so obsessed, I ignored my father and every well-meaning friend and leader and now I have the scars to show for it. There are three things obsession will do to you if you allow it.

1. *It will distract you.* When you begin to fixate on a person or a relationship, you run the risk of being distracted from what is truly important. When I should have been focusing on discovering and developing me, I was distracted and it cost me time, money and too many tears. If the relationship doesn't bring you closer to God, and the goals you have for your life then you're dealing with a distraction. Distractions immobilize us and render us unable to move forward. The thing about distraction is that it will always keep you in cycles and holding patterns. You'll find yourself in the same place you were a year ago - no growth, no development, no goals, just the same mess repeatedly.

2. *It will create a false sense of reality.* When we obsess, we see things that are not really there, and are blinded to the

realities right in front of us. We become obsessed with the thought of someone and totally blind to whom they truly are. I love Tyler Perry's *"Madea"* movies. One of my favourite lines is inspired by a quote by Maya Angelou, *"if someone shows you who they truly are, believe them."* But it's difficult to see the truth when we see only what we want to see. It's difficult to see things for what they are when we create a reality to match the narrative we've created in our minds. When we allow obsession to control our choices in romantic relationships, we fabricate a picture-perfect image of the object of our obsession. Instead of seeing the individual for who they are, we see them for who we would like them to be.

3. **It will bring destruction.** Destruction is such a strong word, but it accurately describes what happens when we allow obsession to drive, not only our fantasies, but our actions too. I'm reminded of Amnon, the first born of King David, who "fell in love" and became obsessed to the point of torment, with Tamar, Absolom's sister (2Sam.13:1-22). The bible says that Amnon was so tormented because of his desire for his sister Tamar, for she was a virgin, and it seemed impossible to Amnon to do anything to her. Amnon was deep in the throes of lust and fixation - obsession.

In this case, as in many others, obsession has a tendency to spill over into entitlement, and that entitlement manifests in the evil desires of the heart. What started as Amnon "loving" Tamar for her beauty, soon became his desire to possess it. Obsession is almost always coupled with the need to possess, to take ownership of. Amnon was so obsessed and fixated on Tamar's beauty that he *had to have her*. He knew that the law would not allow him to have her in any significant way. She was his half-sister, which was incest and directly violated the Law of Moses as per Leviticus 18:9 *"You shall not uncover the nakedness of your sister, your father's daughter or your mother's daughter, whether brought up in the family or in another home"*

Amnon knew the law, he knew the right thing, but his desire and lust for her outweighed rational thinking. He became tormented at the thought of having her. I imagine that his mind was filled with thoughts of her every day. He probably imagined what it would be like to kiss her, to hold her, to sleep with her, and these thoughts so consumed him, that frustration and torment took over. What was once just admiration and love, became dangerous, and made him dangerous.

As the story goes, advised by Jonadab, Amnon feigned illness - he pretended to be sick, he employed deception to get Tamar close to him, so he could take what he wanted. He raped Tamar. He violated the beauty he once loved. He ruined it, and when he was done the bible says he hated her more than he had loved her.

"Then Amnon hated her with very great hatred, so that the hatred with which he hated her was greater than the love with which he had loved her. And Amnon said to her, "Get up! Go!" – 2Samuel 13:15

After Amnon's desire for ownership, and his entitlement to take what he wanted was met, his obsession suddenly dissipated, and everything he had loved, he now hated. The result was that Tamar was ruined and Amnon was killed by Absalom as an act to avenge his sister. There was such great destruction in the wake of Amnon's obsession, that not only affected him and the object of his affections, but the ripples were felt down the lineage of David. It can be said that the opposite of love is not hatred, its obsession. All obsession when acted on, whether in thought or deed, ends in destruction.

My unhealthy attachment ended in the death of my spiritual life. I was a child of God, my obsession at the time was not and he had no intention of becoming one. Open to it maybe, but his actions betrayed his words. And because I was obsessed, I was blinded to this reality, and created my own reality and as a result my love and passion for Christ, His Word and His Spirit died more and more with each willful act of disobedience and obsession.

DON'T HATE THE PLAYER HATE THE GAME

This very annoying phrase was first coined by Rapper Ice-T's 1999 song "Don't Hate the Playa". It became the anthem and excuse for every wannabe Casanova, wanting to relieve himself of any guilt of wrongdoing, claiming, *"Don't blame me, this is just how things work."* And is this not what we've made dating? A game? The problem with this game, is that there are no set rules, and the goal posts are always changing to suit "the playa". To quote "Lady Whistledown" in the popular Netflix series, Bridgerton:

> *"All is fair in love and war, but some battles leave no victor, only a trail of broken hearts that make us wonder if the price we pay is ever worth the fight."*

Our romantic emotional connections vary, from full on dating, to situation-ships, to hook ups, to one-night stands, to "friends-with-benefits", to "no-strings-attached", and the "I'm-not-looking-for-anything-serious" approach, the problem is that the outcomes often leave us devastated, and we need to ask ourselves why this is. Dating only became a thing at the beginning of the 20th century. Prior to the early 1900's, courtship was the way you met your potential spouse. This was a private and unemotional matter, - a process whereby a woman would have many potential suitors who were then shortlisted, by her family, according to their financial and social status until they found the most suitable match for marriage. Before this there was no such thing as young lovers going out on a date.

By 1910 the era of the "gentleman caller" came into play. A young man would follow the proper protocol for calling on a young lady, again, if her family invited him back after his first visit, he would be free to visit her again during the hours specified by her parents. But this era was short lived, and by 1920 the calling protocol was outdated. By the mid 1920's dating became the norm and with this came the change in relationship dynamics; the family and the home no longer determined the rules of engagement, now the gentleman paying the bill called the shots.

By the 1930's, courtship and dating were literally on the opposite ends of the same spectrum. Courtship had rules and formalities, and dating was less restricted and more personal. Courtship was seen as a fundamental part of a well-functioning society while dating was a fun alternative. Courtship only had one potential end, and that was marriage, dating presented men and women with several potential ends to their relationship. The focus of dating was falling in love rather than finding a society approved match.

By the 1950's "going steady" was the term used to describe an "exclusive" relationship. Dating was now more about youth culture, than about family expectation. Then, came the sexual revolution of the 1960s, which grew from a conviction that the erotic should be celebrated as a normal part of life and not be *"repressed by family, industrialized sexual morality, religion and society."* There were no more rules or formalities; self-interest and self-expression gave rise to the "hook up" culture. Each era was becoming more depraved and debaucherous then the last. By 1991, the World Wide Web introduced us to online dating - the remote practice of searching for a romantic partner on the Internet via a dedicated website, with the aim of creating real-world relationships. Now there are apps that show you, in real time, people within a certain mile radius of you, who are ready to just have sex with you. And it gets worse. There are multiple dating websites for married couples. Yes, married couples who wish to start an affair! There is a whole "community" that's open to every type of relationship so long as there's consent. One of the most famous sites for couples to look for an affair together is Ashley Madison.

The site unashamedly asserts on its homepage; *"Have an Affair today on Ashley Madison. Thousands of cheating wives and cheating husbands signup everyday looking for an affair.... With Our affair guarantee package we guarantee you will find the perfect affair partner."*
To say that this generation has options is an understatement. They have a smorgasbord to choose from - from your garden variety, heterosexual connection, to same sex, to multiple partners, to married partner, to one time partner, and that's excluding the connection type; friendship, relationship, companion, escort to an event, just sex, role

playing, Cosplay, BDSM and even professional Cuddlers. Whatever you can think of, is just a click away.

Before the onset of dating the paradigm was that love was as a *result* of marriage. Dating introduced love as the *prerequisite* of marriage. And now we're in an era of custom-made connections to suit our own depravity and preference - a whole lot of freedom and no responsibility. But, even amidst all of that, dating is not all bad - it can be a good thing, if done correctly. But who decides what's correct when it comes to dating, because there are no rules unless we create them; and even if we do create them who's to say we will obey them, and who do we answer to when we don't?

There are people "thriving" in relationships, who are still not able to define what they are. Facebook gives them the relationship option of "it's complicated" - and complicated it is. The best of the 6 definitions I found for dating is the following:

> *"A form of romantic courtship typically between two individuals with the aim of assessing the others suitability as a partner in an intimate relationship or as a spouse. The result of dating may at any time lead to friendship, any level of intimate relationship, marriage or no relation."*

You may ask if it's necessary to define what dating is, or more specifically what your dating relationship is. The answer to that question is yes! Because the definition of your dating relationship determines its purpose, and its purpose will give you the framework and guidelines you operate within. Without it you're in no man's land, you go with the flow, and by that, I mean, anything goes. As Christian Author Andy Stanley says, *"going with the flow will lead you to places you don't want to go."*

I've looked at the evolution of dating and have found that what started out one way has now morphed into multiple strains and variants. I found an article by April Maccario describing 25 variants of dating. Here are 10 of the most relatable.

- Casual Dating

- Platonic Dating
- Blind Dating
- Speed Dating
- Open Dating
- Swinging
- A Fling
- Sexual Dating
- Long Distance Dating
- Exclusive Dating

There's a lot going on here when it comes to dating and without realistic expectations and clear communication one can easily create room for confusion and disappointment.

Last year I watched an episode of Red Table Talk where Willow Smith openly confessed to being in an open or polyamorous dating relationship, which means having multiple emotional and romantic partners at the same time. How the times have drastically changed. What was previously considered offensive, distasteful, unthinkable, and scandalous has now become the norm, and a "necessary option".

Willow goes on to explain, that the reason she chooses Polyamory is because it gives her the freedom to create a relationship style that "works for her". She explained that she didn't just want to enter a conventional monogamous relationship just because other people said it was the right thing to do. When her grandmother challenged her on the sex issue, her push back was that the main reason for failed monogamous marriages is infidelity.

She gave an example of why polyamory works, stating that if you're not a person with a high sex drive but your partner is, it would be unfair to expect them to not have sex just because your libido is low. Unfortunately, yet unsurprisingly, that seemed to settle it for the ladies around the Red Table, leaving me disturbed and unsettled. But it doesn't stop there. There are more variants. The following are phases of a dating relationship that by nature remain undefined - once again creating more confusion.

- *Vibing;* this is described as attraction, a mutual sense of connection and energy. This is where there *is* "something" but *we're* nothing; we're just "vibing" or "feeling each other."
- *Friends with benefits;* this is the friendship relationship that caters to sexual favours and intimacy with no official romantic *relationship* status.
- *Netflix and chill;* simply means to watch Netflix with someone you're interested in with the expectation of eventual engagement in sexual activity.
- *Hook up;* To have sex with someone you don't consider a significant other. Usually, when said by modern youth it means to make out, and when said by people between the ages of 20 and 35 it generally means to have sex; and if it's an older person who says it, it usually means to simply spend time with somebody.

Online dating variants, however, have been getting the spotlight lately. Online dating allows us ease of connection; for example, you'll think twice about sharing your vulnerability and deepest thoughts or motivations with someone staring you in the eye, but there's a certain kind of carelessness that comes with not having to face the response of the person on the other side of the chat or direct message (DM). You are somewhat safeguarded from possible rejection. It also allows a false sense of vulnerability, in that you can misrepresent yourself, or develop a more confident persona, and next thing you know you're sexting and sending nudes. This type of "connection" can become addictive and keeps you at the mercy of your screen and the next "ping". Online dating also has its own language, and if you're a millennial you might recognize it. If you're not a millennial but find yourself "back in the game" for whatever reason, you would do well to familiarize yourself with these terms.

It could mean the difference between *playing the game* or *the game playing you*.

There are quite a few, but I've chosen the 10 most relatable:

- *Benching*; taken from sport when players are sitting on the sidelines; this refers to a person you view as merely an option.
- *Breadcrumbing*; the sending of flirtatious text with no intention to follow through. The difference between this and benching is that the person throwing the "crumbs" wants you to believe you're an option but they have no intention of choosing you. *Breadcrumbing* is often used by exes after a breakup.
- *Cuffing*; this is the seasonal pull to enter a relationship, usually in the winter months
- *Freckling*; this is the seasonal relationship usually referring to a summer romance. *Cuffing* and *freckling* can happen in an online setting or in person.
- *Ghosting*; the ultimate online breakup. This is the abrupt ending of all communication.
- *Caspering* is the soft version of *ghosting*; it's the slow fade of the relationship.
- *Cloaking*; If *caspering* is the soft version then *cloaking* is ghosting on steroids. *Cloaking* is when you're ghosted but then you're also blocked on social media platforms.
- *Haunting*; is when you've been ghosted but the person still continues to watch your socials and even like your pics and posts.
- *Pocketing*; is when the person you're dating actively keeps you hidden, also known as *stashing*.
- *Roaching*; Usually when you see a cockroach there are many more - this is the same principle. It's when the person you're dating is seeing or sleeping with multiple partners.
- *Vulturing*; this is when someone suspects that a relationship might break up soon and they start to position themselves to swoop-in, in order to date or sleep with one of the partners.
- *Hardballing*; this is when you're upfront with the person you're wanting to date. You communicate your expectations and expect the same from them. I like this one.
- *Whiteclawing*; this is when you date someone you find extremely attractive but they're very basic or boring.

So, I haven't been part of the dating scene for 12 years and research on this chapter made me feel so out of touch with the realities our generation faces on a daily basis, on all levels. This is overwhelming. Needless to say, my heart breaks for anybody navigating the relationship landscape, especially those doing the chasing. It gets crazier with every trend. Recently, I stumbled across a TikTok trend called Vabbing. This unconventional seduction method sounds more like an animalistic practice; it is the application of vaginal fluids to key areas on the body as a fragrance in order to attract the opposite sex. This is the exact equivalent of pheromone releasing. Pheromones do play a role in mating behaviour, but most studies on pheromones were conducted with animals. Despite there being no real evidence that it works, sexologist Shan Boodram wrote in an article for Refinery29, *"Regardless of if vaginal pheromones truly make a person irresistible or not, the fact that you think it does will cause you to act in a bolder, more confident manner."* Sadly, I'm not even making this stuff up. There is a literal frenzy in securing a partner, albeit for just a few hours or for the night.

If I'm honest with myself, I was no different in my attempt to chase and find what I thought I wanted and needed in someone even though it's an unhealthy attachment. I'm not even going to compare the devices and strategies because we so easily judge others and think we're better because we didn't go to "those" extremes. When I think of where I was in the chains of the chase, let me tell you, it's the same circus, the same monkeys, all performing for the same treat. I stopped at nothing. I obsessed, got distracted, created a false sense of reality, and opened the flood gates of destruction in my life.

I share on the chase for this reason; the common threads through every dating variant - from classical dating to polyamory - is the illusion of freedom, the poison of impurity and indulgence of self. This is a three-strand cord, and it is not easily broken. It will take a repentant heart and a complete renewal of the mind to break the chains caused by the motivations for modern dating.

We think we're free when we do whatever we want, and we think we can do whatever we want with our lives and the hearts of others. It's an illusion. Freedom is not doing whatever you want; freedom is defined by Merriam Webster as *"the quality or state of being free, such as: the absence of necessity, coercion, or constraint in choice or action. Liberation from slavery or from the power of another"*. In light of this definition and in the context of dating and relationships, we are only truly free when we do not hold ourselves to the mercy of every expectation and necessity to find a partner, to play this game by its given rules and agendas, or to fill the void and sting of loneliness with the careless and casual use of the heart of another.

Steven Covey says it this way, *"...only the disciplined are truly free. The undisciplined are slaves to moods, appetites, and passions."* And this statement is consistent with scripture - our freedom is sustained when we exercise self-mastery (Gal.5:13; 1Pet.2:16; 2Pet.2:19).

Motives are important; they will either validate or cancel your actions. When our motives are impure it disqualifies even actions that appear to be pure. So, when a guy love bombs, chats until the early hours of the morning and does and says all the right things but his motive is to dishonour purity in his own life and in that of his love interest, he disqualifies himself. To the men, being the ultimate "gentleman", to gain her trust so that you can have your way with her, is drinking the poison of impurity. You disqualify yourself (Prov.16:2; Heb.4:12; James 4:3; 1Thes.2:4). And this applies to the ladies as well. To indulge self is to tie a noose around your neck. The more you try to serve yourself, your wants, desires, and passions, the unhappier you become. I know that this statement is contrary to popular opinion. Culture and the influencers today are shouting for you to indulge *yourself*, to do what *you* want, to do what's best for *you*, to do what makes *you* happy. They are screaming immediate gratification. Have you noticed that even with this mindset we are unhappier than we've ever been? Our problem is swinging between two extremes. For a long time, we followed the extreme of "others first" and that got us stressed, frustrated, and tired, now we think that the opposite end of the pendulum – "self-first" - must be the way to go.

Have we considered a better way? God first is the best way. When God is given His rightful place, all else falls into place, both self and others.

> *"For whoever wishes to save his life [in this world] will [eventually] lose it [through death], but whoever loses his life [in this world] for My sake will find it [that is, life with Me for all eternity].* **- Matthew 16:25 AMP**

The principle here is that when we focus on what's truly important, we experience the life we long for; and this is applicable to our "chase" dilemma. When we seek God first, that's when we chase after the Lover of our souls, and we are promised that we will not only find Him, but we are found by Him and found to be in Him.

> *"But first and most importantly seek (aim at, strive after) His kingdom and His righteousness [His way of doing and being right – the attitude and character of God], and all these things will be given to you also.*
> **- Matthew 6: 33 AMP**

> *"You will seek Me and find Me when you search for Me with all your heart. I will be found by you, declares the LORD, and I will restore you from captivity..."* **– Jeremiah 29:13-14**

Everyone is worrying, plotting, strategizing, and chasing after things and people who cannot fulfill their deepest desires and the intimate longings of their hearts. But it's when we pursue God and all that pertains to Him that He will give us what we need.

CAUGHT IN THE ACT

I was prisoner to the illusion that freedom meant doing what I thought I wanted to do, and what I felt I "needed" to do. I loved God but I loved myself and my desires more and I know this because I served my self-interest over God's will for my life. Like the Galatians I used my freedom in Christ as a cover up for my impure motives (Gal. 5:13). I indulged self and justified my unhealthy attachment, an unequally yoked relationship - with a "but I can change him" mentality. Famous last words. RIP Dominique's spiritual life and relationship with God. God did not call me or any of His children to be sacrificed on the altar of impurity so that their unsaved boyfriends or girlfriends could come to know Christ. Here's what you must understand; your relationships are not mission fields. You do not have to compromise on the will and purposes of God for your heart, life, and body to win a love interest to Christ. You might have things and interests in common, but when you do not share the same essence and values where it matters most, you are unequally yoked.

> *"Do not be unequally bound together with unbelievers [do not make mismatched alliances with them, inconsistent with your faith]. For what partnership can righteousness have with lawlessness? Or what fellowship can light have with darkness? What harmony can there be between Christ and Belial (Satan)? Or what does a believer have in common with an unbeliever?"* **- 2 Corinthians 6:14-15**

The reason I did relationships according to culture and my selfish interests, was because Jesus was my Saviour, but He wasn't my Lord. I trusted Him for my salvation but refused His sanctification - and here's the game changer - sanctification determines how the believer does life and specifically how we conduct relationships. How I conducted relationships compromised my faith, values and calling, and as a result I continued in cycles and holding patterns.

And to reiterate, my holding patterns were:

- The illusion of freedom
- The poison of impurity
- The indulgence of self

I did relationships my way and it kept me from growing and knowing. I didn't mature. I experienced a lot but gained no real maturity; attained a fair amount of knowledge but no real understanding. So, when someone tells you that you need to be in a romantic relationship as defined by the world so that you can learn how to relate to the opposite sex, run! It's simply not true.

There are cycles and patterns associated with unhealthy dating variations especially when entered into too early. Here are some I discovered the hard way.

- *Identity Distortion;* Identity is a powerful aspect of everyone's life, more so the believer. If they don't have a fundamental understanding of who they are, and more importantly, *Whose* they are, it's easy to assume a distorted or false sense of identity. Because I entered romantic relationships from the age of 12, without a clear understanding of who I was, I became a chameleon. I took on the personality, mindset and value system of who I was in relationship with. When you don't know who you are, you don't know what you have and can very easily lose out on what God has for you.
- *Crippled Emotional Development;* The landscape of dating has become extremely volatile. When we are young, our emotions are strong and powerful – almost all consuming – but they are extremely fragile. There are patterns of emotions that usually come with how we conduct relationships in this generation and generally involve heartbreak, disappointment, resentment, anxiety, fear, depression, jealousy and unforgiveness. Without the right people and tools needed to navigate these difficult emotions, we can leave the relationship immature, crippled and in bondage to these emotions.
- *Trauma Bonding;* This usually occurs between a person and the person who abuses them, and an unhealthy attachment to the abuser is developed. This can go one of two ways:
  1. This can happen within the relationship where one partner abuses the other, usually when there's a huge age gap, or
  2. A bond between the trauma victims can develop. This happens when both partners were abused and within the relationship, they find comfort in one another and start to believe that no one else will understand them or love them the way their trauma comrade will. This

bond is escalated especially in case of sexual or emotional trauma.

- *Blurred Lines;* When there are no non-negotiable's or boundaries, the relationship becomes a free-for-all and this often results in insecurity and conflict. For example, when children know there are rules, boundaries, and routines they feel secure and safe. But the minute these key elements of development are taken away, you find an insecure and unsure child. When they're older, they begin to push the boundaries and critically think and act around the measures put in place for their growth and safety. This is the natural progression of human development. These healthy elements of human development are still the same in adulthood; when the lines are blurred, we are prone to insecurity and the anxiety that comes with not knowing boundaries.
- *Caught in the act;* What modern dating has done is to trap us with the notion that we can have the act of marriage without the covenant and blessing of God needed to sustain and support it. We want the perks of marriage but not the vow to forsake all others. We turn away the responsibility and accountability that comes with marriage as long as we can have accessibility, shared resources and illegitimate intimacy, among other benefits of marriage. We all want to love and be loved; we all want to be with someone who sees, hears and understands us. The problem is that we are willing to do anything, even if it means dropping our standards and settling. The sad reality is that while it might feel and look real, a dating relationship can never be a marriage and must not be treated as such.

I was caught in the act. I didn't know who I was. I didn't know what I had or wanted. I couldn't think or act independently of who I was in a relationship with. Being crippled emotionally, I couldn't move, grow, or progress because I didn't honour the times and seasons for relationships in my life. I didn't have the mentors or tools to deal with difficult emotions and so I did what everyone does where purpose is unknown – I abused myself and others.

> *"Where purpose is unknown [or ignored,] abuse is inevitable."*
> **- Dr. Myles Munroe**

It is important to note that the blame game did not serve me well when I was faced with the truth about the game and the player, I compelled myself to be. I remember crying out to God one evening asking Him to forgive me for my willful disobedience and to give me the opportunity and strength to surrender my heart and life fully to Him and His will. I was tired of the way I was functioning. I was tired of doing things my own way. I wanted God's way for my life and relationships. After that prayer, I wiped my tears and said amen.

GAME OVER

Every New Year's Eve our Pastor would deliver a prophetic word for the new year, and it was a highlight for our youth group, and especially for me. I wasn't where I was supposed to be with God, but I was enamored by the reality that God is a good Father and He has a good plan for our lives regardless of how bad the world, people and circumstances can sometimes be.

> *"For I know the plans and thoughts that I have for you, 'says the Lord, 'plans for peace and well-being and not for disaster, to give you a future and a hope. Then you will call on Me and you will come and pray to Me, and I will hear [your voice] and I will listen to you. Then [with a deep longing] you will seek Me and require Me [as a vital necessity] and [you will] find Me when you search for Me with all your heart. I will be found by you, 'says the Lord, 'and I will restore your fortunes and I will [free you and] gather you from all the nations and from all the places where I have driven you, 'says the Lord, 'and I will bring you back to the place from where I sent you into exile.'* **– Jeremiah 29:11-14**

I had reached the point where the light and darkness in my unequally yoked relationship were ready to face off, and it wasn't going to be pretty. I told him (my then significant other) that I wanted to attend the New Year's Eve service at our church, and I would like for him to go with me. Needless to say, a church service was the furthest thing from his mind – he wanted to be in the club, and he wanted me to go with him – and why wouldn't he want me to go with him? I had compromised before, and this time would be no different, right? Well, *I* said no, and *he* said no. So, I got my bag and asked him to drop me at the church service and of course, an argument ensued. Unfortunately for me, we were home alone, his mom was working the nightshift, and his siblings were nowhere to be found. I mustered the courage to tell him that I would be finding a way to the service without him, but as soon as I said that I was forcefully locked in his room, and he made clear that If I didn't go with him to the club I wouldn't be going anywhere. Was this what I really wanted?

My mind flashed back to when my father was unsaved and battled with alcoholism and would physically, emotionally, and mentally abuse my mother. I remember one incident when one of his friends had to physically restrain him, giving my mother enough time to pick herself up from the floor to clean away the blood and brush her hair back. This boyfriend never hit or abused me, but he didn't want me to go to church, something my father did countless times. He would come to our church services intoxicated looking for my mother. One time in particular he made such a scene – swearing and threatening to forcefully remove her from the service – which hurt and embarrassed me. Then I remembered the prayer I prayed a few weeks prior. This was my opportunity and God was giving me the strength to surrender my life and heart fully to Him. I made a choice that night and I chose Jesus. I walked into the New Years' Eve Service one hour late with yet another broken heart. I hate clichés but somehow this one hits different; sometimes God will allow our hearts to break to save our souls. Through Christ Jesus, God the Father not only saved me from sin and future destruction, but I believe that night, He saved me from myself.

chapter six
Boy Meets Girl

"Before you find your soulmate, you must first discover your soul."
~ Charles F. Glassman

Oh, how I wish I could write this chapter and tell you of how healed and transformed I was the day after that pivotal New Year's Eve service. Yes, God can perform miracles, instantaneously healing people from sickness, disease, and addiction. God can do in a heartbeat what it would take a lifetime for you and I to accomplish. But God didn't choose instant relief for me. The truth is I was broken, I felt damaged, and my reality was that the path God had for me to healing and restoration was a process – a long process. But true to form, I tried to heal myself with more relationships. Surely a relationship with a saved guy would restore me and give me an opportunity to redeem what I lost in all those years of serial relationships?

My reasoning made complete sense to me because doing things my own way was my default mode. What reinforced my thinking was getting a call from my youth leader. He shared with me, how he and the rest of the leaders were waiting for my breakup so that they could appoint me as a leader in youth, because they felt I had so much to offer.

While my youth leader's intentions were good, and it gave me an opportunity to engage youth ministry on a higher level, it also positioned me to scout the playing field and focus on my next target.

Dominique, don't you learn? Evidently not. I pursued a fellow youth leader and got caught up in a church loved triangle – not once but twice. It was a mess. I didn't want him to have to make a choice to be with me – I wanted to be the *only* choice – and when he finally got around to choosing me, I declined his request for a relationship; despite already being emotionally involved with him. Then a remarkable thing happened, I met someone who pursued me. Different. And it felt good. He bought me flowers, started picking me up from work. He wasn't my type, but he got my attention. We talked for hours, exchanged theological perspectives, our deepest thoughts, and our hopes for the future. I secretly wished that my fellow youth leader would pursue me like he did. He wasn't like anyone I'd been with before, and before I knew it, I was smitten; captivated by his pursuit. He then asked me to be his girlfriend. I challenged him and asked what the difference was between being a friend and a girlfriend? He looked at me knowingly, gently kissed my nose and said, "this, is a friend." He held my gaze and lowered his eyes to my lips and said, "*this,* is a girlfriend." He pulled me close, and suffice to say, he kissed me like I had never been kissed before. Being pursued was new to me and therefore I was convinced that he had to be "the one". The relationship escalated quickly. His mind, his conversation and affection were all I needed. Even our handholding was intimate. We were saved, loved Jesus, led youth groups, did nights of praise and worship, and prayer but our relationship started to look like every other relationship I had, slowly but surely. It was worldly, carnal, and selfish but we put Jesus on it, like a band aid.

My problem was that I was trying to use Jesus as a band aid on this relationship as if it was a wound, when in fact it was an infection - deep within the inner recesses of my heart. When we broke up, it felt like someone had torn my heart apart chamber by chamber. I couldn't eat, and I couldn't sleep. Sometimes I had to remind myself to breathe. I could literally feel my heart pounding in my chest. I would grab my chest at night and quote scriptures through clenched teeth. I cried every day. I needed to know why he didn't run after me when we broke up. I needed to know why he let me go. I wanted - no I needed - closure. For where I am today, I will tell you that I now think closure is vastly overrated, but at the time I didn't. I also realized that I was the common denominator in every relationship - unsaved and saved. The problem was me; I was the problem. To quote Taylor Swifts, Anti Hero: *"It's me, hi, I'm the problem, it's me."* This is a revelation that demands a response. When you are the problem, it's vital that you deal with you, and when I say I was the problem it's not a case of my identity but rather what I carried. I carried deep rooted issues that needed to be faced and dealt with, because these issues wouldn't just "go away".

I once counseled a young man who refused to admit that he was the common denominator in the situations he created, and then played the victim in. I could see it and would ask the leading questions to help *him* see it. Being confronted with the truth of his own doing was just too much for him, so he hooked up with a friend and left for another city. Two months later he was back home again, realizing that not even a thousand kilometres could separate him from his issues, because wherever he went, he carried the issue.

Deep rooted rejection, my history of sexual abuse and a misguided desire for love helped me create a distorted view of what I thought romantic relationships should look like. Add that to our postmodern culture and you'll have created a monster. And I took that monster with me into every relationship. What I didn't get and what I need you to get is that that your relationship with Christ is the most important relationship you will ever have. It is our relationship with Christ that determines the quality of every other relationship we will ever have. Christ is the blueprint that builds our capacity to have and steward healthy relationships with others. Notice how Jesus was always in relationship with others; with God the Father, with His earthly mother, His disciples, sinners, even now He's in relationship with His bride, the church, and with us. Everything you will ever want to know and apply in relationships is found in your relationship with Jesus. A few more "saved" relationships later and I was finally ready to surrender to making my relationship with Jesus my priority.

TIMES AND SEASONS
When your relationship with Jesus becomes your focus there are some mind blowing, life changing lessons you will learn, and the

lesson of times and seasons is one of them. God honours times and seasons. The enemy, on the other hand does not. The enemy operates in patterns and cycles, resulting in delay and stagnation or haste and prematurity, note the end goal is always destruction and bondage. He wants you in chains. The enemy has no desire to see you grow, be fruitful or successful. Times and seasons are so important that God does nothing without it. A healthy baby, a successful business, a godly relationship, healing, transformation, restoration, you name it, has a time frame attached to it. The gardener will tell you, plant too soon and the cold could damage tender plants, plant too late and risk missing the window of optimal conditions for blooming. Timing is everything. I've seen this reality play out in conflict, in crisis and in life in general; the right thing said or done at the wrong time manifests as the wrong thing, no matter how you try to justify it. I've counseled people and advised that, many times it's not a matter of right or wrong but a matter of timing. Understand this dear reader, the best things in life take time. The microwave, fast food, broadband, high velocity, overnight success mentality has duped us into thinking that we can have value *and* quality now - it's a lie. The difference between a McFeast Deluxe and fine dining, among other things, is *time*. It takes 30mins to conduct a wedding ceremony but a lifetime to build a strong marriage - again the difference is time. Take any industry, any area of discipline, any worthy cause and those in-the-know will tell you, vision, discipline, hard work and other fundamentals compounded over *time* resulted in their impact and success. Never underestimate the power of time and timing in your life and relationships. The right thing done at the wrong time can still translate into the wrong thing.

> *"But when the fullness of time had come, God sent forth his Son, born of woman, born under the law, ⁵to redeem those who were under the law, so that we might receive adoption as sons."* **Galatians 4: 4-5 ESV**

God the Father sent God the Son when the fullness of time had come because had Jesus been sent a generation or two earlier, the world would not have had the capacity, infrastructure, people, or materials needed for the mission. When you study the conditions for Jesus' incarnation you can only say wow!

> *"Yet God has made everything beautiful for its own time. He has planted eternity in the human heart, but even so, people cannot see the whole scope of God's work from beginning to end."* **- Ecclesiastes 3:11**

And here's the key, everything in your life will always be connected to a season. Some events, difficulties, victories, losses, relationships, even people are seasonal. To everything there is a time and a season (Eccl. 3:1-8). The turning of this key is dependent on knowing their times and seasons. When you know the time and season you will be able to either unlock or walk through an open door into all that God has for you.

For many of us, this is why there are some doors that will not open for us, so we quote things like *"while this door is closed, I'll praise You in the passageway."*

No dear, know the time and the season of the thing or person and watch doors open or walk past that door to the next. And yet not every doorway is meant for you, just like not every relationship is meant for you. Keys and doorways are powerful and should be handled with care. Doorways are symbols of access, opportunity, and entrance, alternatively they could represent barriers, rejection and exits.

There is a season where doorways you enter, or pass determine your destiny in a big way. This season is called *Singleness*. Nothing causes more confusion and frustration than this season right here. It's been demonized and used as a weapon to emotionally suppress, oppress, and shame a generation into small, closed minded and selfish living. We made it to be something it's not - it's feared, unwanted and rejected. Because of generational myths and mistakes, we do everything we possibly can to avoid and sidestep it. For some reason, we believe the lie that singleness is not part of Gods plan, when really, it absolutely is – for a season. we have bought into the lie that we are "incomplete", and so we find ways to find fulfillment, and fill a "void" that God had not deemed needed to be filled. Marriage is then seen as the Promised Land - a heaven on earth – and while this is

Gods desire for marriages, it becomes quite the opposite when entered with the selfish motive of escaping singleness. I love being married, but it's hard work.

This brings me to the perspective of those who have given into the notion that marriage solves everything. Can we correct the misconception that marriage is evidence of wholeness and holiness? Adultery is the rebuttal to that kind of wayward statement. Can we rectify the distortion that those who are single are burning with lust and are automatically sinful? A lot of single women are finding it increasingly difficult to find a sense of belonging in the church. The truth is, if they are not married, do not have kids, and they are no longer students, there is nowhere for them to go. Exiled to "Women's Ministry" they are often marginalized, left out and not catered for. It's a given that the male to female ratio in churches is quite unbalanced, with it often being 1 man to 4 women. With these odds, those who really wish to meet and marry a Godly man already within the church structure is greatly diminished, leaving them to be the pursuers and finding interesting ways to "getting noticed". The rest are left to find a suitable spouse outside the confines of the church. Unfortunately, without the validity of being married, often single women don't feel accepted in the Christian context. Well dressed, driven and articulate women especially, are seen as a threat to marriages, and thus single women are banished to a "no-mans-land", where they are "too old" for Christian messages on abstinence that is targeted and geared toward teens and, too single for messages about intimacy aimed at married couples. The churches solution has been to abandon them, or, like drug peddlers, push them onto any and every available man, as though her singleness was some sort of plague to be cured by the taking of any man that will have her. The church needs to stop. Well-meaning moms in women's ministry need to stop. A man's singleness is not a threat, an impediment or disability, a women's singleness shouldn't be either. Yes, we desire singles to be married, should *they* desire that, but it's not a matter of "the sooner the better", so that they're "not a threat" to marriages in the church or elsewhere, or so that they don't "burn with lust". There are many motivations and reasons why there's a push to have singles married off. In an article written by Katie Gadinni for Relevant Magazine,

Gadinni states that *"the pursuit of marriage wasn't just because women wanted to get married - some didn't. It was because marriage afforded women a certain visibility, even authority within the church, that they otherwise lacked."*

While it is true that marriage is Gods design, we need to stop exhorting marriage so much that it becomes the "preferred status" and even the qualification for active ministry. Marriage has become the idol to which we sacrifice singles, and the tool with which we demonize those who choose to remain single. Can we please stop making idols and demons of our relationship status? Singleness is not a disease and marriage is not a cure. Both singleness and marriage, when put in their proper place can be both beautiful and valuable life stations.

I've counseled with many people, especially young women who were struggling with the pressure placed on them to marry. Something as simple as the constant, *"when are you getting married?"* question, has caused so much shame and guilt on singles, as though they had control over this "very basic thing". These comments have left women especially, feeling like there is something wrong with them, or that they are unlovable. If you are single, allow me the opportunity to exhort you in your singleness; you are worthy you are valuable, and you are wanted. You are not unlovable, and there is a place for you within ministry and within the body of Christ. If you are a well-meaning mother within the church especially, please be cognizant of our precious singles. Embrace them, utilize them. These valuable people will prove to be an invaluable ministry tool, and under the correct mentorship, can change the narrative of the stigma surrounding singles in church.

Let's honour those who choose to wait, and are in a waiting period, because they are the ones who have taken up the courage to say: it's better to marry late than to marry wrong, or to marry for the wrong reasons. The divorce rate is too high, within and outside of the church. Let's help normalize singleness as a productive and full season, not as a problem to overcome. If I knew then what I know now I would not have been so wasteful with my season of singleness.

And yes, I had a season of singleness but my perception and exercise thereof were misconstrued. I also viewed the season of singleness as unwanted, to be feared, a necessary evil to endure. It felt like a penalty, almost like punishment, and at times, it felt like it was the last chance to do what I want before I get married and spend the rest of my life with just one person. Singleness is also not your season for rebellion, and breaking boundaries, and living loose, and bucket-listing all the things that "marriage would constrict you from doing" and doing them with great haste and all caution to the wind. I got it twisted. I focused more on what I felt about the season than what was true about it. Feelings are good and must be validated but they make poor leaders. Feelings are real but they are not necessarily true. Here's what is true about the season of singleness.

It's a Season - The season of singleness is just that, a season. It has a beginning and an end. Contrary to popular belief, you are in a season of singleness from the age of consent to the day you get married - the day when God blesses the coming together of two bodies and more specifically, the coming together of two hearts and lives. The beauty about seasons is that they have been set in place by God and therefore have a purpose.

> *"While the earth remains, seedtime and harvest, cold and heat, winter and summer, and day and night shall not cease."* - **Genesis 8:22 AMP**

The season of singleness comprises of many things from growing, learning and discovery but the overarching theme of singleness is a time of sowing. Anything we put time, effort, energy and focus into is an act of sowing. Even our thoughts and words are seeds and when we act out our thoughts and speak out our words, we are sowing. In the season of singleness, our habits, pursuits, goals, words, and actions are seeds we are sowing. Singleness is the season that prepares us for our next season.

It's a Gift - Generally speaking, a gift is not something we work for or earn, it is something we either receive or reject, and like traditional gifts they are wrapped. We spend an exciting amount of time unwrapping our gift, we squeal with excitement, shaking it, trying to estimate how much it weighs or guess what it is. Layer by layer we unwrap until finally we get a sneak peek. And if the giver knows us well, it's usually something we love. At this point we throw our hands up in the air and hug their necks until they can't breathe.

> *"Every good and perfect gift is from above, coming down from the Father of the heavenly lights, who does not change like shifting shadows."*
> **- James 1:17 NIV**

Singleness works the same way - we either receive or reject it - and because God our Father is a good father, and He knows what we need we can unwrap this gift with the full knowledge that what's on the inside will bring us joy. Singleness is a time of discovery, discovering God, ourselves, and others, and how we all fit together. The beauty is that our singleness is also the gift we give to others.

It's an opportunity - the opportunities in the season of singleness are endless. Opportunities for growth, capacity building, travel, and many times it's only in the season of singleness that we are able to take advantage of life changing and once in a lifetime opportunities that may arise. And as we know the opportunity of a lifetime must be seized in the lifetime of the opportunity. There is a freedom that singleness offers, to be able to take larger risks, and explore deeper things, and the bounce back is much swifter, with less baggage. The truth is that there are just some opportunities and life events that are best suited to be pursued in singleness. When you get married and have a family your life changes, your priorities change, your habits change - or *should* change. Your time, resources, space, and body are not your own. Your concern is for your spouse and family.

> *"I would like you to be free from concern. An unmarried man is concerned about the Lord's affairs - how he can please the Lord. But a married man is concerned about the affairs of this world - how he can please his wife - and his interests are divided. An unmarried woman or virgin is concerned about the Lord's affairs: Her aim is to be devoted to the Lord in both body and spirit. But a married woman is concerned about the affairs of this world - how she can please her husband. I am saying this for your own good, not to*

restrict you, but that you may live in a right way in undivided devotion to the Lord." – **1 Corinthians 7:32-35 NIV**

The mistake I made in singleness was thinking of it as living my life in a deficit, when in fact it was a necessary journey I had to go through; a season given as a gift to all of us. It was a time to fully concentrate on discovering my Lord Jesus Christ and who I am in relation to Him and others. Singleness was not just a season I stepped into when I got sick of the cycles and patterns of heart break, frustration, and bondage, and decided not to date for a while, no, even as a little child, as I was wading through my everyday connections with all those around me, I was sowing even in the unknown. Paul taught the church in Corinth concerning marriage and singleness that given the time they were living in; marrying was right but the person who chose singleness did better (1Cor.7:37-38). According to the principles we glean from Paul's admonition, it would be foolish of us to undermine the purpose and power of singleness. Can ours be the generation to redeem singleness? Can we restore the dignity and blessing of singlehood? Not over and above marriage but rather alongside marriage as a season of sowing, a very precious gift, and a divine opportunity to be, and do all God has called us to?

Singleness is not *not* dating or not being in a relationship with someone. The truth is even when you're seeing someone, you're single. Until the day you marry you are single. Actively dating or being in a relationship doesn't alter your marital status. You are considered single until you get married. This is evidenced by the fact that filling in any legal or government documentation, you still tick "single" regardless of your relationship status. Only few and far between, do those forms even give an option for "engaged", but even then, you are still considered single.

About the time I started on my journey of "no dating", a lot of other young people my age were doing the same thing and I believe this was because we were seeing that there was something grossly wrong with how we were doing relationships. I remember admiring the young men jumping onto this trend. And then, as with all things that are man-initiated, I observed a boastful attitude about these seasons of singleness – we were loud and proud. Some young men committed to 1 year, the brave ones committed to 2 years, but because our perspective of singleness was askew, we were setting ourselves up for failure.

After a few months I saw some of the young men fall back into old habits and ultimately backslide, and they were viewed as weak. Those who went the distance were perceived to be the strong ones and were idolized. Then something interesting happened, when the duration of their singleness was completed, they ended up marrying the very next person they dated. In one particular case it was a shotgun wedding, because the bride was pregnant.

I share this to say this, the season of singleness is not something we do to prove a point or enter because we're done playing games and have "become serious" about finding the one. It's so much more than a Christian trend; it's a time and a season assigned to us, to build capacity for our next season, whatever that may be.

NOT A MATTER OF WHO, BUT A MATTER OF YOU
The quest to find "the one" has eluded many a searching heart. I know because it's something I struggled with for a long time. I feared that I would miss the one person God had set aside for me and dreaded the thought of sabotaging the one shot I had at my "happily-ever-after." Added to the fear of missing out on that encounter, was the fear of "how would you know if he's the one?" What would the signs be? Would God show you? Would God tell you?

Youth ministries dealing with dating and relationships would encourage young people to make a list of all the qualities and characteristics they wanted to see in their future spouse and ask God to send them someone that ticked all the boxes. Thinking back, I just laugh. Some of the advice I heard was to conduct the date as an interview. A date was seen as an opportunity to gather as much information about the person as possible to gauge if he or she was possibly the one. The challenge with that, is that a date or dating doesn't always offer us enough time to see whether the answers to the questions we ask are honest and aligned to who the person really is, because let's face it, a date and its many variants can be used as a show room to put your best foot forward. Everything about how we date is set up in such a way as to present the best self and to get what we want in the shortest possible time. It's all about motives and instant gratification. It's when we accept our single season, for what it truly is, that we discover that it's not a matter of who the one is but rather who you are, and second to that, it's about you becoming the one you would want to spend the rest of your life with. The person you're becoming is who you will have to live with for the rest of your life, whether you're single or married. Let's put it this way, a husband or a wife can leave tomorrow but you can't walk out on you. So, in your season of singleness focus on you not who. Allow me to shake things up for you a bit about the legendary "one" for you. The "one" is not some mystical magical person that appears when you have done all the right things; the "one" is the person you choose. I know, it sounds somewhat unspiritual, but in truth, God will not make any decision for us. Can He lead us? Of course! Will He guide us, show and reveal things to us, if we allow Him to but we have free will and God will not overstep that boundary. The onus is on us to make an informed and wise decision concerning who will be our One. It is when we allow God into our decision-making process that He will lead and guide us in the way that we should go.

We must not be so foolish into thinking that we don't have a choice in the matter. The abdication of responsibility is this generation's downfall. The first thing Adam did when he disobeyed God is blame God for giving him the woman, Eve. Eve then follows suit and blames the serpent. Don't do that.

> *"Then the man and his wife heard the sound of the Lord God as he was walking in the garden in the cool of the day, and they hid from the Lord God among the trees of the garden. But the Lord God called to the man, "Where are you?" He answered, "I heard you in the garden, and I was afraid because I was naked; so I hid." And he said, "Who told you that you were naked? Have you eaten from the tree that I commanded you not to eat from?" The man said, "The woman you put here with me – she gave me some fruit from*

the tree, and I ate it." Then the Lord God said to the woman, "What is this you have done?" The woman said, "The serpent deceived me, and I ate." -
Genesis 3: 8-13

Own your decision and the responsibility that comes with your choice. Any two people in this world can be "the one" for one another regardless of their background, ethnicity, personalities and all the other measurements we use to determine compatibility. The ability to do this lies in God's ability to bond them.

When two people are in Christ, rooted and established and Christ is in them, purifying and sanctifying them, they will be the one for and to one another. This is why your choice of life partner is key – it's pivotal – and should not be entered into lightly, but again *who* should not be your focus. When you focus on you and all that pertains to you, you will build capacity, wisdom and insight when making your decision for "who".

WHEN GOD DIRECTS YOUR LOVE STORY

I messed up my self-proclaimed season of singleness because I didn't understand its purpose and power. I thought that not dating or engaging the opposite sex was the definition of a "single season". My motivations were completely out of alignment with the will of God for my life; first I tried to self-heal by immersing myself in relationships that didn't work, then I tried self-healing by completely cutting relationships off. And here's the lesson in my mistake, the very thing you're trying not to do, becomes the very thing that you do. So, I tried not to do relationships but wherever I turned it was right there. And so began the cycle of guilt and shame even in my so-called season of singleness. Paul helps us make sense of this conundrum, which is the Christian life, in the book of Romans. Let's rehash the scripture used in chapter 4.

"I do not understand what I do. For what I want to do I do not do, but what I hate I do." – **Romans 7:15 NIV**

The context of this scripture is that Paul is teaching on the power of sin and the law; he states that the more he tries not to sin, that's exactly what he ends up doing. The principle is this – the more you focus on the negative the more you will step into it. Paul paints a very grim picture, leaving one almost hopeless about the struggle between what you want to do and what you do not want to do, but decides to change his focus. Change your focus. I changed mine. Like Paul, I came to the end of myself! It didn't happen overnight, but there was a moment when I admitted to myself that I couldn't heal myself, I couldn't restore or redeem myself. I needed help.

"I've tried everything and nothing helps. I'm at the end of my rope. Is there no one who can do anything for me? Isn't that the real question? The answer, thank God, is that Jesus Christ can and does. He acted to set things right in this life of contradictions where I want to serve God with all my heart and mind, but am pulled by the influence of sin to do something totally different." **– Romans 7:24-25 The Message**

I was in my final year of bible school, sitting on a bed in the home of a family that took me in so that I could do ministry in a community I felt called to serve. I entered into a sweet time of intimate worship with the Lord, and almost without thinking, I asked Him for a word concerning my future husband. Before I could stop the words, they were out of my mouth. I cannot explain to you why I felt apprehensive to ask for a word concerning him – should that not be our disposition, knowing that our Father knows our future and watches over His word to perform it? (Jer.1:12). Should we not allow Him to speak about our future, unknown to us, but known to Him?

I will never forget what I sensed God saying. It was inspired by Psalm 92:12, which says, *"The righteous shall flourish like a palm tree, he shall grow like a cedar in Lebanon."* I grabbed my pen and journaled His promise to me.

"He will be like a palm tree, firm and steady. Though the winds of life blow hard against him, he will remain standing. He will be evergreen, loving you all the days of his life, but give him time, he's still growing and so are you."

I know, I said that we choose the one, and that God will not make the choice for us, but the beauty in it is that God knows the end from the beginning (Isaiah 46:10) and in His foreknowledge of our lives and choices He is able to give us a word we can hold onto when we ask Him. I wrote what I sensed was my promise and I closed my bible and journal and said amen. Little did I know that my journey with the one I would choose started 2 years prior to this moment. I was in my first year of bible school and I remember we were getting ready to minister at a local church. I had no desire to attend the service because it was a very conservative church, and I didn't feel like wearing a skirt. I lied and said I wasn't feeling well, but, The Holy Spirit, true to His nature, convicted me and I asked God to forgive me. He did, and I confirmed with our student leader that I would be in attendance. I entered the church and immediately noticed the "sound guy", and the reason I did was because he had the coolest hairstyle. For now, let's just call him *Sound Guy*.

Without thinking much of it, I greeted him and gave him my CD because I was ministering in dance that morning. Halfway through the service I felt led to change my song selection and I located him and requested the song change. After the service I forgot to collect my CD, but he didn't, *Sound Guy* made sure I got my CD back, and thereafter we were whisked to another location to enjoy the meal the church had prepared for us. Midway through a delicious lunch I got the strange feeling that someone was watching me, I followed the direction I sensed the gaze coming from and there, as large as life was *Sound Guy*. I felt my cheeks go warm and my ears followed suit with a tingle. I looked away and was immediately overwhelmed with a sense of self consciousness. I thought that I may just be imagining things, so I stole a glance, and no it was not my imagination – our eyes met again. My head was saying *"no, not again"*, but everything else was saying *"here we go again"*. I felt a bit annoyed, because while I liked the attention, I didn't like feeling "shy"; I didn't like feeling like a juvenile 12-year-old, so I decided to take control of the situation. I looked back at him, and resolved not to look away, I was going to own the stare down – talk about being 12 again…

Not long after, I was compelled to look away. I seemed to have met my match. The room got small very fast. I remember journaling that night, wondering about who this guy was; I was intrigued and curious, but I was adamant, I would not chase. I would not do things the way that I was used to. I had broken up with my default mode and committed myself to doing things in a way that honoured God and reflected His work of sanctification in my life.

I couldn't get *Sound Guy* out of my mind. There was something about his masculinity, thoughtfulness in returning my CD and his audacity in the stare down. I put my pen down, and thought that thankfully, I'd probably never see him again.

The next day I ran into one of my fellow students who asked for my number, stating that it was for his friend – we'll call my fellow student *Mutual* – I felt my cheeks and ears get hot! I asked rhetorically who his friend was, knowing exactly who he was speaking of. Without missing a beat, he stated emphatically, "My friend, Ricardo, the Sound Guy". I acted confused, like I didn't know who he was speaking about. *Mutual* described him to me using words like "tall, well built, cool hair" to which I feigned not knowing who he was speaking about at all, and then asked why he would want my number. Before *Mutual* could answer, I ran into my next line of questioning, the one answer of which, would determine the next step; I asked if *Sound Guy* had a girlfriend. The answer was yes, and that sealed it for me. I said no, I would not give him my number. Not one to give up or disappoint his friend, *Mutual* replied, *"He's not looking for a girlfriend, he's asking for your number because he wants to be your friend."* This was the strangest thing to hear, because in my mind he was either a player in the game or a complete idiot. Usually guys with motives, who claim to want to be your friend, conceal the fact that they have a girlfriend or girlfriends. I was intrigued by the honesty, but my answer was still no. *Mutual* didn't stop. He asked me daily, and daily I said no. After about two weeks of this consistent hounding, I eventually gave in, and gave my number – curiosity got the better of me. I expected *Sound Guy* to call immediately but to my chagrin, he did not. He called me *two weeks* after receiving my number.

Score: *Sound Guy* 1 – Dominique 0

Well. Hello. Different. He genuinely wanted to be my friend. He communicated – in no uncertain terms – his commitment and loyalty to his girlfriend. There was no funny business. A believer himself, in fact a pastor in training, his speech was always encouraging and uplifting – no dates, no oversharing, no ambiguity, no confusion – none of the "it's complicated" or "situationships" – just a sincere, platonic desire for friendship. We texted now and then, called when necessary, and I could call on him for prayer. I was confused by his clarity.

I moved from intrigue and curiosity to attraction. And here's where I learnt the game changer: **You don't have to be in a romantic relationship with everyone you're attracted to.** I learnt this when I disclosed to him my attraction to him, and he redirected me to our original intent and purpose – *friendship*. I do believe, that if I had continued to push he would have cut me off. So, I stopped feeding into my attraction, because what you don't feed, dies. I was deflated, but not for long. I learnt to value his integrity and courage to go counter cultural with relationships. We were friends and I valued him.

Score: *Sound Guy* 1 – Dominique 1

A BETTER WAY

During my final year at Bible School, I was in the throes of exams, and I received a text message from *Sound Guy*. I had to read it a few times to make sense of it. It read, *"Please pray for me, I broke up with girlfriend."* I was conflicted. I responded with my commitment to pray for him, but I had to pray for myself first. I prayed that I would honour him like he honoured me; that God would help me pray His will and not mine, for *Sound Guy*. At this point in my life, I knew where the danger lie. Had this text message come 18 months earlier, I would have seen this as an opportunity to swoop in and act on my attraction – but God.

Dear Reader, I want to reiterate, we are called to pray for one another not prey on one another. I made up my heart to honour him as my friend. So, after I prayed for me, I prayed for him and continued to study. When I shared this with my roomie at the time, - we'll call her *Small One* – she immediately tried to get me to reach out to him. But I knew there was a better way. We remained friends.

Twelve months later I graduated and came back home. I was not the same girl. I was wiser, stronger, still prone to mistakes but intentional about my pursuit of God and accountable in my walk with Him. I accepted the fact that any and every relationship I have is dependent on, and a reflection of my relationship with Jesus. The building blocks needed for healthy godly relationships are built and forged in relationship with Jesus. Faithfulness, trust, devotion, passion, forgiveness, and intimacy are cultivated by knowing and being known, loving, and being loved, by Jesus.

Everything we need to make relationships work, romantic or otherwise is found in Jesus. If you can't remain faithful to Jesus, how will you remain faithful to anyone else? If you can't forgive others, it's because you haven't fully accepted the complete forgiveness found in Christ. How will you walk in true friendship if you haven't discovered Jesus as the friend that sticks closer than a brother? There was a better way to doing relationships and I wanted it.

Then, one day, there came a knock on the door. A good friend of mine came to visit me and she brought some friends along, and *Sound Guy* was one of them. God has a sense of humour and I just laughed. I didn't know what to make of this, but welcomed them in. It was the first time *Sound Guy* visited me at my home, and it wasn't the last. I then reminded God of His promise to me and opened my heart to the possibility that *Sound Guy* could *not* be the one. I learnt that it's important that we don't make the mistake of being so consumed by finding the one that *that* becomes all we see. So, I asked for confirmation. We spoke about who we were becoming as individuals, but overall, our conversation revolved around God and His call on our lives. He matched my energy on all levels, from his relationship with God to his vision for life. Everything about our relationship, as it grew and evolved, made it evident that we were heading toward an exclusive relationship, and he made no secret of his pursuit. But I needed to know if the promise I received from God a year prior referred to him. As a matter of testing the word I received, I asked him, if he could be any tree what tree would he like to be? And his response, almost immediately, was "A palm tree."

Being taken aback, and at the same time trying not to show any signs of giddiness, I asked why. I needed to know why he didn't say the mighty oak or precious olive tree; why he specifically chose the Palm tree. He explained that a palm tree is 100% more likely to withstand the storm. Its flexibility allows it to face gale force winds and overcome. I felt a gentle nudge, and at that moment confirmed my own desire for an exclusive relationship. He was as clear about a relationship as he was about our friendship. It was his consistency for me. He, unequivocally, defined the relationship as *exclusive and godly*, with the end goal of preparing for marriage. This time around, I was not confused by his clarity. And so, I purposed to approach this relationship differently. I wanted to, as my mentor encouraged me, *"touch nothing without adorning it."* She taught me that, if and when, I walk away from something or someone and it or the person is not better than when I found it or them that I have failed as a leader and more importantly, a decent human being.

So, I came with a *"build beautifully"* mindset. What this meant was that should things not work out with *Sound Guy* that I would have built in such a way that I would not hang my head in shame or regret because of the things did or said while in the relationship. Instead of asking what I could get, I asked what I could give; Instead of asking how my needs could be met, I asked how can I be fulfilled? I came to a stage in my life where I accepted the fact that only Jesus truly satisfies. I responded to *Sound Guy's* pursuit with a changed perspective.

God has called us to build up and not break down. We are like our Father; He is both Architect and Builder of all things beautiful. Imagine every relationship we entered was a building of your making, what would the landscape of our lives look like? Like any building needs a foundation, so does any relationship. In fact, the most important part of any building is the foundation. It's true for buildings and it's true for relationships. A foundation holds up what's built on it. Without a solid foundation you will experience serious damage to the building. In fact, the foundation is so important in building that it needs to be done right the first time because if something goes wrong further down the line, it's sometimes impossible to fix. Contractors advise that it's worth the time and effort to ensure that the foundation is done correctly from the start. And this is true for relationships.

"For no man can lay a foundation other than the one which is laid, which is Jesus Christ." **– 1 Corinthians 3:11**

If you're a child of God and your relationships - romantic or otherwise - are built on anything other than the foundation of Christ, you'll have a relationship prone to cracks. You need a foundation that can bear the weight of the challenges that come with building a strong relationship. And this is not to say you won't have challenges with Christ as your foundation, what I am saying is that the foundation of Jesus allows us to build and know that your relationship will stand even when the challenges come.

Not attraction, or emotions, and not even our shared vision or values can give us the foundation our relationships need. It's Christ as a foundation or nothing, and unfortunately if Christ is not the foundation, our building is in vain - this is true for our lives, our faith, and our relationships. We also need an expert Builder. If the foundation is Christ, then the Builder must be God, because nothing of significance can be built unless God builds it first.

"Unless the LORD builds the house, its builders labor in vain. Unless the Lord watches over the city, the watchmen stand guard in vain."
- Psalm 127:1

And us? What role do we play? What do we do? We, dear reader, are what the bible calls living stones (1Pet.2:5). Not only are we doing the building but we're also being built up. We are called living stones because of God's indwelling Holy Spirit. We have life and power. But this becomes compromised when we build relationships on anything else other than Jesus, and when we try to build without God building ahead of us.

When God directs your love story it will not look like mine, it will look like yours. What I've shared in this chapter is not a blueprint, it's not even a model. God is the standard and blueprint for your love story. He knows you better than you know yourself; He knows your end from your beginning, and He knows what you need. He has even budgeted for your mistakes and is able to redeem every wrong turn or poor decision for His glory.

So, let's not make the same mistake that countless authors on relationships and readers before us have made, let's rather look to God who establishes our times and seasons, instead of focusing on the 'who' rather allow the Holy Spirit to work on you and all that pertains to you. When God gives you a promise, He will remain faithful to His promise. Jesus shows us that there is a better way to do relationships.

Jesus changes everything. And nothing in our lives is exempt from His life giving, life changing and transformational power, not even our romantic relationships. And here's why this is a good thing: it means that we get to honour God with what He values, and one of the things God values is relationships. We have an opportunity to glorify God with our relationships. I learnt this when I met the one, I would choose.

chapter seven
Sexuality By Design

"Our sexuality is not our soul, marriage is not heaven, and singleness is not hell."
~ **Jackie Hill Perry**

I want to ask that all those who have been misinformed, hurt, and shamed by the incorrect and incomplete teachings of sex and sexuality in the church - please forgive us. In an attempt to preserve sexual purity, we have instead demonized sexuality, and as a result we have a generation unable to reconcile their sexual perceptions and experiences - good or bad - with the word of God, rendering God's design for sexuality outdated and irrelevant in their lives. The truth is, our sexuality was not an afterthought when God created us - in fact it was worked into the very fabric of who we are as human beings.

Sex and sexuality are a part of us, but it's broken, because we are broken and what we must accept is that we are all sexually broken. We are all affected by the consequences of sexual brokenness. You might feel exempt from this statement, because you're a virgin or you're not sexually active or you're married and faithful to your spouse but, because of our limited understanding of God's design for sexuality, we have all been overpowered by the three major enemies of sexuality.

- *Enemy #1: The enemy of our souls* is also the enemy of our sexuality. He has taken what God declared good and a gift to us and has perverted it, stripping it of honour and beauty. The enemy will stop at nothing to break down this precious gift. He will attempt to destroy it and everything God created by any means possible (1Pet.5:8).

- *Enemy #2: Our sinful nature* has tainted our sexual desires so much so, that once our sexuality has been awakened it will stop at nothing to be fulfilled. There is a battle between the *sinful nature* and the Spirit (Gal.5:16-21), and this battle seems to be fiercest in the area of sexuality.
- *Enemy #3: The pervasive culture* of our times assaults our sexuality daily. There is often no respite, and this has the potential to cause anxiety and frustration (1Jn.2:15-17). The most well-meaning Christians find themselves in the lion's den trying to navigate sexuality in our culture, and unfortunately, they are not Daniel, and they find themselves devoured.

It was all of these things that distorted the truth about my sexuality, and because of distortion it caused uncertainty and insecurity. This usually causes us to stumble and fall. I did. We have young people in this space, raised in the church, being taught incorrect and incomplete teachings, not seeing sexuality clearly as God designed it and stumbling and falling as a result.

I counseled a young girl, dealing with the issue of her sexuality. When we discussed sex and sexuality, she was completely shocked to learn that sex and our sexuality is a gift from God. I literally had to ask her to close her mouth. She confessed that she thought sex and sexuality, in her own words, "was created by the devil." And can we blame her? We've been tossed between extremes on the topic, like a ping pong ball, from one generation to the next we are polarized on this issue.

What was taboo in one generation is a free for all in the next, and then we are thrust into "Purity Culture?" That in turn starts a cycle of shame and blame and we sit with a generation that thinks their sexuality is a switch to be turned on, only on the wedding night. As counselors we bear the burden of picking up the pieces of broken *sexpectations* - expectations about sex - if I knew then what I know now...

But God always uses what the enemy intends for our destruction; God used my experiences to teach and shape me so that I could be the voice and support to others; the voice that I needed as a young woman navigating the murky waters of sex and sexuality in a dark and depraved generation. The enemy doesn't want us to know that there is a purpose and a plan for our sexuality. It's his best kept secret in a sexually charged generation. When I discovered that God designed and has a purpose for our sexuality, it changed everything. Seeing God as a good father with a good plan, despite a bad world and my own sexual brokenness, changed the way I saw myself! And that changed how I related to others. I went from internalizing my sexuality to submitting it under the Lordship of Christ. I embraced God's design for sexuality, and it gave me freedom, victory and a sense of joy that I cannot even begin to describe to you. Here are some of the truths I have embraced:

- God created sex and it is good.
- I have God given sexual desires and they are good.
- God created me, and my sexuality is a part of the package.
- I *have* sexual desires. I *am not* my sexual desires.
- My sexuality is a part of who I am, it is not my identity.
- Sex and sexuality have a Designer.
- Sex and sexuality have a design.
- Sex and sexuality have a purpose.
- Sex and sexuality are part of a good plan God has for us.

Our problem is that we have assumed that our sexuality is our identity, and we've allowed our world and lives to revolve around it. This means that however we view sex and sexuality contributes to how we view ourselves, and until we have a clear view and understanding of sex and sexuality, we will always find ourselves handling it, and ourselves, incorrectly. It's time to redeem our identity and by extension sex and sexuality.

BORN THIS WAY

A few years ago, I was called by an educator who was struggling to understand a young student in her class. The young student was a boy about 7 years old and effeminate. Firstly, effeminate was not quite the word she used, and secondly, she was uncomfortable with seeing what she knew to be a little boy, acting like a little girl. She then concluded that God created him and therefore he must have been born *that* way. She basically called me to affirm what she decided was true for this precious boy - that God created him gay.

"Born This Way" is a song by American singer Lady Gaga, and the lead single from her second studio album of the same name. The song was inspired by 90's music which empowered women, minorities and the LGBTQIA+ community. Gaga states that "Born This Way" was her freedom song. "Born This Way" has sold 8.2 million copies worldwide, making it one of the best-selling singles of all time. I find it interesting to note that the "Born This Way" album was released on 11 February 2011.

Did you know that the number 11 has biblical significance in that it's the number associated with disorder, chaos and judgment? Now I'm no conspiracy theorist, but I know that nothing in the music industry happens by coincidence. When you watch the music video, coupled with the lyrics you'll understand what I mean. Jon Bloom puts it this way:

> *"'Born this way' is a pop anthem of Western culture, a musical declaration of sexual independence. Gaga is singing a mainstream manifesto, a dominant cultural belief about self-identity: I am my sexuality (my sexual desires and self-determined gender identity), I am beautiful, and I was born this way."*

When we take on our sexuality as our identity and attribute it to God's doing it has the potential to result in disorder, chaos, and judgment; especially when our sexuality is elevated above God's design and purpose for it. The truth is that as children of God when we depart from God's design and purpose for our sexuality we depart from God. In response to this educators' concerns and subsequent conclusion, I took a deep breath and responded by saying that "we're all born this way, but for reasons very different to that of Lady Gaga." I went on to explain that we are all born with the capacity to sin, rebel and commit horrendous acts against God's design for our lives and more specifically, for our sexuality. And there's nothing beautiful about this. We don't have to look far to see the effects of our capacity to commit acts that depart from God's design for sexuality. I say *our*, because we all have been born with this ability, and this little boy? Well, let's just say we ended that phone call with more questions than answers because there's no one size fits all answer as to why he was effeminate. You'll probably come for me, and that's ok, but the TRUTH is he was not born gay; he was born with the capacity to sin, to turn from God, to be influenced by sin, and life often presents the opportunity to divert from God's purpose and intent for our sexuality. I remember being sick to my stomach at the news of a grown man raping a 9-month-old baby. The scary reality is that South Africa has become synonymous with child rape in the world today. I mention this because as humanity we have the potential to do the most basal, animalistic, and depraved acts. Mother's prostitute their children, fathers rape their daughters, and siblings and family members molest the vulnerable. We must not be ignorant of how low we can go. I say *we* because sexual brokenness is not a 'them' problem, it's a *us* problem. It affects us all.

Our problem is that we don't understand same sex attraction and where to place it, so we put homosexuality - which is ultimately the departure from God's design for sexuality - in a special little box apart from sin, and convince ourselves that surely people who self-identify, who are transgender or practice homosexuality are "born this way", when it simply isn't true, while still not being so simple. The truth is we were all born *this* way, with the ability to depart from God's design for life, and this departure can range from white lies, gender confusion, body dysmorphia or dysphoria to grave acts of perversion and everything in between, which is why we must be *born again* (John 3:3). When we're born the first time, in our natural physical state, we are born under the power of sin; it's our default mode. Sinful desires come naturally, which is why you don't have to teach a child to lie, steal or to do the opposite of what you ask. It's our natural state. Children naturally gravitate towards disobedience. The bible says in Proverbs 22:15 *"A child's heart has a tendency to do wrong, but the rod of discipline removes it far away from him"* which is why we must train and teach them to be obedient. But when we're born the second time, sin no longer has power over us. Although we have the potential to sin, we are now under the Lordship of Christ and His Spirit empowers us to live out our lives and sexuality in a way that honours God and His design for our lives. When we are born again, we are new creations, and we enter into a new way of life.

Now I realize I'm making this sound so much easier than it really is. It's difficult dealing with same sex attraction, transgenderism and the gender dysphoria that usually comes along with it, but it must be dealt with. Unfortunately, the church has not been a safe place for followers of Christ who struggle with sexual brokenness, and this is mainly because of our inclination to box sexual brokenness and not accept that it affects us all in some way, shape or form. The truth is that whether you're experiencing same sex attraction or opposite sex attraction, as a Christ follower we have a framework and design for our sexuality that cannot be argued away.

I remember being alarmed by a popular talk show host advocating a solution to the transgender enigma. He categorically stated that the brain of a biological male, who feels like a woman trapped in a man's body, looks like that of a woman. Now, I'm not a neuroscientist but I know enough to know that the brain makes connections between thoughts, feelings, and experiences. Thoughts, trauma, and habits have the potential to change your brain. So, to assert that the brain proves that someone is born transgender is absurd. There are too many variables to make that conclusion. There is no imperial evidence that shows that we are born this way or predisposed to same attraction, homosexuality, or variance in sexuality. To further complicate matters, there is no data that can qualify the surgical and medical intervention involved in transitioning from one gender to another. As complex as the reasons for sexual brokenness are, so also are the outcomes. Christians who struggle with sexual brokenness, who have surrendered their lives to the Lordship of Christ, all have a unique narrative, and we will rob ourselves of the gift that is their lives by viewing them as problems to be solved, when in fact they are people to be loved.

When God calls us, He calls *all* the parts of us, the good, the bad and our sexuality to Himself. It is when we come to Him that He makes us a new creation and sanctifies us according to His purpose.

For me, same sex attraction started with being molested as a child and ended with intentional discipleship, which was the renewing of my mind and surrendering my sexuality to God's design. And yet, I am not the standard, this is not everyone's narrative. I think of Jackie Hill Perry, author of "Gay Girl, Good God", who turned her back on a homosexual lifestyle, although still experiencing same sex attraction, but having the grace of God to marry and have children. And there's Greg Coles, author of "Single, Gay and Christian", who has committed himself to celibacy. Their testimonies help us see that God has a design for our sexuality and it translates differently for everyone, but the standard is the same. We must trust God to do what only He can with our sexuality.

I AM MORE

A Tik Tok trend that was making the rounds was asking women who were in relationship with "high value" men, to state what they're bringing to the table. One woman, knocked the ball out of the park, in response to this question and stated, "*I am the table.*" She owned her value. With these 4 words she declared that she is more than just what she brings to the table. It's not just about what she brings to the table, but it's about who she is. This is true for men too! As children of God, you and I are more - so much more than our sexuality. We must resist the temptation to allow our sexuality to define our identity. It is our identity that determines our sexuality. Truth be told, healthy sex and sexuality only makes up 10% of our adult lives as opposed to the 90% picture that culture and society paints for us - and isn't this why we fall out of love? Because love and sexuality have become synonymous and interchangeable, when they couldn't be more distinct. While they are, by implication, an extension of each other, we must preserve their distinction. We are more than our sexuality; we are more than our desires and we are more than the roles we play in relationships. We *are* the table. Understand your value and worth so that others don't have to determine it for you. Right now, in the world there is a gender war - a battle of the sexes - but if we know our value, we will not have to break one another down to build ourselves up. This is true for any relational dynamic, not just between the sexes. We put our sexuality in perspective when we accept that our sexuality is not who we are but forms a *part* of who we are. You are not just enough... you are more!

I AM NEW

As a child of God not only were you created in the image of God, assigned a gender by God way before your conception, and given a mandate, (Gen.1:27-28) but your new nature was created to be like God.

> *"Put on your new nature, created to be like God — truly righteous and holy."*
> **– Ephesians 4:24 NLT**

Our desires may have been corrupted in the Garden of Eden when Adam and Eve disobeyed God's command to not eat of the Tree of the knowledge of good and evil, but Jesus died and was crucified on a tree so that you may have new life, and a new nature consistent with God. I find it interesting that the disobedience that broke our communion and relationship with God involved a tree, and the obedience that purchased our salvation and redeemed us also involved a tree. Jesus is a first fruit, and believing in Him grants us ever lasting life. Jesus came to redeem what we lost in the Garden!

Wow!

You being a new creation, changes everything. It changes how you see and engage your sexuality. You did not evolve, you are not here by mistake or coincidence, a big bang did not bring about your existence. God created you twice - first in Adam and then in Christ - and because of this you are no longer a slave but an Image bearer, reflecting the glory of your Creator.

I AM CALLED

Make no mistake, we were created by a God who calls. Before we came to know Christ Jesus as Lord we are described as having been far off, separated from God because of sin. We were called to be children of God, and we answered, not because we were entitled in any way, but because we needed a Saviour. He then filled us with His Spirit and gave us a new identity, nature and aligned us with our destiny. But He doesn't just stop there, does He? He then calls us deeper, higher, closer. He calls us to live our lives according to His purpose and plan. Now check out God's faithfulness, He not only calls us to live our lives according to His purpose, but He also gives us the desire to do so (Phil.2:13). But we are not all called the same. Embrace this reality, while we are all called as children of God, we are called differently to live out that calling (2Tim.2:20-21). I remember being called into full time ministry; it was glorious but scary at the same time. No matter how I tried to stifle or suppress it, it was etched in my heart and mind. The more I tried to ignore it, the stronger the sense of calling became. That's because it is often our sense of calling that keeps us moving in the right direction. We might not be where we want to be, but answering God's call on our lives gets us there, step by step. We are not lost or alone. We are called.

I AM CAPACITATED

God is not like Pharaoh, who doubled the Israelites' work quota but did not give them the resources they needed to fulfill their duties. Pharaoh not only expected them to go out and find what they needed to do their work, but He also expected them to get it done, within 24 hours (Ex.5:6-14). God is different. He is as Addison Bevere describes as *Other*. He is not like us or anyone else. God will not expect something of us that He did not already do or is not willing to do - and the life of Jesus is our case in point. When God calls us to Himself, He doesn't bible bash us and set us up to fail. No, He gives us what we need to enable us to live up to the high calling of being His child.

In the book of Acts, Jesus told the disciples that they would be His witnesses starting from where they were to the uttermost parts of the world, but they had to wait on the Holy Spirit who would give them the capacity to live up to what Jesus called them to do (Acts 1:8). And this is the same for you and I. God has a will and we have been capacitated to live up to it.

"It is God's will that you should be sanctified: that you should avoid sexual immorality; that each of you should learn to control your own body in a way that is holy and honourable, not in passionate lust like the pagans, who do not know God; and that in this matter no one should wrong or take advantage of a brother or sister." **- 1Thessalonians 4:3-6**

Will we always get it right? No. However, we are without excuse. We have been given everything we need to live a godly life.

"By His divine power, God has given us everything we need for living a godly life. We have received all of this by coming to know Him, the one who called us to Himself by means of his marvellous glory and excellence."
- 2 Peter 1:3

I AM COMMISSIONED

Webster's Revised Unabridged Dictionary defines the word commissioned in the bible as *the act of granting authority to execute instructions pertaining to a trust*. What the enemy does not want us to know or understand is that we have been given authority to execute the instructions we've received pertaining to everything entrusted into our care. Whether it be the trust of the gospel, to baptize, teach and disciple (Matt.28:16-20) or relationships that are to be treated with all purity (1Tim.5:2), or even our bodies; honouring God with them (1Cor.6:20). What we must get on the inside of us is the reality of our authority, and authority dear reader is a powerful thing.

I live a stone's throw away from one of the most important roads in South Africa, the N1, it is the road that links Cape Town with Johannesburg and Pretoria and continues to the Zimbabwean border. When I stand on my front porch, I can see cars driving as fast as 160km p/h or as slow as 40km p/h depending on the traffic on the day. Should I decide to one day stroll over and try to stop traffic no one would take me seriously, in fact I run the danger of losing my life at worst and at best, being seriously injured. But, a Traffic Officer, on duty and in uniform, will bring that national road to a standstill with just the lifting of their hand. Why? Because they have the authority to do so. How things work is that when we are under the authority of Christ, we have authority over everything that tries to hinder His purposes in our lives. Not many people know and understand this, neither did I.

I AM CHRIST'S LOVE LETTER

"Clearly, you are a letter from Christ showing the result of our ministry among you. This 'letter' is written not with pen and ink, but with the Spirit of the living God. It is carved not on tablets of stone, but on human hearts." – **2 Corinthians 3:3**

Not only do our lives tell a story, but the Apostle Paul describes our lives as a letter from Christ Himself, communicating to a lost and broken world the power of His love – and look at Jesus! He doesn't write it on stone tablets as law but on our hearts as grace, extended to all who encounter us. Many have stated their case and opposed the bible, finding fault and accusing the holy scriptures of error but there is no one who can argue with a life transformed! No one can refute a heart unchained.

How do you argue with the evidence? I've cringed at sincere believers arguing their way into the lives of unbelievers, quoting scripture left, right and center, giving long winded theological lectures, often in "Christianese" without subtitles. Don't get me wrong, engagement on this level has its place but I believe that there are times when our lives should speak loudest. We must not fail to realize the power of living our story of redemption, especially in the area of our sexuality.

When I say that we are Christ's love letter, I mean that our lives should speak of His presence and power; it should be evident, obvious, apparent and plain for everyone to see. I remember years ago I volunteered for an organization as a mentor to a group of at-risk youth in a school on the Cape flats (strip of low-lying land in Cape Town, South Africa). These students were rude, testy, and scary to be around, but I showed up week after week, loving on them and doing my best to live out the curriculum I administered to them. The catch was that I was not allowed to preach, use religious jargon, or mention the name of Jesus – a daunting task, but one I took on. Now before you judge and quote Romans 10:14, what good is a message that I have no audience for? To have remained in the school I had to abide by its rules. So, what I passionately preached on a Sunday morning in church, I would need to live out loud and proud without saying a word. But the loophole was this, if the students asked me a question concerning my faith I would be allowed to answer. Slowly but surely, I saw the layers of aggression and hurt peel off as I started building solid relationships with the students in my care.

There was one girl in particular, very quiet and unpredictable, that seemed to watch my every move. One day we were alone, and she cornered me, she wanted to know what was different about me. She asked me questions like, "why are you so caring?" and "why do you treat us all the same?"

The reason why they called our organization into the school was because of racial tension among the students. She wanted to know how I managed to see past colour and the socio-economic barriers that seemed to divide her class. And before I could answer, she claimed to know the answer. She said, *"You're a child of God, I can see!"*

The greatest sermon you and I will ever preach won't necessarily be with words but with our actions. What a sexually charged, but sexually broken world needs right now are lives embracing God's design for sexuality, bringing healing and restoration to divine masculinity and femininity.

THERE'S A PURPOSE AND THERE'S A PLAN
Myles Munroe said, *"Where purpose is unknown, abuse is inevitable."* I would also like to add to this quote by also stating that *where purpose is ignored abuse will ensue.* Purpose is our handle on life; it's what gives

us a reference point for all things. No one plays cricket with a crystal vase, the purpose of the vase determines what it will be used for, and *not* used for. Correctly handling anything will require an understanding of its purpose - this applies to people too. We have purpose, and by extension, so does all that pertains to us. When we willfully use our bodies, minds, or sexuality for anything other than the purpose it was created for, we run the risk of breaking the crystal vase - in a manner of speaking.

Something shifts in our relationships when we handle ourselves and others according to purpose and more specifically, our purpose in relation to others. And I get it, I grew up immersed in faith and the church community and faced the frustration of not knowing what my purpose was, or so I thought. I've had long and in-depth conversations with young people perplexed about not knowing their purpose, and just listening to their questions and frustrations gave me the language I needed for my own struggle with purpose. But things changed for me when I realized that instead of being caught up with the unknown, I can lean into the known. A good question to ask is, what has God already revealed to me about my purpose? God is not playing games with us, He wants us to know, but He also knows us; He knows that too much too soon can harm us and so He incrementally leads us into a life of purpose. God calls us to what He has already revealed about our purpose, and it's right there, in black and white. It's when we lean into what we know, by showing faithfulness and obedience in the known, that God then builds capacity within us for the unknown. What you don't know about your purpose will be revealed when you're faithful and obedient with what you know.

This is true for our sexuality too. God has revealed to us the *"knowns"* about the purpose of our sexuality and it gives us a reference point for the unknown. Our season of singleness is the absolute best time to lean into the known about our sexuality. It creates the bedrock our souls and bodies need as we face the unknown. When we are fixated on the unknown without having the solid foundation of God's purpose for our sexuality, we end up opening Pandora's box.

Once the unknown about sexuality is awakened before it's time, it's difficult to deal with it. It is possible, but it is difficult. It starts with exhortation and revelation.

> *"I have the right to do anything," you say – but not everything is beneficial. "I have the right to do anything" – but I will not be mastered by anything. You say, "Food for the stomach and the stomach for food, and God will destroy them both." The body, however, is not meant for sexual immorality but for the Lord, and the Lord for the body."*
> **– 1 Corinthians 6:12-13**

Paul addresses a mindset that we often have; sometimes this mindset is motivated by what I call "uber-grace" which is the incorrect understanding or teaching on grace. It's the Christian that thinks that because we're under grace we can do anything we want. This mindset can be motivated by carnality which influences the carnal or soulish Christian to be lead and governed by their emotions and desires. Either way, Paul responds with wisdom. Because truth be told, if you know enough scripture it's easy to manipulate yourself and others by justifying your actions. Yes, I've done it many times; I've quoted scripture out of context, to ease my conscience and to "protect" myself against the call to accountability.

Paul makes four key statements:

#1 - Not everything is beneficial.
#2 - We are not to be mastered by anything other than Jesus.
#3 - God has power over our needs as well as our bodies.
#4 - The Body is not meant for sexual immorality but for the Lord.

But the Apostle Paul has more to say on what God has revealed about our sexuality.

> *"Do you not know that your bodies are members of Christ himself? Shall I then take the members of Christ and unite them with a prostitute? Never! Do you not know that he who unites himself with a prostitute is one with her in body? For it is said, "The two will become one flesh." But whoever is*

united with the Lord is one with him in spirit."
– 1 Corinthians 6:15-17

Paul points out the sanctity of our bodies, but in this era, we are indignant when it comes to the "my body, my choice" argument. Categorically, Paul, states that our bodies belong to Christ, and that, who we connect with sexually, matters, because we become one with that person. We might wonder why Paul refers to a prostitute in his argument against sexual immorality. He did this because sexual immorality and prostitutes were rife in Corinth - the temple of the love goddess Aphrodite was in Corinth. This temple employed prostitutes as priestesses and sex was a part of the worship ritual. Paul's strong admonition is still revenant today, as children of God, we are to have no part in sexual immorality, even if it is acceptable and popular in our culture.

Paul makes more key statements:

#5 - Your body is a member of Christ himself.
#6 - Culture does not determine the exercise of your sexuality.

"Flee from sexual immorality. All other sins a person commits are outside the body, but whoever sins sexually, sins against their own body. Do you not know that your bodies are temples of the Holy Spirit, who is in you, whom you have received from God? You are not your own; you were bought at a price. Therefore honour God with your bodies."
– 1 Corinthians 6:18-20

If you were ever confused about God's purpose for our sexuality, I don't think it gets any clearer than this. Here's what it's not: - our sexuality is definitely *not* for sexual immorality. We are taught to flee from it. But what do we do? We do everything but flee, we compromise, Netflix and chill, justify and like spoken word poet, Janett...Ikz [pronounced "Genetics"] so passionately states, *"we flirt with the ideology of 'can you just tell me how much I can get away with and still be saved?'"*

I needed to learn how to flee, not try to understand, or try to be tolerant or try to be strong and resist but flee. That's it. That's the TED Talk. Run! We must run from sexual immorality, because sexual immorality seeks to bypass the purpose for our God-given sexuality rendering us and others abused and used. It is in our human nature to try to find a loophole, we try to get technical about sexual immorality creating lists of what's allowed and what's not. We try to see how close we can get to sexual immorality and still be saved. In the New Testament the word sexual immorality is derived from the Greek word Porneia. It's the same word we get the word pornography from. Porneia means "whoredom", "fornication" and "idolatry" all of which are forbidden under the law and even under grace. In essence sexual immorality is the surrendering of sexual purity and primarily involves any type of sexual expression outside of a biblically defined marriage (Matt.19:4-5).

Paul then goes for the jugular:

 #7- Flee from sexual immorality.
 #8 - Whoever sins sexually self-harms.
 #9 - You are not your own, your spirit and body belong to God.
 #10 - Honour God with your body.

When God commands that we exercise purity, it is not for His sake but for ours. When we surrender our sexual purity to sexual immorality, we harm ourselves, because the truth of the matter is you can't touch my body without touching my soul, my mind, and my spirit. As humans we are so interconnected that sexual immorality doesn't just sit in the body but like an aggressive cancer, spreads through every facet of who we are. Sexual expression outside of a biblically defined marriage is spiritual suicide, it will kill you softly. But even in the direness of this, there's an even greater danger - what you dishonour, you lose. When we dishonour God with sexual immorality we lose our connection with Him, with the body of Christ and with ourselves. For everything that hell is, the most is distressing thing, is that it's the absence from the presence of God. Sexual immorality kills your prayer life, fills your worship with carnality and isolates you from godly voices and spirit filled communities. It chains your heart to ungodliness. It's not just our connection to God that we lose, we almost always lose the very relationship we exercise sexual immorality in - at worst - and at best, we lose respect, trust, a sense of security and connection. This is why couples who fornicate run a greater risk of losing the relationship. Even though sexual immorality is trending, it still puts hearts and relationships at risk. Data shows that divorce is 1.31 percent higher for couples who cohabitated before marriage. I point this out to show that there are principles that govern the purpose and plan for sex and sexuality, and we cannot circumvent those principles, because, more often than not, we lose what we dishonour.

But there's hope because our sexuality has a purpose and there is a plan. We've concluded that the purpose is not sexual immorality, and the plan is not 50 shades of grey. Not the world or our culture created sex and by extension our sexuality, God created it; He holds the patent to its original design and original intent. Understanding the purpose and following the plan will lead us into a life - and relationships - that will glorify God and be a reflection of God's love to a dying world. Scripture points us to at least 4 aspects of purpose when it comes to God honouring sex and sexuality.

"God blessed them and said to them, 'Be fruitful and increase in number; fill the earth and subdue it. Rule over the fish in the sea and the birds in the air and over every living creature that moves on the ground."
- Genesis 1:23

This first scripture points us to the concept of *procreation*, which basically means to produce offspring after our own kind - in layman's terms - make babies. Marriage is the blueprint for bringing life into this world. I find it very fitting that Jesus would enter this world through the birth canal - and in the most scandalous way. The virgin was with child and expected her fiancé to believe that her pregnancy was conceived by the Holy Spirit. Thankfully God Himself informed and confirmed her narrative. It carries us through the glares, gossip, and false accusations.

We serve a God who honours human life above every scandal devised by sinful people. I've always felt like a mistake, but being unchained means we accept that people often make mistakes, but God does not, in fact He can take an unwanted baby and transform her into a God-fearing lady. God can take a disaster and make her a pastor. God takes our scandals and gives us stories of mercy and grace.

To any person, who feels like they were a mistake, or were told that they were a mistake, I want to say this to you: there is no such thing as an illegitimate child. Children born of unions not formalised by marriage have traditionally been described as 'illegitimate' children". Another meaning of the word illegitimate is *"not authorised by the law; not in accordance with accepted standards or rules", from the Latin for 'not lawful'*. But those are not Gods standards. God is the one who gives life and causes children to grow within the womb of their mothers. It was God who decided that you need to be here, it was Him who made room for you and gave you the breath of life. God does nothing outside of HIS own legitimacy, and He is the standard for lawfulness, and outside of His authorization none other is needed. He didn't accidentally plant you in the womb of your mother, nor did he accidentally allow your heart to beat with purpose that He placed there, and He did not accidentally allow you to be carried to term. Your existence here is by divine right. The only illegitimacy that comes is that on the behalf of the parents, who acted outside of legitimate bounds, via fornication or rape or whatever other means. But you dear soul, are not a mistake. Your space and place in this life was already carved out before God ever even said "let there be light!"

Let me assure you, babies are not the only purpose for sex and sexuality. There's more. There is the purpose of *union* between husband and wife. Sexual intercourse has the power to make one flesh, of the husband and wife – and by one flesh I mean that two separate individuals are now considered and seen by God as one. We know that God honours legitimate oneness; in fact, God is moved to bless it. Jesus bases his teaching for marriage on this scripture, which is why Paul warns against casual sex. There is something powerful that happens when a husband and wife are intimate, they are engaging in the physical representation of a spiritual reality, the oneness of their lives, physically, emotionally and spiritually.

The height of intimacy is oneness, and this is the purpose and blessing of the married life as God intended.

> "May your fountain be blessed, and may you rejoice in the wife of your youth. A loving doe, a graceful deer - may her breasts satisfy you always, may you ever be captivated by her love." **- Proverbs 5:18-19**

The third aspect of the purpose of God-designed sex and sexuality is *pleasure*. Yes, I said pleasure. God made room for sensuality in our sexuality, and that is evident in the writing of the book of Song of Solomon. The Bible says that all scripture is God breathed. All Scripture.

> "All Scripture is breathed out by God and profitable for teaching, for reproof, for correction, and for training in righteousness, that the man of God may be complete, equipped for every good work".
> **- 2 Timothy 3:16-17**

Song of Solomon is no different.

Believe it or not, God delights in us enjoying sex and our sexuality. Feeling twitter-pated, flirting, foreplay, passionate kissing, caressing, climaxing, the orgasm - All God's idea. Many people have a hard time processing the purpose of pleasure God has for you, so if this is you, allow me to bring this idea closer to home for you. The words "sexual pleasure" and the words "God ordained", don't usually fall into the same sentence, but that is only because we have taken sex outside of the sanctity of marriage and from behind the closed doors of the bedroom, and exploited it on Television screens for the viewing pleasure of just about anyone. The innate "wrongness" we feel when it comes to sex, sexual desire and seeking sexual pleasure, as children of God, is usually rooted in hedonism. Hedonism is the pursuit of pleasure and sensual self-indulgence, but the pursuit thereof, as the *primary goal and aim of a life*, supplanting all other goals.

Every movie, every series, every form of entertainment, has a sex scene as the culmination of the shortest romantic pursuits in human history, leading us to believe that the end goal is always sex. As Christians we know that this is not right, and thus feel guilty or bad for wanting to enjoy sex, or for looking forward to it, or for seeking sexual pleasure in it. It's like a voice in the back of the head that says "men only want sex" and "women are prudes", so with that as the underlying theme, keeping sex holy, and still fun and enjoyable seem like a very weird impossibility.

When we're single our desire for sex is demonized and suppressed. Now that sounds like a contradiction because as Christian singles, we've been led to believe that we ought not have any "desire for sex". But it also begs the questions that, if sex is for marriage, why do single men and women have such strong sexual desires? Why doesn't God take these longings away until He brings a spouse? And why would He care if we have sex with someone to whom we're not married? Firstly, we need to understand that God created sexuality to help us understand covenant love. Covenant love goes beyond romantic feelings or even the joy of close friendship. This love is based on a promise that cannot be broken, and this is God's love for His people. The overarching message of the Bible is God's covenant love — that a holy God pursues us with sacrificial, passionate love to bring us into fellowship with himself. Your sexuality is a profound tangible reminder of this truth.

For most single men and women, sexual desire represents a major struggle. They want to know how to push "pause" on sexual feelings, because their sexual drive seems to create so much drama, temptation, and shame, it's often viewed as a bad thing. You will find singles desperately trying to live for God and honor him but begging Him to take their sexual desire away as it serves as hindrance to pursuing the mark of the high calling in Christ Jesus.

But we should all remind ourselves, that sexual desire is a gift from God. We shouldn't ask God to take one of his gifts away from us. What we should want God to do, is empower our discipline and strength to be obedient. We must remember that sexual desire is not only a good thing, but a God thing. The Creator intentionally gave you the longings you have to share your life and body with another person. With our knowledge of both the world's standard and of biblical truth, the enemy has warped our desires so that they either represent selfish pursuit or shameful restraint. Our sexual desire was created to remind us that we were made for intimacy. Not for a hookup or for sexual release looking at a computer screen, but for the sacrificial, life-giving intimacy *represented* by the marriage covenant.

In the absence of this understanding and discipline, we experiment, cross the line, fornicate - and if you share my narrative - we internalize our sexuality and our sexual brokenness. Alternatively, you might have had a painful and traumatic experience with sex, you may have been exposed to pornography too early to understand its danger or molested and violated. Your trauma robbed you of the experiencing the beauty of God ordained sexual pleasure. Whatever the case may be, by the time we step into our God ordained season of marriage our perspective on sex is hardwired and we can't accept that we can and should enjoy sex and our sexuality as God intended. Somewhere, somehow the devil twisted and tainted it, and left you with a mass of mess to unravel and work through.

> *"Husbands, go all out in your love for your wives, exactly as Christ did for the church — a love marked by giving, not getting. Christ's love makes the church whole. His words evoke her beauty. Everything he does and says is designed to bring the best out of her, dressing her in dazzling white silk, radiant with holiness. And that is how husbands ought to love their wives. They're really doing themselves a favor — since they're already "one" in marriage."* **- Ephesians 5: 25 - 28 MSG**

The fourth and final aspect of the purpose of God-designed sex and sexuality is *instruction or teaching*. Through the marriage and by extension the intimacy and oneness between husband and wife we have an object lesson on the relationship between Christ and the Church, his Bride. We learn how to be loved and how to love in an intimate marriage relationship. And it doesn't end there, let's track with the message translation.

> *"No one abuses his own body, does he? No, he feeds and pampers it. That's how Christ treats us, the church, since we are part of his body. And this is why a man leaves father and mother and cherishes his wife. No longer two, they become "one flesh." This is a huge mystery, and I don't pretend to understand it all. What is clearest to me is the way Christ treats the church. And this provides a good picture of how each husband is to treat his wife, loving himself in loving her, and how each wife is to honor her husband."* -
> **Ephesians 5:29-33 MSG**

Christ's relationship with the Church is the point of reference God uses to show us how husbands ought to love their wives, and how wives ought to honour their husbands. What's more, is that through our oneness, a broken and dying world may recognize His love. It's usually when we don't understand the purpose of sex and sexuality that we deviate from the plan. And yes, there is a plan. Where's the plan, you ask? I've learnt not to ask this question if my bible is closed, because the truth is you will not find it anywhere else. What kept me in chains is that I looked to everyone else except the author and perfector of the plan for my sexuality.

> I looked to me.
> I looked to friends.
> I looked to media.
> I looked to culture.
> I looked to the world.

And all these sources took me further and further away from God's plan and left me with a ball and chain in a prison of my own making. One of the few things I learnt about God's plan is that it always liberates - every other plan imprisons.

So where is this plan? It's where it's always been. God's plan is not hidden, it's in His Word and the beauty about His plan is that contrary to popular belief it never becomes outdated, irrelevant, or obsolete. The enemy wants you to believe that, but he's a liar! We've allowed ourselves to become caught up and polarized on issues around cultural things and trends such as dating, singleness and the presumed purity culture. God's plan is bigger than the little arguments we have in Christian circles about sex and sexuality. His plan supersedes any trend, cultural norm or plan we might have for our sexuality. Not only is His plan in plain sight, but God's plan is also personal, it speaks directly to you and every dynamic pertaining to you. It is when we walk in relationship with God that we can understand His purposes and more specifically his very personal plan for our sexuality. Following God's plan will not only require understanding of purpose but also empowerment of the Holy Spirit. When it comes to His plan, as awesome as we are, we cannot do it on our own.

"For it is God who is working in you both to will and to work according to his good purpose. **- Philippians 2:13**

Not only did I not look to God for His plan, I also depended on myself to follow "a plan" which I now know was a fabrication of my broken imagination. In hindsight I can see how I deviated from God's plan. Like me, you too may have gone your own way, did your own thing, made your own plans, and tried in your own strength, to follow some sort of plan to live out your desire for sex or to express your sexuality. You're not alone. I totally understand the frustration, guilt and shame that comes with insisting on or ignorantly following our own way. In my case, I insisted on my own way to God's plan - and I have the scars to show for it. I wish I could call them battle scars but they're not, they're self-inflicted wounds that I could have done without. And the self-preserving argument is always that it was a lesson learnt. No dear reader, there are some lessons we can learn from others; there are some mistakes you don't have to make. Only the arrogant can make the same "mistake" they've seen others make and think that the outcome will be vastly different.

Only the foolish think that consequences don't pertain to them. I was arrogant and foolish. I thought I could manage outcomes. God will not be mocked. When we insist on our plan for sex and sexuality you can be guaranteed of bondage and chains. This is a reality. But there is another reality we must consider when we talk about God's plan for our sexuality, and that is that even when we deviate from His plan we can return to the original plan and intent. You might believe that you've crossed the line, or you've gone too far; you might have believed the lie that you've missed a detail or turn and will have to forfeit God's plan for you, but - and I consider myself blessed to be able to share what I'm going to write next - God is a good Father and He has a good plan even in a dark world with broken people and cringe worthy circumstances. We can turn or return to the original plan. And what's beautiful about God's plan is that God is a Mastermind. His plan budgets for our mistakes and wrong turns. His plan accommodates our arrogance and foolishness. His plan is fool proof and it's been tested for mistakes and weaknesses. When we love God and answer to His call, He can make his plan work out for our good.

Our sexuality has a design and a Designer, it also has a purpose; understanding of its purpose will reveal God's plan and God Himself will enable us to follow His plan. I dare you to live out your sexuality by design and not default.

PART THREE

chapter eight
Love, Lust & Stilletto's

"Lust doesn't care if you're married or single. You may be Solomon in wisdom or David in praise or Abraham in faith or Joshua in war, but if you're not Joseph in discipline you will end up like Samson in destruction."
~ **Evangelist Ayanfeouluwa**

To love and be loved is one of the greatest human desires, in fact it is safe to say that it is more than a *want*, but a *need*. We *need* to love and be loved. I think that's because we were created with love in mind. And receiving anything less than love drives us to search for it in all the wrong places. I know this to be true because that was my story. I searched for my idea of love and found myself in spaces and relationships that could not satisfy what I felt was an ache in my heart.

The more "love" I got the more I wanted. Like an addict I could never get the high like the first time and so I needed to get more and more and more and was willing to compromise everything valuable to me and sadly even myself for it. I was in love with my idea of love. Addicted to the dopamine that came with romantic love, I was willing to lie, manipulate, steal, and cheat. I lied to myself, I manipulated others, I stole from my future and ended up cheating myself out of true love. I chased my idea of love like my life depended on it.

Throughout history, many harmful, inhumane, and unethical psychological experiments have been conducted on children and infants. Although the children were not physically and willfully harmed during the experiment, the outcomes were still dire. Going as far back as the thirteenth century, where the German King, King Frederick, wanted to discover what language a child would naturally grow up to speak, if the child was never spoken to. Today, common sense today dictates, that if a child is never spoken to, they will never learn to speak, and thus there would be no primary or first language. Frederick however, lacked this basic common sense and conducted an experiment whereby he took babies from their mothers at birth and placed them in the care of nurses and caregivers, who were forbidden to talk *to* them, or talk in earshot of them. Added to this, he also implemented a second rule, which forbade the caregivers from touching them, picking them up, comforting them etc. The results? Well needless to say, with regard to speech and language, the results were inconclusive, (as the infants died before they were even able to develop their speech) but it did reveal something quite definitive and significant with regards to human nature, and our need for touch and emotional connection. In the 1930's similar experiments were conducted under Nazi rule, where infants were placed into 4 control groups.

> **Control group 1:** The infants were well fed, well taken care of, spoken to, loved, and cuddled, touched, picked up etc.
> **Control group 2:** The infants were well fed, all other needs taken care of, but not cuddled, picked up or held.
> **Control group 3:** The infants were loved, picked up, cuddled, taken care of, but were extremely rationed on feeds and sustenance.
> **Control group 4:** The infants were also extremely rationed on feeds and sustenance, but were also not touched, picked up or cuddled, or comforted.

It is rumored that again in 1944, a similar case study was conducted on 40 newborn infants in The United States. Taken from the article "US Experiment on infants withholding affection" – author unlisted, the aim of the experiment was to determine if individuals can survive on meeting the basic physiological needs alone. No emotional connection or affection would be given to the infants. Half of the newborn infants were placed in a special facility where the caregivers would feed them, bathe them and change their diapers and but nothing else. The caregivers were not allowed to look at or touch the babies more than necessary, they were also not allowed to communicate with them. The study shows that all their physical needs were met with careful and thorough care, and the environment was kept sterile.

By the 4th month, the horrific experiment was stopped because, sadly, at least half of the babies had died. Furthermore at least two more died even though they had been rescued and taken out of the experiential environment. Here's what makes this experiment so sad; there was no physiological cause for the babies' deaths; they were all physically healthy. What's interesting is that before each baby died, they would stop baby babble and basically stopped trying to engage with their caregivers. It is noted that when they generally stopped moving, stopped crying, or even stopped changing facial expressions; they would die shortly thereafter. Even the two babies who were rescued died in the same way. They were rescued too late.

The result of all these experiments, reiterated what Italian historian Salimbene di Adam recorded in 1248! *"They could not live without petting."* The babies literally died for want of touch. The infants within the four control groups had similar fates.

In the first control group, the infants thrived and went on to live normal healthy lives. In the second control group the infants succumb to sicknesses, a weakened immune system, depression and eventually died.

In the third control group, the infants, although extremely malnourished, lived longer than the infants in control group two. They seemed to fight to live. In the absence of feed, they seemed to gain strength from physical touch and healthy emotional connection.

Today, modern medicine calls this phenomenon, "failure to thrive." Humans undoubtedly flourish under the influence of love, and we gradually die without it. The infants in control group four all died within *hours* of the experiment.

As disturbing and sad as these inhumane experiments were, it revealed, scientifically and conclusively, our need for love, affection, comfort, and the touch of another human being. It also showed the resilience of the human spirit to thrive, and choose life, even in the absence of physical nourishment. It was love and touch that gave the babies in the third control group hope to hold on just a little longer.

I have said it earlier, but allow me to reiterate - *we need love*, not just our idea, opinion, or philosophy on it, but we need the love we were created by and for. As a child, I didn't have the language to express it but somehow, I knew I needed it. Something that tripped me up quite a bit after that fateful confrontation with my father was that I realized that I had never heard my mother say that she loved me. I searched the recesses of my mind, trying to find some recollection of her confessing it, but there was nothing, not even a vague memory. That is not necessarily evidence that she didn't or doesn't love me because everyone who knows my mom knows she loves me and fiercely so. I would even venture as far as to say that she *likes* me a lot. I have no doubt in my mind that my mother would gladly and willingly lay down her life for me, but it took a lot of prayer and processing, on my behalf to accept that even though I can't remember her saying it and even though she might never say it verbally, I find great solace in the fact that I *know* that she does love me. The fact that she has shown it in her actions, and expressed in a billion different ways, the unending extent of her love for me, is more than enough for me.

I am utterly convinced that it is fundamental to introduce children to intentional true love, as soon as humanly possible; it is the bedrock their lives will be built on, anything less than intentional true love is sinking sand. And isn't this the reason our generation is in the state that it's in? We have been sold versions of love that have left our souls' bankrupt. Love has been reduced to nothing more than a feeling, a fall, it's been defined as blind, and heck, we're so powerful we can even "make" love?! No pun intended.

I'm often filled with regret when I think about how I gave others my sub-standard version of love. I genuinely thought it was the real thing, in giving and receiving, and that's the problem; we think we know what love is, but do we really?

NOT WHAT BUT WHO

1 Corinthians 13 is the most quoted chapter, especially for wedding stationery or in the sermon before the vows. And why wouldn't it be? It's inspirational, and it's beautiful; it's poetic, and it is exactly what love is in that honeymoon period, of the "in-love" euphoria. But it's also a command:

> *"Love is patient, love is kind. It does not envy, it does not boast, it is not proud. It does not dishonour others, it is not self-seeking, it is not easily angered, it keeps no record of wrongs. Love does not delight in evil but rejoices with the truth. It always protects, always trusts, always hopes, and always perseveres. Love never fails."* **- 1 Corinthians 13:4-8a**

Yet, even in all that truth and beauty the divorce rate climbs, hearts are chained, and homes are broken. Such a poignant scripture reading and still gender based violence is at an all-time high - trust is broken, bodies are violated and the vulnerable are not protected. Women in South Africa - and I believe the world at large - are more likely to be assaulted and killed by a husband or partner, and it seems like love has failed. Like the *Black-Eyed Peas*, I beg the question, "Where is the love?" The truth is, that despite what we see around us, love is indispensable. Paul is utterly persuaded that despite being gifted, in all manner of gifts, without love, he is nothing. He comes to the conclusion that any investment on his part, without love, gains him nothing (1 Cor.13:1-3). We cannot live or be without love. How can we get something so important so wrong? Could it be that the reason for that is because love is not a matter of what but a matter of *Who*.

Love is *not a what.*
Love is *not an it.*
Love is *not a feeling.*
Love is *not an experience.*

Love is *not sex*.
Love is *not an affair*.
Love is *not blind*.
Love is *not a fall*.
Love is *not pain*.
Love is *not a happy ending*.
Love is *not what we thought*.

What I'm about to share with you has the potential to forever change your life and relationships. It may change the trajectory of the very relationship you find yourself in or determine the next relationship you step into.

Love is a *Person*.

> *"Everyone who confesses that Jesus is God's Son participates continuously in an intimate relationship with God. We know it so well, we've embraced it heart and soul, this love that comes from God. God is love."* – **1 John 4:15-16a**

When God gives us love, He gives us who He is. God is love. Love is not only something God feels or does, it's who He is. However, it's at this point right here that we can be so right and yet be so wrong. You might ask, *"but how is this transformational?"* *"How will this change the trajectory of my relationship or future relationships? I've known that God is love for years"*. Yes, but have you *known* God? To know God is to know Love.

I once had a very interesting conversation with a young believer who was head over heels in love and in a relationship with a young man who was "spiritual" but not a born-again believer - apparently, that's a thing. They would speak about God; he would even encourage her from the bible and was very supportive of her walk with God. Faith in Jesus Christ just wasn't "his thing". The fact that she was unequally yoked with an unbeliever didn't seem to bother her and I soon discovered that this was because he claimed to *love* her.

Their reasoning was that God is love. In her mind it made perfect sense, if her boyfriend loves her and God is love then surely God is in their relationship?! That is quite a reach and a lengthy stretch of biblical truth - that's not how things work. I took a minute to help her see that if he doesn't love God, he can't claim to love her. Unfortunately, this kind of thinking is not uncommon in this generation. I've seen it over and over again and it's harmful. It puts our relationship with God in jeopardy. Yes, it's *that* bad. It borders on idolatry and here's how:

"God is love" and "love is god" have become synonymous with each other, and if you're not careful, you begin treading that line of thinking they are same thing. We must resist the temptation to make an idol of our rendition of love. True love starts with God and not our understanding of what we think it is. It's so easy to worship our idea of love, even our idea of God, which is idolatry. When we do this, we put what we feel or think above God. People think idolatry is bowing down to an idol made of wood or stone and because most people don't do that anymore we think we must be safe. Not true. Idolatry is more than just worshipping an idol; it is the worship of anything that takes God's place in our lives. But there's more, it is the worship of a god we create in our own minds or in our own image (Ex.20:4).

This is the reason we find ourselves in bondage in relationships because our idea of love has taken God's place in our lives. Someone who does not know God cannot love you in the true sense of the word. They can feel for you, show affection towards you and can even be loyal but their love is dependent on self, their needs, emotionality, sexual desire, philosophies and ideologies - bluntly put, they're loyal to their need for you and what you can give them - the height of selfishness. Their "love" is dependent on what you do, and how you make them feel about themselves.

You see, because someone who doesn't know God has not received love and therefore cannot love. Until you encounter the God who is love, you can try but you cannot love. Only someone who has experienced the love of God, can love God, and love others truly. We love because God first loved us (1John 4:19). We truly love when we know God, and have experienced His love.

Relationships between people who do not seek to know God and love Him are what I call Kamikaze Relationships ("Kamikaze was a Japanese aircraft in World War II, loaded with explosives and making a deliberate suicide crash on an enemy target" - Dictionary.com). It's the kind of relationship that will self-destruct or not reach its full potential or destination. I'll take it a step further; marriage is not for all people, marriage is for people who seek to know and love God, because people devoid of God have not experienced unconditional love and therefore do not have the capacity to love fully. I said what I said, or rather wrote what I wrote.

On a serious note, though, this is why people are falling in and out of love, are unhappy in their marriages, are having affairs, move from one relationship to another, are addicted to pornography, are addicted to substances and abuse, hurt and humiliate one another - this list can go on. God's love is not externally motivated like ours often is. Nothing in us or because of us, makes God love us. Nothing we can say or do can make Him love us more. His love is not conditional; failure to adhere to terms and conditions will not make Him love us less. The Apostle Paul asks and answers his own question with a bold statement about the love of God.

> **Q:** *"Who shall separate us from the love of Christ? Shall trouble or hardship or persecution or famine or nakedness or danger or sword* - **Romans 8:35**
>
> **A:** *"No, in all these things we are more than conquerors through Him who loved us. For I am convinced that neither death nor life, neither angels nor demons, neither the present nor the future, nor any powers, neither height nor depth, nor anything else in all creation, will be able to separate us from the love of God that is in Christ Jesus our Lord."* - **Romans 8:37 - 39**

God is not moved to love us because of who we are or what we've done. Not our beauty, brains, gifting, or income bracket causes Him to fall for us. Not our worship or church attendance gives Him butterflies. Nothing externally motivates or stirs His love for us. God is love and therefore He loves. Nothing in all creation can separate us from His love. While it is true that there are things that can cause us to have a broken relationship with God - we might even feel far from Him - there is absolutely nothing that can separate us from His love. He loves us regardless.

God doesn't just say that He loves us. God's love is a verb - a doing word - demonstrative in nature. But before we break that down, it's interesting to note that there are several words for love in the bible, 4 Greek words to be exact. The Greeks were deep thinkers, philosophers, and thankfully they were able to express the distinctions between the various expressions of love.

#1 *Storge:* This expression of love is pronounced *Stor-jay* and describes family love. It's the bond of affection that exists and grows between parents and children, brothers and sisters and extended family members. We see this all over the bible, mainly because God has a father heart and ordained families to be a reflection of his heart for our identity, legacy and growth. One can't help but see how the family unit is being broken down and distorted. Storge is under attack.

#*Philia:* Pronounced *Fill-ee-uh* is described as the powerful emotional bond seen in deep friendships. The root word for Philia is phílos, a noun meaning "beloved, dear ... a friend; someone dearly loved (prized) in a personal, intimate way; a trusted confidant held dear in a close bond of personal affection." Philia can be defined as experience-based love.

Our understanding of friendship is so warped it's not even funny. In this generation we have what we call a *Frenemy* - someone who pretends to be your friend but is your enemy. We have lost Philia and are unable to form deep friendships. And this is so important because Jesus said Philia would be an identifier of his followers (John 13:35): *"By this everyone will know that you are my disciples if you love one another."*

#*Eros*: Pretty sure we know how to pronounce this one. It's where we get the word erotic or erotica from. Eros is the Greek word for sensual or romantic love. Eros wants satisfaction—to have the object of its desire. Contrary to popular belief, this expression of love is a gift from God reserved for marriage and it is within marriage that eros love is to be celebrated and enjoyed. It is to our disadvantage that Eros has become the poster child for love. We foolishly equate love with sensuality or romance, ignorant of the fact that it's an expression of it, not the be all and end all of love.

The fourth and final expression of love is, by definition, the ultimate expression of love. It's the love above all loves, unrivalled, unmatched, unstoppable, undeniable, unforgettable, irresistible, it truly is the greatest love of all. The late Whitney Houston who gave us hits like, "I will always love you" claimed that the greatest love of all was learning to love yourself, which sounds about right, but doesn't do justice to the love I'm about to share with you.

#Agape: If you've never seen this word before, it's pronounced *Uh-gah-pay*. It is described as the divine love that comes from God. Agape love is perfect, unconditional, sacrificial, and pure. It is a love of willful, intentional choice and does not come about because of attraction or obligation. It is more than just a feeling, it's an act of the will, a decision taken to love despite how one feels or what one desires. It's the kind of love that loves despite not being loved back.

The litmus test for love is if you'll love whether somebody loves you back. Trust me, I know - been there, done that. I thought I was ready for love, I thought I was able to love, but my inability to continue to love when not being loved back proved that my love was conditional and dependent on what I got in return. And when love was not reciprocated or returned in a way that I could understand I got angry, bitter, resentful, hurt, and depressed. All tell-tale signs of a lesser love.

Without giving too much of my age away, while other girls were binge reading Mills and Boon, I was engorged on the writings of Francine Rivers. One of her books that that has made a lasting impact on me, is *Redeeming Love. Redeeming love,* a modern-day story of trauma, pain, hope, healing, and a love that redeems. The book is classified as fiction, but there's nothing fictional about a love that redeems. Redeeming Love is inspired by the Biblical Book of Hosea whose central theme is the redeeming love of God towards sinners. It is originally the true story of Gomer and Hosea. Rivers' adaptation of this complicated love story resonated with many audiences the world over. The novel sold over three million copies worldwide since its publication in 1991 and has been translated into 30 languages. Many Christians are familiar with the name and even story of Hosea as a minor prophet, but few are familiar with Gomer, his wayward wife.

Gomer is described by God Himself, as promiscuous. While promiscuity in this generation is overlooked, accepted as the norm, and celebrated, back then it was not. It was an indictment against her.

To be clear, the word *promiscuity* has lost the gravity of the sin denoted to it. In plain English, Gomer was nothing more than a common whore who was unselective, indiscriminate, and casual in her approach to her blatant and open sexual relationships. She had no standards of morality of which to speak, and she was the epitome of making her way through life on her back with her legs spread. Many biblical scholars, in wanting to bring accuracy to her description, deny the fact that she was ever a prostitute. Prostitution implies payment for the peddling of ones' wares. Prostitution can come about by choice, or circumstances beyond ones' control, but Gomer didn't ask for payment, she didn't expect payment and she didn't need payment. She chose to recklessly give herself to anyone who asked - rich, poor, dirty, clean, servant or master - anyone! I don't mean to labour this point, but I want you to understand the gravitas of the position Gomer placed herself in, only then will you understand and fully appreciate the message of redemption.

Cue Hosea. In stark comparison, Hosea is described as a man of God; his name literally means "Salvation"! The Talmud - the central text of Rabbinic Judaism and the primary source of Jewish religious law and Jewish theology - claims that he was the greatest prophet of his generation. In fact, Hosea was a man in such right-living with God that God chose him as His own personal mouthpiece, speaking on God's behalf. Hosea had the seal of God on him, marked by his holiness, and righteousness before God. Why then, would God reward him, by instructing him to do the unthinkable? God instructed Hosea - the prophet, the man of God, the one called and anointed of God - to do what? To marry Gomer!

One would think that given Hosea's loyalty and devoutness to God, that he deserved a wife of honour and good reputation, one that would stand by him as he proclaimed the word of The Lord to His people. But no, God chose a wayward wife for Hosea; and immediately one would think that He did so, so that Gomer might change under the influence of Hosea's love, right? God told Hosea - in advance - that Gomer would commit adultery and the children in their marriage would be conceived through unfaithfulness (Hosea 1:2). Hosea completely understood the terms of his impending marriage, and still took Gomer as his wife. True to Gods word, Gomer kept wandering into the arms of other lovers. She was unfaithful. And yet the Lord told Hosea to keep going after her again and again and bring her back home. I'm thinking what in the world?

"When the Lord began to speak through Hosea, the Lord said to him, 'Go, marry a promiscuous woman and have children with her, for like an adulterous wife this land is guilty of unfaithfulness to the Lord.'
- Hosea 1:2

The English Standard Version says it best: *"When the Lord first spoke through Hosea, the Lord said to Hosea, 'Go, take to yourself a wife of whoredom and have children of whoredom, for the land commits great whoredom by forsaking the Lord.'"*

God is not one to mince words, or to be politically correct. The New Living Translation elaborates on God's purpose and intent with His seemingly strange instruction to Hosea.

"This will illustrate how Israel has acted like a prostitute by turning against the Lord and worshiping other gods." - Verse 2b

Hosea and Gomer were to be an illustration, an object lesson, a case in point. In many ways Israel was like Gomer and through Hosea marrying Gomer, God wanted to show His chosen people how unfaithful they were.

- They rejected God and His ways.
- They forgot God and did not acknowledge Him.
- They practiced prostitution and worshiped other gods.
- They conceived and gave birth to illegitimate children.
- They aligned themselves with ungodly nations.
- They ended up in bondage and slavery.

Their adultery was both physical acts of immorality and an inward decay of idolatry. Like Gomer, the Israelites were adulterers at heart and because of it they broke covenant with their Husband. The outcome of their unfaithfulness was separation from God. But it doesn't end there. It wasn't just about Israel's unfaithfulness, but also about Gods faithfulness despite it. God wanted to show Israel the measure of His love.

Sometime after the birth of Gomer's third child she becomes enslaved in prostitution. So, Gomer goes from the promiscuous girl to the adulterous wife (and mother), to prostitute and sex slave. The truth is that on many levels, like Israel, you and I are a lot like Gomer. And this reality has a past, present, and future. We readily and so easily relate to Hosea - chosen, anointed, called, and set apart; the man who has "kept the ways of the Lord"- but somehow feel we are so far removed from the bad girl Gomer. We tend to do this with God's leading men and women, because who can resist the temptation to self-identify with the hero or heroine in our bible reading? We're always the persecuted but elevated Joseph, the overlooked but anointed King David, the courageous Deborah, unstoppable Esther, or loyal Ruth - never Gomer, Rahab, or Delilah. Why?

Because in our minds we're never as bad as someone else, are we? We are never the villain of the story. We console ourselves with the fact, that we never went *that* far, or got into it *that* bad; we didn't hit rock bottom or end up on a podium naked for auction. The truth of the matter is that we all have sinned and fallen short of the glory of God. I am reminded of the quote by Dieter F. Uchtdorf *"Don't judge me because I sin differently than you"*.

We might not have sinned like Gomer, but we all have sinned and because of our humanity we have the capacity for the lowest of sins.

"But each one is tempted when he is dragged away, enticed and baited [to commit sin] by his own [worldly] desire (lust, passion)."- **James 1:14**

Until we understand at least half of the depth of our depravity we will never value the height of our salvation. Despite Gomers clear desire to be a prostitute, to live a life of concupiscence, God instructs Hosea to go and love his wife yet again Yes, even after her adultery. I encourage you to open your Bible to Hosea 3:1-4 and read it for yourself. Yes really, go and read it. What you will discover is that when Gomer was at her lowest, unable to cover her guilt and shame, unable to justify or rectify the irreparable damage left in her wake, completely helpless and hopeless, lost and utterly abandoned in the arms of a lover who was prepared to sell her for next to nothing - God sends Hosea to do for her what God longed to do for Israel - but what more than that - what God, at the time was getting ready to do for you, for me, for all humanity. Hosea buys his wife back for 15 shekels of silver and a homer of barley. The song "I've come to take you home" by The Crabb Family singers, I think, accurately and wholly displays the story of Hosea and Gomer, and his desire to have her back - not only His obedience to God, but His very own desire to find and redeem his wife.

"Go plead with your mother, were the words of Hosea
As he sent his children to extend his mercy
So they journeyed down the old path that lead to much destruction
All the while their loving hearts were hurting
Their hope was crushed inside as their compassion was denied
The woman they so loved seemed like a stranger
Heartbroken and alone they took the long road home
For sin now reigned and all hope seemed gone to change her

One day the word was told, some slaves were being sold
A restless love sent Hosea seeking, one by one they brought them in
So beaten down with sin, within his chest his anxious heart was beating
All at once she caught his eye, from his lips the bids were high
She could not believe the voice that she could hear
Would he through judgment take her life, forever end his pain and strife
What would happen as she saw him drawing near her

I've come to take you home, I know that you've done wrong
But for you I'd give my life
Through the sorrow, pain and strife I couldn't let you go
Let's leave the past behind
Love conquers one more time
He took her hand and said, there's a new day just ahead
I've come to take you home!"

This song depicts the love and longing of a husband, and even the desperation of Gomers' own children. This is literally what it was. Hosea was a man, a mere mortal like you and I. It was not that he went through the motions and just blindly did as God had instructed, devoid of any emotional connection. No, Hosea loved Gomer. He had to. I believe that God gave Hosea such a deep incredible love for Gomer; the kind of love that would send him to bed in tears as he cried out for Gomer to return to him; the kind of committed love that could not let her go, no matter how many times she walked away, no matter how many men she entertained - all Hosea could see was that this was *his* bride. A sacrificial love, that he would give up his own comfort, his reputation, his life to go seeking for Gomer. He would give to his hurt to buy her back. Make no mistake, Gomers' infidelity toward Hosea, dug deep into him. It hurt him, it embarrassed him, it broke him, and still for the love he had for her, he went to bring her home, because *he* was still her husband.

What God instructed Hosea to do was an illustration of the love God has for His people. Through Hosea, God would reveal - albeit just a shadow of - the depths His love would go. A love that would look past our tendency towards unfaithfulness at best, our sinful nature at worst, and see our need for redemption; a love that would act despite the reality of being rejected; a love that would redeem regardless. In His bid to reiterate His ongoing love for us, God moves from illustrating through Hosea, to demonstrating His love through Jesus.

"You see, at just the right time, when we were still powerless, Christ died for the ungodly. Very rarely will anyone die for a righteous person, though for a good person someone might possibly dare to die. But God demonstrates His own love for us in this: While we were still sinners, Christ died for us." -
Romans 5:6-8 NIV

Dear Reader, God's love has been demonstrated, not by our comfort, answered prayers or fulfilled dreams. Resist the temptation to associate God's love with getting what you want or think that you need. Take captive any thought that downgrades God's love to *only* making a way for you or providing for you. While these things might make us feel good, they do not demonstrate or prove that God loves you. Rebuke every lying thought that says that God's love is something that must be earned or is a reward for good behaviour. God's love does not have key performance areas.

The reality of God's love for me hit me right between my eyes while sitting in the room of a then-boyfriend. I was coming down from what I call a "performance binge" - when you do all the right things, you know to do; you pray, you read your bible, you attend church, and exercise your spiritual gifts. Basically, when you go through the motions of your faith and pat yourself on the back. And coming down from that is when you fall back into old thinking patterns, habits, and the things you used to do, specifically those things that bring bondage.

The "performance driven" life is fueled by pride, and it cannot sustain the life and relationship with God that He has called us to. I was a mess. I sat there in my guilt and shame, empty. I couldn't stop my tears even if I wanted to. In that moment I wasn't the hero of my story. I was fully aware of the fact that I was Gomer! Unfaithful Gomer. In need of love, not the watered down, distorted, and misrepresented version I was chasing after. I needed Him - Love.

And oh, how God loves us! There was a moment in my sobbing when light pierced through the darkness. I began to worship, inaudibly at first. Then in broken whispers I sang a song I had sung hundreds of times before, but this time I sang it with the eyes of my heart wide open.

> *Nothing you can do*
> *Can make Him love you more*
> *And nothing that you've done*
> *Can make Him close the door*
> *Because of His great love*
> *He gave His only Son*
> *And everything was done*
> *So you would come...*

I became alive to the fact that God loves me unconditionally. And His love lifted me to realize that even in my mess I wasn't separated from His love. He still loved me. Period. My unfaithfulness separated me from His presence yes - but He never moved. That's the difference. His love was not determined by how good or bad I was but was demonstrated by the sacrificial death and resurrection of Jesus Christ.

Hosea paid 15 shekels (half the going rate for a slave by the way, see Exodus 21:32) but Jesus gave His very life to not only demonstrate the love of the Father but as a ransom buying us back us from sin, eternal judgment, and the power of darkness. It is when we have encountered and walked in the love of God that we can truly love others in all its various forms, because the love of God is what anchors the expressions of love.

To my brothers - real talk. Unless you can love her like Christ loved the church, don't confess your undying love to her. Quit talking about what you will do for her or to her, saying foolish things like, "I'll make you my queen" and "There's nothing I wouldn't do for you." Those are the very definition of "sweet nothings"- they are sweet, but they mean nothing. It's not about what you will do for her, what matters is what you are willing to sacrifice for her. What are you willing to die to so that she can live in your love and not be chained, smothered, or oppressed?

To what lengths will you go to find her where she is and bring her up to where she belongs? Are you willing to forsake all others, will you leave the 99 and walk with her in oneness? If not. Do not, I repeat, *do not awaken her love.* King Solomon, in all his vast wisdom cautions this in the Book Song of Songs - and I paraphrase - *"Do not arouse or awaken love until it so desires…. for love is as strong as death, its jealousy unyielding as the grave… Many waters cannot quench love; rivers cannot sweep it away…* Song of Songs 8: 4, 6, 7

MY KINGDOM COME MY WILL BE DONE

Now, allow me to introduce you to the nemesis of all relationships, romantic or otherwise, my once friend, and now foe - lust. Unfortunately, we met a long time ago and our friendship was built on deception, betrayal, and broken promises. It took me a while to see that lust was an imposter. At some point I believed that lust was love, until the cracks started showing. And here's the thing; unless you accurately identify lust, you will not be able to deal with or overcome it.

Lust is a destroyer.

To be clear, let's not make the mistake of confusing lust with sexual desire. Contrary to popular belief, there's a difference between lust and sexual desire. The challenge with the teachings of the purity culture is that it taught that sexual desire is wrong, ungodly, and sinful. The gist of this message was that, in order to have an awesome sex life when married, you would have to switch off, and suppress all sexual desire while you're single. As we unpacked earlier, a half a truth is still a whole lie.

And so, I concur with Jesus, "wisdom is vindicated by her children." We have an entire generation who are victims of the over promising and under delivery of incomplete teachings of the purity culture. An entire generation thought that the sexual desire switch could just be flipped back on, on their wedding night. What we thought was wisdom has come back to haunt us.

Here's the whole truth, sexual desire is God-given and when experienced and exercised according to God's framework for our sexuality it honours God. At its core, sexual desire is not evil or ungodly unless we allow it to be. Sexual desire is not sin although it has been tainted by sin. Sexual desire is a healthy part of our humanity and plays a very important role in our relationship with God when submitted to the Lordship of Christ and our divinity. Yes, I wrote "our divinity." Our bodies are the temple of the Holy Spirit. The Spirit of the Living God dwells inside of us, and this reality alone has the power to break chains on our sexuality. Sexual desire that honours God is beautiful and should be experienced with thanksgiving, it should be celebrated and treasured. So, it does beg the question, how is sexual desire celebrated in singleness? (Spoiler alert, the answer to that question is dealt with extensively in Chapter 11.) (Check Chapter 11)

Lust on the other hand is ungodly, unholy, deceptive, and capable of serious damage. Lust is a sin. Lust is the sinful desire and willful fulfilment of that desire, sexual or otherwise. Sexual desire becomes sinful lust when that desire stirs you to act in a way and at a time that disregards and dishonours all else for the sake of self-gratification. Lust is more than a feeling, desire or craving it is also the exercise of the will towards doing what you want, when you want - "do what thou wilt"- A foundational teaching and doctrine of the Church of Satan - Lust is both the desire and action towards self-gratification. Lust cannot honour God or others.

Lust is irreverent. It holds no regard for standards, holiness or the will and purposes of God. Lust worships the god called Self, and will sacrifice others, even self, on the secret alter of empty promises. Lust screams, "It's all about me! I want what I want, and I want it now!" Two things lust will do:

    #1 *Lust Dishonours*: Lust will act on sexual desire outside of marriage or will act on sexual desire in marriage but with someone other than a spouse. Listen lust does not discriminate; the victim is irrelevant, as long as lust gets what it wants. Let's take the example of sexual desire exercised outside the context of marriage: what lust is actually saying is, "I want you to satisfy my sexual desire, but I do not want to enter a covenant of marriage with you first; I want to use you for my sexual pleasure devoid of the marriage commitment needed to sustain a sexual relationship." This is the literal embodiment of dishonor.

#2 **Lust Disregards:** Lust ignores God or anyone else on the path to self-gratification. Lust pays no mind to the will and purposes of God. Lust sows and doesn't care that it will reap. Lust will pay no attention to red flags, objections, or a call to accountability. Let's take the example of lust unabated: what lust is really saying is, "God who?"- a dangerous disposition, because you and I both know that God is not mocked.

Lust is dangerous; it will destroy relationships, romance, and potential. Lust wants to destroy you, your vitality, spiritual fervour, your dreams and visions, your goals and desires - and lust is pervasive; it has the potential to infect us all. Money, power, sex, food, control, you name it, lust will consume you. This is why when lust has a stronghold in one area it usually has its tentacles in other areas as well, often less visible, but it's there all the same.

You must understand that once you're in a relationship with lust, nothing is on your terms anymore. Morning affirmations, positive self-talk, power declarations and summoning all your will power, will not free you from its death hold. Self can't cast out self. And when I speak of self, I'm not speaking of the new creation, created to be like God in righteousness and true holiness (Eph.4:24). Lust runs rampant in the part of you called the flesh which gives way to sinful desires that war against the Holy Spirit. The flesh is the part of us we are called to put off; to die to. Samson was gifted, anointed, set apart, a Nazarite from birth, and yet lust owned him.

Yes, you can be anointed and still be tempted to lust. You can be called *and* gifted, and still be carnal. Romans 11:29 says, *"For the gifts and calling of God are without repentance."* This means that God won't change His mind about what He has called you to do. If God has called you, that calling is still there, whether or not you have obeyed, or are living a sinless or sinful life. This is a scary reality that we must deal with decisively if we are to be unchained. As blood washed, born again and spirit filled believers, we are not immune to the vices of the flesh.

Imagine being remembered for what you could have been?

Samson had enemies but it was his *inner-me* that destroyed him. We tend to blame Delilah for his downfall, but let's be honest, the only power she had was the power Samson gave her. And that's the thing with lust, whether it's the lust for power, money, or sex, it's always going to find someone to blame. When the deed is done, notice how it's always the words or actions of others that "made them do it". Lust is not someone else's fault, regardless of what the other person said, did or wore, we make the decision to allow lust to reign.

> *"The temptation to give in to evil comes from us and only us. We have no one to blame but the leering, seducing flare-up of our own lust. Lust gets pregnant, and has a baby: sin! Sin grows up to adulthood, and becomes a real killer."* **- James 1:14 The Message**

Yes, allowing lust to reign is our decision. Child of God don't be deceived into thinking that you don't have power over lust, or control in how and where it enters. When you were out in the world it had power over you, but now that you're in Christ it goes against your new nature. In fact, in order for lust to be in your life it needs an opening that comes with your approval. For lust to operate, it needs your sign off. Would you believe me if I told you we can say no, we can deny access, we can refuse lust's seduction?

I think the real question is, why don't we? I think it's because lust *feels* so good. Lust makes us feel alive, powerful. All our senses are activated, and we feel free to go for what we want, what we deserve. Lust delivers in the moment, satisfaction is guaranteed - that is, until the sweetness turns bitter and what was once the absolute thrill, drives us to self-loathing. And so, to keep us from coming down we pursue the next high, only the next high requires more and more and more. Lust is insatiable. We are never truly satisfied. Chained by lust is a scary place to be; it's dark, and it's a mess. Sometimes the thought of never breaking free can be crippling. There is a tendency to give up on ever breaking free. It's a vicious cycle. When counseling people chained to this formidable enemy, the common denominator is the fear of being found out. Prisoners of lust fear being exposed. That's why it's so difficult for them to reach out for help. They're afraid of what others will think of them and the things they've done.

It is my life's mission to unchain them, to set the captives free; to create safe spaces and extend merciful grace. To reach them, even in the darkness, even in the mess, to open the prison doors and teach them the truth about the chains that bind them, because that's what Jesus did for me. It is imperative that they know that it's not what I think about them that matters but what their heavenly Father thinks of them, how He loves them and what He was willing to do for them. I must make sure they understand that their chains are broken in Jesus Name.

Dear Reader, it's the truth you *know*, not the truth you don't know, that will set you free. We must *know* the truth. Now, we can learn about lust in real time from the plethora of media houses just waiting for us to click; we're literally a button away from lust on steroids. The problem is that they paint a glamorous, picture-perfect lie; they sell us lust with no consequences, no repercussions, no fine print.

When I said that Samson was destroyed by his inner-me, I was pointing us to the *cause* of lust. It comes from within. When we are selfish, self-centered, and self-reliant, we are prone to lust. Self is the blue pill that ensures that one remains in the fabricated reality of the Matrix of lust. Yes, that's right, his heightened sense of self manifested lust. It started with sexual desire - which in and of itself is not a bad thing, it's part of our human experience - but add to that a sense of entitlement, and we've got a hot mess.

Entitlement is the Achilles heel of our generation. The belief that we deserve what we want is what trips us up every time. Are we worthy and deserving of love? Of course, we are. The problem is that we want it on our terms. Being entitled should not be confused with self-awareness, self-love, or self-care. These are good and have their place in our walk with God, even though we tend to make good things bad.

I've cringed at many teachers of the bible who have taught that we are to die to self by being disconnected from our feelings, dreams, desires, and preferences. While their intentions I believe were good, the outcome of their teaching brings us to the unspoken unhealthy ideal of becoming, as Peter Scazzero points out, "non-persons" when we become Christians. We are not called to die to the good parts of who we are, but rather those sinful parts.

> *"True, Jesus did say, 'If anyone would come after me, he must deny himself and take up his cross and follow me' (Luke 9:23). But when we apply this verse rigidly, without qualification from the rest of scripture, it leads to the opposite of what God intends. It results in a narrow faulty theology that says, 'the more miserable you are, the more you suffer, the more God loves you. Disregard your unique personhood; it has no place in the kingdom.' We are to die to the sinful parts of who we are - such as defensiveness, detachment from others, arrogance, stubbornness, hypocrisy, judgementalism, a lack of vulnerability - as well as the more obvious sins described in scripture. We are not called by God to die to the good parts of who we are."* **- Peter Scazzero**

Self-awareness, self-love and self-care is not the same as selfishness or to be self-centered. And so, we have this trend infiltrating the minds of younger Christians, that to get what they deserve they should become selfish. While this sounds about right, it's a set up for lust; the sinful desire and willful fulfillment of that desire, sexual or otherwise.

Lust dishonours others and disregards God; Lust chooses self over others at the expense of our relationship with God. Don't do it; don't follow this harmful trend. Don't become selfish for the sake of self, become Spirit filled and sanctified, because God always gives us what we need and deserve. It's when we distrust God that we choose self at the expense of our relationship with God and others.

Samson was not self-aware, exercising self-care or walking in the good of his authentic self. No, Samson was selfish, self-centered, self-reliant, and entitled. This created quite the platform for lust in his life.

Lust pursues immorality; lust looks for an immoral way to fulfill a sexual desire. It will make plans and is very ready to exploit an opportunity when it arises. That's why lust in someone else will often catch you by surprise. Lust is strategic, and the goal is always sexual immorality. It starts with a thought, a look, a touch, a word, a kiss but the end goal is always immorality. When lust pursues, it has already committed the deed in the mind, and where the head goes, the body follows. Samson, although anointed and appointed, set apart from birth intentionally pursued immorality.

Lust blinds to red flags; while it might be evident to us that Delilah was "Satan's cousin", this was not as obvious to Samson. Whether he was blinded by lust consciously or subconsciously we can't tell, because some of us can outright ignore red flags. All we know is that not once, not twice but thrice this man falls for the same trick! An anonymous quote comes to mind, *"once bitten, twice shy, third time a fool."*

If we still believe that "love is blind" then we have gotten it all wrong; it's not love that's blind, love rejoices with the truth, and to rejoice with the truth you must be able to see and recognize the truth. So no, it's not love, but lust that is blind. Because you want what you want, when you want it, you will walk into your assassination with your eyes wide shut.

Lust makes you comfortable in a hostile environment; Not only does Samson not see the red flags in the "little games" she played, but he is also now comfortable with someone who has agreed to have him trafficked; sold into bondage. This man is so comfortable that he falls asleep on the lap of his handler. Because of lust he was not discerning at all. Even in danger, Delilah had the perfect lullaby, she was the epitome of a beautiful nightmare and lust made this possible.

Sometimes the reason we can't rebuke the enemy is because we're sleeping with the enemy, literally and sometimes figuratively too. We are always more susceptible to the enemy when we're sleeping spiritually; when the eyes of our hearts are closed, we can't see the truth.

Lust wears you down; Samson had a form of godliness but denied its power in his life. Outwardly he walked out the laws of covenant with God but inwardly he was consumed with lust, and so he put up with Delilah's manipulation in wanting to know the secret to his strength. The bible says (Judges 16:16-17), *"With such nagging she prodded him day after day until he was sick to death of it. So he told her everything..."* Day after day his discretion regarding who God had called him to be was worn down and brought him to the point where he threw his pearls to the pigs. He shared the secret to his strength with someone who did not understand its value, and how could she? She knew Samson but because of lust she was not introduced to his God.

And as you know, every cause has an effect. Out of the many effects we can explore with Samson and lust, there are three I would like to mention here.

#1 He lost his strength.
"When Delilah saw that he had told her everything, she sent word to the rulers of the Philistines, "Come back once more; he has told me everything." So the rulers of the Philistines returned with the silver in their hands. After putting him to sleep on her lap, she called for someone to shave off the seven braids of his hair, and so began to subdue him. And his strength left him." - **Judges 16:16-19**

What's scary is that after lust had its way with Samson, he thought he could carry on with business as usual (verse 20) and this is sins' deceitfulness, we think that nothing will change when we allow lust in. Delilah called on the Philistines like she had done three times before and Samson thought he would shake himself free like he did before, but there comes a point in every lust cycle that you must face the effect and consequence of lust. Samson's strength left him and so did the presence of God, and because he was sleeping, he didn't know.

He found out when he woke up, and by then the Philistines were upon him. Don't be fooled into thinking that lust will allow you to carry on as per usual, no, there's always a price to pay. Once the enemy has what he wants it will be used against you and the problem with spiritual slumber is that while you're sleeping you can't protect what's been entrusted to you.

#2 He lost his sight.
"Then the Philistines seized him, gouged out his eyes and took him down to Gaza." - **Judges 16:21a**

The first thing the enemy did was subdue Samson; the second thing was to gouge out his eyes. How ironic - the enemy took the very thing that started this mess, his eyes. Our desires are heightened by our senses, and in Samson's case, what he saw, he lusted after and as Jesus taught, a lustful look is considered a done deal in the heart (Matt.5:28). I can't begin to imagine the pain Samson must have endured.

Samson, now blind, finally has his eyes opened, in a manner of speaking. With his eyes gone, his vision and focus are finally restored. Sometimes it takes a painful experience to help us see what's truly important. I will say though, we don't always have to wait for something bad to happen, and we don't always have to "lose our eyes" to see clearly. Samson didn't look to lust but could finally see himself for who he truly was, a weak man in need of God. I believe that what the enemy meant for his destruction, God used to help Samson see God for who He was - all powerful and still in control.

#3 He lost his freedom.
"Binding him with bronze shackles, they set him to grinding grain in the prison." - **Judges 16:21b**

Samson was bound with bronze shackles; much stronger than the ropes he snapped off so effortlessly before. He was no longer in a place of comfort. Samson lost his freedom and was now a prisoner. Lust always imprisons. In fact, note to self, the inner-me will always hand you over to the enemy.

Notice how lust always robs you of your freedom to go to God, instead of running *to* God, it convinces you to run *from* God and to overthink in a prison of your own making. When lust is present in your life you lose the freedom to reach out to godly voices in your life. You isolate yourself from friends, family and fellow Christians who will pray for you, walk with you and hold you accountable. Lust takes our freedom by force.

Fortunately, Samsons story does not end in tragedy but in triumph. Lust wants you to think that it's over for you, that you're finished. This is not true. Samson may have been, dishonourable, entitled, overcome with lust, he may have completely disregarded God the sake of his "love" interest, but God's love, His plan, purpose and promises still stand. Samson's transgressions and iniquity couldn't knock God off center, it did not catch Him by surprise. God never abdicates His throne. In God's foreknowledge and wisdom, He knew what it would take to get Samson to where He needed to be. What almost destroyed Samson God used to effect judgment on the enemies of God.

> God will take our mess and give us a *message*.
> He can take our test and transform it into a *testimony*.
> From a disaster, God can make a *Pastor*.
> He can take an unwanted baby and turn her into a *God-fearing lady*.

God's track record speaks for itself, He can redeem anything and anyone at any time. Because of lust, Samson was half the man he was created to be, blind, in bondage and grinding grain in a Philistine prison, But God...

"The hair on his head began to grow again after it had been shaved."
- Judges 16: 22

Samson's hair began to grow again, his supernatural strength returned and this time he was not going to be caught sleeping. The rulers of the Philistines assembled to offer a sacrifice to Dagon their god for delivering Samson into their hands.

The narrative shows that there were thousands of his enemies gathered in one place. I'll tell you now, if you're willing, God always makes room for a comeback. Samson was blind enough to see this God-given opportunity. While his enemies were entertained by his blindness and bondage, Samson positioned himself in prayer and positioned himself for purpose; he asked to be led to the central pillars that held up the arena - sometimes pain will position you - and Samson exerted his strength one last time, so much so that he killed more Philistines in his death than while he lived. You've heard it said that your greatest ministry is often birthed from your deepest pain; I'll go further to say that your greatest impact in relationships romantic or otherwise is determined by your willingness to die to self.

WHAT'S LOVE GOT TO DO WITH IT

We are all familiar with Tina Turner's hit song, where she asks the question: "Who needs a heart when a heart can be broken?" right? No, wrong. Love, and by extension, your heart has everything to do with it. Agapè underpins all of life and that's why it's so important that we get the various expressions of love right, because when we get it wrong, we not only miss our purpose and life's calling but it will also impact the generations that will come from us. Too much hangs in the balance for us to get love wrong.

It is by the love we have for one another that the world will know that we are Christ's disciples. This is one of the many reasons why love is under siege, because when we truly love we are most like God. When we are filled with love, we are who we were truly created to be, and will do all that we were called to do. And yet, we've gotten it so wrong that broken men will use love for sex and hurt women will use sex for love. We are wired differently, and we know that and unfortunately, we've learnt how to use our differences to our advantage - an advantage that has become our disadvantage. Men know that women are moved by how they feel.

A woman needs to feel secure, wanted and adored. Persuasive words, convincing actions, and time and attention move her to feel, and to feel deeply. Women know that men are moved by what they see; a man wants to see you satisfy him with respect, servitude and very importantly, sex, and so women will use seduction, strategies and sex to bag the love she longs for. Love has become a dangerous game we play. Russian roulette has nothing on our game of love. And that's because we've gotten it wrong, thinking that Eros is *it*.

Erotic love is not love unless it is undergirded with Agapè. Unless we have experienced the God Who is love, we will make a god of eros. With our broken version of love, eros will always be the end goal and because of this brokenness, the end will always justify the means. By "means" I mean, the lies, the games, manipulation and fornication. To get to eros, broken men and women will do whatever it takes, and then one day decide they want to play the game with someone else, or with more than one person. I think our problem is that we are willing to settle for the broken version of love, which is eros devoid of agapè.

> *"It would seem that Our Lord finds our desires not too strong, but too weak. We are halfhearted creatures, fooling about with drink and sex and ambition when infinite joy is offered us, like an ignorant child who wants to go on making mud pies in a slum because he cannot imagine what is meant by the offer of a holiday at the sea. We are far too easily pleased."*
> **- CS Lewis**

Could it be that the thrill of our chase for love is absolutely nothing compared to what God is offering us? Could it be that in pursuing eros we're missing out on the best? Could it be that God is not offended by our strong desire for love but that you and I have a "me-problem", in that we are truly as CS Lewis says, *"We are far too easily pleased."*

Whatever you do, do not settle. Do not settle for the caricature of love we've accepted as truth, because it couldn't be farther from it. Don't settle for anything devoid of agape, because if your love interest can love and be loved by God they can love and be loved by you. If they have the capacity to love God, they will have the capacity to love you.

This is where *Sound Guy* blew my mind. Firstly, he was the first man I met that was so comfortable with his sexuality that he didn't need to prove it. When we started dating, I knew he was attracted to me because he didn't make a secret of it, I read his eyes, they told me everything. They still do.

It was his self-control for me. *Sound Guy* taught me how to respect and master my flesh. A common mistake young Christians make and some older ones too, we tend to overestimate our ability to disciple the flesh. We want to cast out the flesh and disciple the demon. Pastor Robert Morris, Senior Pastor of Gate Way Church makes this statement, and the point is that we need to know what we're up against so that we can deal with it effectively. *Demons can't be discipled, and the flesh can't be cast out. Know what you're dealing with and deal with it effectively.*

Sound Guy knew what he was up against and proved to be man in control, because he was under control. He was in control of himself because he was under the control of the Holy Spirit. I'd never seen that measure of self-control in a romantic relationship, and I thought it was beautiful. Were there times we were tempted to open negotiations on non-negotiables, to adjust boundaries? Like one elderly woman responded to a rebuke from her pastor about her live-in boyfriend, "*I'm not made of stone.*" So, to answer the thought in your mind, yes of course we were tempted, but God always provided the way out. Sometimes *Sound Guy's* self-control would leave me breathless, but here's what sucker punched me. I was curious; I wanted to know how he knew I was the one he wanted to choose. His response, "*I want to spend my life with someone who loves God more than me, and I found that in you.*" It didn't take me long to figure out he was looking for that quality in me because he desired to love God more than me. And to this day I wouldn't want to have it any other way.

This is where I learnt that love is not only a decision, sacrifice and demonstration, love is also a motivation. It's a reason, not an intention. There's a difference. Too many people enter romantic relationships with only good intentions. But good intentions are not enough. Good intentions can get the romance started but it cannot sustain the relationship. Intentions need a motivation.

An intention is a desire. A motivation is the reason why. Your *why* will keep you going when your desires pack up and leave. Because of their fickle and temporal nature, intentions soon become regrets. Intentionality is often noble but without the *why* factor of love, your good intentions will lead you all the way to hell. I've cried and counseled people who had good intentions but sat with their heart in their hands because they failed to check in on the motivation, whether it was strong enough to carry the desire. And here's the key to unchaining your heart when it comes to the motivation of others. Motivation is a heart thing, and that's God's domain. We spend too much time, effort and tears trying to change the hearts and the motivations of others. Everything about them shows that they're not the one we should choose but we commit ourselves fully to *making* them the one. We try to make them better, to make them love us, to make them change. But it's a matter of motivation, and motivation is a matter of the heart, and that's God's domain. Stay in your lane.

The only motivations you are responsible for are your own. Start there. David prayed and asked God to check if there was any wicked way in him (Ps.139:23-24). In prayer God showed me the motivations of my heart. And when I say prayer, I mean the kind of prayer that has the bible open, the dialogue not the monologue kind. Effective prayer is not just speaking to God but pausing long enough to hear Him speak back and shining His light on the inner recesses of our hearts.

Prayer and circumstance often reveal what's really in our hearts. Tests, difficult situations and people have a way of revealing the truth about us, our hearts and motivations. Whether you're single, married, divorced or in a "situationship", (ok, we'll include the "it's complicated" persons) it's important to make sure your motivation for relationships romantic or otherwise has as its foundation agapè, if not, you're setting yourself and others up for chains.

God is more interested in the motivations that lead to our actions (1Cor.4:5). This reality ought to change our focus from what we do, to why we do it.

Now for our next challenge: Because we cannot see the inner motivations of others, we are unable to judge their motives. When I say judge, I don't mean in the capacity of God on judgment day, when He will judge the world and mankind to eternal death or eternal life, I'm referring to the judgment all believers are to exercise when it comes to making quality decisions on the kind of people we will align ourselves to (1Cor.2:15). While we can't judge their hearts we can discern their fruit, because a tree is known by its fruit (Luke 6:43-45).

A good friend and I were chatting about how single women must remember men are not known by their words or kisses, they are known by their fruit. They are not known by the *feels*, but by what they produce! And this is true for women as well. Single gentlemen, she will be known not by her hips or lips, and yes, we know her hips don't lie, but can she pray? Can she worship? Is she led by the Spirit? Does she show honour? Can she work her gift? Can she produce? Think a little further than your stomach and ego; can she impact your life and the lives of others in a way that matters for eternity?

While we can't see a person's motive, unless it is revealed, we can discern their fruit. And here are a few ways to do that, there are more, but these should start you on your way.

(a) Time; Notice fruit doesn't grow over night, and like the process of growth, takes time; it will take time to begin to see their fruit. This microwave, fast food, hook-up culture generation will try to convince you that you don't have time. Our culture will create FOMO (fear of missing out) by implying that if you don't act now, you'll miss out on the opportunity for love. Don't get me started on the "biological-clock-is-ticking" gorilla tactic used to create fear and

anxiety in the hearts of young women. Nothing reveals fruit like time - the longer the better - the more time you're willing to give, the more will be revealed.

(b) *Observation;* a lot of people look, few people see, but the wise watch. If you're going to get to know someone by their fruit, you are going to have to be observant. And observation comes with proximity. You will have to get in their space. Spaces like work, play, family - wherever they're comfortable. Like Jesus, He saw a fig tree in the distance but had to get closer to see if it had any fruit (Mark 11:12-25). From a distance He recognized that it was a fig tree, but up close He found it to be fruitless.

Let's pause here for a moment. This story of the fig tree that Jesus curses, has left many bewildered and wondering why Jesus would curse it. The passage states unequivocally that it was not the season for figs, it was in late spring, and most fig trees haven't developed mature fruit, so why then, did Jesus' deal so harshly with it? Well, the scripture reference starts the fact that Jesus spots a fig tree "in leaf", meaning that it *looked* as one in full bloom. This tree draws Jesus' attention because it already had a full covering of leaves. It was an early bloomer. Its foliage signals that it should have early figs.

With that expectation, Jesus inspects the tree. He is immediately disappointed. All leaves, no fruit. All expectation, no satisfaction.

It is here that Jesus curses the tree and makes it wither from the roots, never to yield fruit again. Just like this fig tree, there are many who *display* characteristics that they do not *possess*. It is easy for a man or woman to act like they have integrity, to act like they have a relationship with Jesus. They just need to say the right things, quote the appropriate scriptures, raise their hands in church, etc., but upon closer inspection they bear no fruit.

In Matthew 17:16 Jesus states that we shall be known by our fruits. Known, not recognized. From afar one can recognize a fig tree, just like Jesus recognized this one, but then cursed it, when there was no fruit to back up that it was indeed a fruit bearing tree, available for sustenance. This tree was "putting on a good show." And that made it all the worse. It's one thing to lack fruit out of season. It's another thing to lack it while pretending you have it.

Our personal lives can look "in leaf." The lives of those we wish to partner with romantically, may look "in leaf", but looks can be deceiving, because although the leaves look good, the root may be withered. There may be no fruit of holiness and no intimacy with God. The leaves only come to fool us.

You've got to observe them in their natural habitat not just on dates. Why? Because even a predator is just entertainment in a glass cage. What I mean is that everyone puts their best foot forward on dates but given enough time and proximity they'll snitch on themselves. Observation will require you to be objective and to think critically about what you're seeing in the life of your love interest - whether its fruit, or just leaves. It is important, that you don't observe *in* the relationship, but that you observe *before* you commit to the relationship, because one of the grave dangers is that fruitlessness leads to judgment - Jesus cursing the tree - and when you yoke yourself to someone, you become part of that judgment when it comes. And then there's:

(c) *Perspective;* there's nothing like good ol' fashion perspective to help you discern fruit. And the interesting thing about perspective is that what you see is determined by where you stand.

The most common example is to have two people standing at the opposite ends of the number 9. For the person looking from the top, they see a 6, the person looking from the bottom sees a 9. Perspective is determined by a number of things but when it comes to fruit, allow the perspective of someone closer in proximity to inform yours. There is no perspective quite like that of a family member, a longtime colleague, a close friend or someone from whom they cannot benefit in any way. No and this is not snooping, or trying to catch someone out, this is you getting perspective, so that you can make an informed decision about the depth of your involvement with them. Someone with nothing to hide will not object to you doing your due diligence, and in fact, they would be wise to do the same with you.

Often times people will keep you away from their family and friends, and those who know them intimately, and this is not because they wish to keep *you* a secret but are themselves the secret they wish to keep you from finding out. They are not "protecting the relationship", they are keeping you from knowing their true fruit.

Yes, and I get it, sometimes people low key hate, and will say untrue things to slander the person or just to throw you of course, which is why your discernment is vital, but on the flip side, if everyone is seeing the same thing then you better take note. We need to hone the art of differentiating between personality and character. Too many times we confuse the two. Personality implies who we seem to be, how we portray ourselves; character represents who we really are. The personality of an individual may change with time. However, the character lasts longer.

For example, someone may be described as a "nice person", which is the very reason people get into relationships with other people, because they are nice people. But even serial killers can have "nice personalities"- in fact in interviews conducted with those around them, the general consensus is "I am so surprised, he seemed like such a nice person!" Personality is who you are when you are with other people. Character is who you are when you are alone. Personality is leaves; character is fruit. Your personality can get you into places, that only your character can sustain you in.

Discernment is a superpower. It is the ability to judge well, and it proves to be critical in navigating the often-murky waters of romantic relationships in a fallen world. Fundamentally discernment is a gift of the Holy Spirit and He gives it to us to judge between truth and error, between what looks good and what *is* good. It is the Holy Spirit who enables us to judge a tree and its fruit; between what people display and what they produce.

Time, observation, and perspective are just some of the ways the Holy Spirit reveals the truth about an individual to us. And if we are honest with ourselves, sometimes there are things we don't want to see, so we reason away realities and justify why we see red flags and not ripe fruit. This brings to mind the popular phrase: "you can put lipstick on a pig, but it's still a pig." That expression is older than my grandfather's grandfather and it means that you can dress something up, but it doesn't change what it is - circumstances do not alter a man's true nature, nor even his manners.

That my dear friend is on us, and not God, because had we taken the time, and done the hard work of observing and gaining proper perspective we would have been able to make informed decisions before committing ourselves to dysfunctional and toxic relationships. When dating *Sound Guy*, I realized that God had wanted to show me all along, how to steward the grace of choosing a life partner. There was a time when young people didn't have a say, in this generation, we have a say; for the most part, we can decide for ourselves, that is grace, and it should not be taken lightly.

The most important decision we will ever make is choosing Christ as Lord and Saviour because that determines whether or not we will have eternal life, and the second most important decision is who you will spend your life with because that will determine the quality of your life. And here's the thing, Jesus is always the wise choice, the question is will you exercise wisdom in your love choice? We must be sure never to rush into emotions or relationships devoid of agapè, and how we do that is by discerning the fruit or what our love interest produces. And here's the baseline for what people produce.

"But the Holy Spirit produces this kind of fruit in our lives: love, joy, peace, patience, kindness, goodness, faithfulness, gentleness, and self-control. There is no law against these things!" - **Galatians 5:22-23**

This is where we start when we speak of a tree is known by its fruit. What they produce is severely diminished if they don't have love. Their fruit must begin with love and love begins with God. The mistake we make is thinking that the fruit of the Spirit is something to attain, something we work towards; something others have to work towards. This is foundational; an apple tree doesn't produce apples by self-effort, it produces apples because it is an apple tree. It doesn't have to try. Bearing anything other than apples would be going against its nature, basically rebelling against its DNA. When something goes against its DNA, one of two things happens - mutation or destruction. The tree will start looking like something it's not or if the error cannot be corrected it will start to destroy itself, essentially self-destruct.

Let me break it down. Saints, we are rushing into relationships, running on the fumes of desire but unsure of the motivation. Instead of checking their fruit, we're justifying their red flags and misusing the baseline of fruit as a goal, settling for less than God's best for us. So, we're okay with thorn bushes trying to be apple trees; we're ok with the mutant version of what their fruit should be, so we post things like "love lives here" while we're in self-destruct mode. To quote this generation: "the fruit is not fruiting!"

What we fail to realize is that we're already loved. We don't have to weaponize the weakness of the opposite gender to get what we think we need. God's love is the measuring line and standard by which we give and receive love. We don't have to settle. We don't have to rush in, narrow minded and blindly. It is time to unmask lust and expose it for what it truly is, we've aided and abetted the inner-me and like Samson, it has chained us. And so, to answer our question, love has everything to do with it. Love never fails.

HOW FAR IS TOO FAR?

I'm not sure how many times I've heard this question from young people and actually tried to answer it. What I do know is that generally when we ask this question we've already gone too far. And again, generally, Christians want to know where the line is so that we can do spiritual gymnastics in trying to get as close to the line as possible and still be regarded as "saved." We want to get as close to sex as possible without facing the consequences or losing our Christian identity. This in and of itself is a delusion. It's a lie that we believe because the truth is, the sin of sexual immorality does not start with the act of sex. We've become so focused on not having the act of sex that we've duped ourselves into thinking that everything before sex is permissible. So, the unspoken rule is, everything goes as long as we're not having sex. Right?

Wrong. There are three realities we must face if we are to start the process of deconstructing this lie.

> **#1.** The act of illicit sex starts as a thought.
> **#2**. You can't touch my body intimately without touching my soul.
> **#3**. The further you go, the more difficult it is to come back.

Firstly, note that all sin separates us from God. Habitual sin causes spiritual death. Illicit sex not only separates us from God, but we also sin against our own bodies. This is why when you indulge in sexual immorality you not only feel disconnected from God but also from yourself; your true self, created to be like God in righteousness and holiness. Sexual immorality makes you an enemy to God and a stranger to yourself. Sexual immorality is lethal in that it not only destroys your relationship with God in the here and now, but for eternity to come. So, when we teach on this, it's not God holding out on you, it's God looking out for you, it is in your best interest not to be chained to sexual immorality. The challenge before us is that sexual immorality doesn't begin with sex, it begins as a seed, a thought. Is the thought sin? Well, just like temptation is not a sin, neither is the entry of a thought. However, it is what we *do* with the thought that brings us closer to sin. "Martin Luther said, "*You cannot keep birds from flying over your head but you can keep them from building a nest in your hair.*" In other words, you can't keep the enemy from suggesting thoughts, but you can choose not to dwell or act on them."

Thoughts begin in your head then affect your body and before you know it, you're moving towards it. Sex is the culmination not the start, and it's the start we must guard against. For the longest time I thought that I didn't have control over my thoughts; I thought that where they lead, I must follow. And what compounded this was that I thought all my thoughts were my own, and added to that I thought that the enemy knew what I was thinking. According to John 8:32, Jesus did not come to play when He said, *"If you abide in my word, you are truly my disciples, and you will know the truth, and the truth will set you free."* Understand that you will continue to be chained to sexual immorality if you don't know the truth about your mind, thoughts, thought patterns, strongholds and your power, because it starts there.

The Lie:
You don't have control over your thoughts.
Thoughts lead… and we follow.

The Truth:
"Guard your heart above all else, for it determines the course of your life." - **Proverbs 4:32**

Your heart is made up of your thoughts, will and emotions, and you have been mandated to guard it, because not only does everything you do flow from it, but your heart also determines the course - and by extension - the direction of your life. No one is placed as a guard without having the capacity to protect what has been entrusted in their care. You have been fully equipped to guard your heart with the power of the Holy Spirit. And what's more; you have access to everything you need to guard your heart. Yes, you have access to wisdom and the power required to guard your heart. Paul takes this a step further and gives us a mental picture of what this process of guarding your heart looks like:

"We demolish arguments and every pretension that sets itself up against the knowledge of God, and we take captive every thought to make it obedient to Christ."- **2 Cor. 10:5**

Can you see how you're like a Samurai Warrior when it comes to your thoughts? You have the power to demolish imaginations. You have the authority take captive every thought and make it obedient to Christ. And the enemy does not want you to know this.

The Lie:
All your thoughts are your own.
Because you thought it... you must own it.

The Truth:
"It was during supper, when the devil had already put [the thought of] betraying Jesus into the heart of Judas Iscariot, Simon's son, that Jesus, knowing that the Father had put everything into His hands, and that He had come from God and was [now] returning to God, got up from supper, took off His [outer] robe, and taking a [servant's] towel, He tied it around His waist." **- John 13:2-4 AMP**

Not all your thoughts are your own. Many times, the enemy has a hand in the thoughts that come into your head. In Judas case it was direct, often it's indirect. I tread carefully here because now we're talking about intrusive thoughts. An intrusive thought is an unwelcome, involuntary thought, image, or unpleasant idea that may become an obsession; it is often upsetting or distressing and can feel difficult to manage or eliminate. The key is knowing what you're up against with intrusive thoughts. If its origin is spiritually dark, you have been given spiritual prowess to overcome the intrusion. However, if intrusive thoughts persist beyond a spiritual response - such as responding with the word, worship or meditating on scripture, we might be dealing with the outworking of your body's chemistry and it might require that you have the humility to ask for help from your pastor, a counselor or doctor. The point is that you can either accept or reject a thought. When a thought is accepted you have given it the right to remain in your mind and thus your heart. When a thought is rejected and replaced with truth, you have cancelled its power and hold over your heart. And yes, you're that powerful, even though it doesn't always feel that way.

The Lie:
The enemy knows what you're thinking...
that's why he has power over you.

The Truth:
"..then hear in heaven Your dwelling place, and forgive and act and give to each according to his ways, whose heart (mind) You know, for You and You alone know the hearts of all the children of men, so that they may fear You [with reverence and awe] all the days that they live in the land which You have given to our fathers."
– 1 Kings 8:38-40

- Satan is *not* omnipresent. He has minions that do his bidding. He can only be at one place, at one time, and it's probably nowhere near you.
- Satan is *not* omniscient. What he knows about you has been filtered to him by demons who have been watching you from birth. Everything the enemy knows about you is learnt information.
- Satan is *not* omnipotent. He is a formidable enemy yes, but a defeated foe all the same. He is an ancient enemy, but His power is limited.

God on the other hand *is* omnipresent, omniscient, and omnipotent. God knows everything, sees everything and is all powerful. Don't get it twisted child of God, if you're going to break the chains of sexual immorality it's going to start with you exercising your power over your mind, thoughts and thought patterns. This is why what you allow into your mind matters; the *inner-me* and the *enemy* can only use what's already there. This means we're going to have to be vigilant about what we watch, listen to and the company we keep. We must guard over what enters our hearts and minds.

Secondly, let's talk touch. Intimacy and what happens before sexual intercourse. Let's say the thought has now morphed into action, and we start telling ourselves that we can get as close as we can, without "actually doing it". So, we do a "dress rehearsal", thinking that it will prepare us for show time. You can imagine my horror, when I realized that the "dress rehearsal" was the real thing, because the show starts when the thought becomes an intimate touch. I said it once and I'll say it again - you can't touch my body intimately without touching my soul. The human touch has the power to touch your soul, the seat of your will, thoughts, and emotions. An intimate touch can create desire and stir emotions; it can also cause trauma and pain. An intimate touch has the potential to affect the soul for better or for worse. What I didn't realize while I was going from relationship to relationship, was that the illegitimate intimacy was compromising my soul. It was unauthorized and not in accordance with God's standard for intimacy.

Finally, understand this dear reader, the further you go with intimate touch, the more difficult it is to come back - not impossible - but difficult. The reason for this is that our human nature, and our physical body, knows it's headed somewhere, and the body is beginning to respond. Every time we are illegitimately intimate and cut it off for the sake of not having sex, we are abusing the gift that is our sexuality, but also creating a craving in the physical body, to reach culmination of what was awakened.

We were not created to cut off but to consummate; every time we stop short of sexual intimacy, we're going against the purpose, plan, and design for our sexuality. And anything that is abnormally used is being abused. This is why we are not to awaken love until it so desires. But when we have authorized access to sexual intimacy through a healthy marriage, we are living out our sexuality as God ordained it. Anything outside that framework is illegitimate and brings chains and bondage; whether you're stopping short or full on engaging in illicit sex, it's the same thing; sin is sin, is sin. This is not God's purpose for your sexuality.

Back in the day the metaphor of baseball was used to measure our proximity to sex. First base was kissing, second base was anything from caressing to groping; third base was a conundrum because the more you entered that playing field the more it resembled no man's land, the proverbial point of no return. Third base was especially dangerous when you discovered that you could climax without penetration. Fourth base, which was referred to as the home run – sex – could easily override or bypass third base. Usually, the progression to these bases happened over time, but with the grand entrance of social media and virtual dating, we are ripe and ready within hours of late-night chats, flirty statuses, profile thirst traps and steamy voice notes. Let's not forget sexting in the virtual foreplay. It is no wonder that boundaries don't stand a chance. This generation has succumbed to the law of momentum; even if you apply the brakes your momentum takes you further. When you're going at neck breaking speed, you don't stop where you applied brakes; you're going to continue down the road, and often it's too far and too late.

KRYPTONITE

Most of us will never forget the nostalgic tagline: "It's a bird! It's a plane! No, it's Superman!" The red and blue, with the striking yellow 'S', is exclusively synonymous with the fictional character that is Superman. This flying demigod from another planet inspired us to hope and know that good will always prevail. As Christians can relate to Superman, being in this world, but not of this world. Superman possesses supernatural strength, being known as the man of steel, not only for his brute physical strength, but also his strength of character. Superman is the epitome of leveraging strength for the good of all. Because of his strength Superman is unstoppable, unbeatable. Although we've seen him get beat down time and time again, we know how the story ends, always. We know Superman gets the girl and saves the day. Yeah! But even Superman has a nemesis, a weakness... Kryptonite. Whenever Superman is exposed to it, he becomes vulnerable and weak, making him like any other mortal man. Kryptonite is a compound from Superman's home planet Krypton and has the power to render the powerful Superman powerless. We know Superman is fictional and so is kryptonite but like John Bevere, Author of the book Kryptonite states, *"Kryptonite is fictional but spiritual Kryptonite is not."*

Sin, and more specifically sexual sin, - everything from lust to illicit sex - is like kryptonite. We are in this world but not of it - powerful beyond measure because of the indwelling Holy Spirit. We are given assignments to leverage our power, gifts, and opportunities to serve God, His people and to extend His kingdom, but exposure to sexual sin, like kryptonite, weakens even the strongest among us. When engaged in it we become just like the world around us. Now to be clear, there is a weakness that God uses to show His strength in our lives, but this is not that. The weakness I'm referring to is the kind that hinders, delays, binds, and keeps us from being and doing what God has called us to. I've heard young people romanticize sexual sin, explaining that, had they not engaged in it they would not have felt and experienced God in the way they did.

While it's true that, *"...the Law came to increase and expand [the awareness of] the trespass [by defining and unmasking sin]. But where sin increased, [God's remarkable, gracious gift of] grace [His unmerited favor] has surpassed it and increased all the more",* (Rom.5:20) we need not go to such great lengths to experience the grace and mercy of God.

Please be careful not to justify sin. Yes, God does use what the enemy meant for evil, and turn it for our good, (Gen.50:20) but that does not mean that He condones or glorifies the sin, as a means to an end. This places our feelings and experiences – specifically our sexuality - higher than God's will for our lives. Remember our feelings and experiences are only reference points when sharing truth. While these feelings and experiences are real, they are not necessarily the truth. God's word is truth and God's word expresses His will and ways. You may validate your feelings and experiences, they are real, and they are yours, but if you're going to be unchained and walk in truth and freedom, your feelings and experiences must be brought under submission to His Spirit filled Word.

Joshua chapter 9, entitled "The Gibeonite Deception" is a case in point. I encourage you to take the time out to read it, but for purposes of this illustration, I will take you through it. Israel was on a mission to take possession of the Promised Land, this meant that they would have to drive out all its people, but the Gibeonites resorted to a ruse (9:4). They disguised themselves as people coming from a distant land, worn out and weary. To escape being destroyed along with all the Canaanite nations, they urged Joshua to make a covenant with them, in fact they pleaded (9:9). Their deception worked, *"Joshua made peace with them and made a covenant with them, to let them live."*

And why did their trick work? The bible makes it clear in chapter 9 verse 15. It was because Joshua and the leaders did not ask counsel from the Lord.

Instead, Joshua and the leaders sampled their provisions - the dry and moldy bread - they examined the cracked wineskins and they looked at their clothes and sandals, that were worn out from the supposed long journey. Joshua knew God's provision because he ate manna, drank water from a rock and his clothes and sandals never wore out, but Joshua knew what forty years in a wilderness felt like. And so, three days after Joshua and the Israelites entered into covenant with the Gibeonites they discovered that they were Canaanite neighbours and ended up compromising on what God had commanded them.

God's counsel trumps our feelings and experiences, it doesn't mean that they're not important, it just means that His ways and thoughts are higher than ours. Where we can be deceived, God can never be. Here are 3 ways kryptonite weakens us:

#1 *Weakens our witness* - we are called to witness to the world of the love and transformational power of God in our lives. A witness either has or carries evidence proving the truth they profess. As witnesses to the world, we carry truth, our lives are supposed to be evidence of God's presence and power. Jesus wants us to be His witnesses - first where we find ourselves - and then to go out and find others beyond our borders, but our witness is weakened when the very thing we are witnessing about is not our truth or reality. When exposed to kryptonite we are muted, unable to testify to the truth because we have sided with the enemy against God and against our own bodies.

#2 *Weakens our relationships* - we were created in relationship and for relationship. Relationships are part and parcel of our spiritual DNA. We are conceived between one male and one female. We are born into a family. Our family forms part of a community. No matter where we go or what we do we will always form part of a relationship in some way, shape or form. When we come to God through Jesus Christ by the power of the Holy Spirit, we enter relationship with God and have communion and fellowship with

Him - our triune God - He is relational. A relationship is the deciding factor for entering the kingdom of heaven (Matt.7:21-23). Kryptonite weakens our relationship with God and others. Kryptonite will cut off godly voices of family and friends.

#3 *Weakens our moral authority* - as believers we have values and standards that determine our behaviour, we are also called to exercise principles of right and wrong in a relative world. This is especially true for leaders within the body of Christ. As leaders we are held up to higher standards - not pedestals - they should be standards. It is our ability to consistently walk in the truth of God's word that gives us the moral authority to speak into the lives of others. The right to speak into the lives of others is not a given, it is earned. We earn it through practicing what we preach; being an example through disappointment, sacrifice, pain, and temptation. But Kryptonite weakens our moral authority. When we fail in the area of sexual morality, we lose the right to speak into others' lives; we lose the right to admonish, teach and correct those we lead or walk with. In fact, we do spiritual harm to ourselves and others when we nurse sexual sin while leading and serving others.

We have a choice to make, we can expose ourselves to kryptonite and become like everyone else in the world or we could surrender to the sanctifying work of the Holy Spirit in our lives and relationships and truly be who God called us to be to one another and the world. So how do we deal with kryptonite? I can't remember how many times I have had to ask myself this question. All the relationship books I read were in agreement on setting boundaries, resisting & running.

What I really wanted was a heartfelt desire to be content with my sexual desires and not ashamed of them. I wanted what *Sound Guy* had - a mastery over his soul, truly satisfied, willing to go the distance and be patient in the waiting. I wanted to exercise wisdom and foresight and not run for the sake of running, but to run with conviction and prudence, because saints, we can only run for so long when we feel forced to run. I wanted to *want* to resist and run from temptation.

I noticed something with Joseph, the beloved son of Jacob. Joseph went from being loved and adored, to being trafficked in what must have seemed like the blink of an eye. He was sold for 20 shekels of silver, headed for Egypt. His crime? Two dreams and a coat of many colours. Joseph was thrown into a pit and sold by his own brothers. I can't even begin to imagine the level of PTSD linked to that situation, but we are told that he was sold again, this time to the captain of Pharoah's guard, Potiphar. Joseph was highly favoured and soon caught the attention of Potiphar's wife, because he "ticked all the boxes".

- Favoured
- Blessed
- In Command
- Successful
- Well built
- Handsome

I've read the account of Joseph and Potiphar's wife so many times before, but failed to notice that what happened with Joseph reveals keys to overcoming kryptonite. We are told in scripture, that this woman tried to seduce him daily, but he refused to go to bed with her or even be near her. And here's why.

> *"But he refused. 'With me in charge,' he told her, 'my master does not concern himself with anything in the house; everything he owns he has entrusted to my care. No one is greater in this house than I am. My master has withheld nothing from me except you, because you are his wife. How then could I do such a wicked thing and sin against God?"*
> **- Genesis 39: 8-9**

Joseph was *entrusted* with everything Potiphar owned - we're talking *everything* in his house and in his field. With everything of value in Joseph's care, Potiphar did not concern himself with anything except the food he ate. To entrust someone with everything you own requires a great measure of *trust*, in their character, in their intentions, in their dealings. Potiphar trusted Joseph with everything. To be clear

Potiphar's possessions didn't belong to Joseph, but he had the aptitude, competence, and integrity to steward it as if it were his own. And this is our story too. We are not our own, we were bought at a price. Redeemed is what we are. Not even our bodies belong to us, everything we have has been entrusted to us. And the mind-blowing fact is that God trusts us with us! Our time, treasure, talents, yes, every opportunity, difficulty, trial, and lesson has been entrusted to us; our families, relationships, networks, and connections have been entrusted to us. We are not the owners, but we exercise ownership by being good stewards. And what's more, everything of value has been given to us according to our ability. God will not entrust something of value to us that we don't have the capacity to steward.

Every good steward understands that everything that has been entrusted must be accounted for. Bad stewards manage things of value poorly, not understanding that one day they will have to give an account of their management of those things. Joseph was a steward who understood that what was put into his care would have to be accounted for.

What does this have to do with kryptonite?

Well, not only did Joseph know what was entrusted to him, he also *knew what was off limits*. In his case, the *what*, was a *who*; Potiphar's wife was off limits. You must take note of the fact that Joseph did not obsess about who was off limits, he occupied himself with managing what was within his limit, with what was entrusted to him. And this is important because this tactic of the enemy is as old as the Garden. The enemy will always manipulate us into focusing on what we can't have instead of everything we can. Which is why this generation is so absorbed with what we shouldn't do that it forgets what we should, this approach makes romantic relationships unsustainable.

The next key to overcoming kryptonite is found in the fact that Joseph *perceived* Potiphar's wife's invitation to adultery *as wicked*. The thing with wickedness is that it's not a weakness or mistake or an error in judgement; wickedness is not something you stumble into. Wickedness involves profound evil, committed consciously and of free will. You *decide* to be wicked. The problem with our generation is that we perceive wickedness to be desirable. And I understand why media houses have attached compelling and relatable storylines to fornication; they've added mood altering music to steamy love scenes between adulterers. Everyone knows someone - us included - engaged in sexual immorality, and we are unable reconcile God's holy, standards and commands with our brokenness. We have created an emotional connection with sin, so we see what separates us from God as desirable.

Until we see kryptonite for what it truly is, we can continue to resist and run but people like Potiphar's wife will eventually wear down our resolve like Delilah did to Samson. By the time Potiphar's wife grabbed hold of Joseph he had already unlocked doors of victory over sexual sin with these keys. Joseph knew exactly *why* he was running; He could not sin against God and against Potiphar in this way (Gen.39:9). He ran from sin; he wasn't running from a desire to sin. There's a difference. He saw adultery for what it truly was.

Flee: *escape, elude,* or *seek safety in flight*. Because of the relationship Joseph had with his God, he had already dealt with the *desire to sin*, by submitting himself unto obedience to the call and command of God. Therefore, fleeing from and abstaining from *every* form of evil (1Thess 5:22) was a no brainer. He didn't need to evaluate or quantify the size of the sin, or the severity of the impending consequence. He just knew the difference between what pleased God, and what didn't.

You don't need to understand to escape temptation, but if you don't know the value of your relationship with your God, soon your running will become a futile exercise, and what you're running from, will wear you down. We ought not just flee/run from sin, but we ought to pursue righteousness.

> "But you, man of God, avoid all these things. Strive for righteousness, godliness, faith, love, endurance, and gentleness."
> **– 1 Timothy 6: 11-12 GNT**

"So then, let us rid ourselves of everything that gets in the way, and of the sin which holds on to us so tightly, and let us run with determination the race that lies before us. Let us keep our eyes fixed on Jesus, on whom our faith depends from beginning to end." - **Hebrews 12: 1-2 GNT**

Running *from* sin, is only one part of the life of the overcomer, the other part is to continually pursue, run *toward* righteousness. The question before us is, can we see sexual immorality in its various forms for what it truly is? With that said, we ought to be careful to not romanticize righteousness. It leads to entitlement. I've seen the disappointment entitlement brings to the life of the believer. We think that because we do the right things that we are entitled to circumstances serving our interests. Job showed us that even the righteous are not immune to trouble. Even Jesus concurred this sentiment when He said: (Jn.16:33), *"In this world you will have trouble. But take heart! I have overcome the world."*

Let's take a step further:
"Anyone who wants to live all out for Christ is in for a lot of trouble; there's no getting around it." **– 2 Timothy 3:12 MSG**

I don't want you to be deceived into thinking that doing the right thing will always get us the outcome we desire or feel we deserve. It's important that you understand this, because being a "Joseph" in this generation and saving yourself for marriage doesn't always guarantee a great sex life in marriage - another purity culture incomplete teaching. There are too many complexities that must be aligned. So then, why save yourself for marriage, what's the end game?

- Because it honours God
- Because it's God's will for your life
- Because it creates a preferred future
- Because iniquity will not be passed on in your bloodline

This list can go on, but what I am saying is: Choose love over lust because it will give you more than just a great marriage or sex life, it will give you the chance to truly *live*, in every sense of the word. Joseph ran from Potiphar's wife and what was his repayment for being a good steward, knowing his limits, evading sexual immorality and wickedness? Prison. Dear Reader, his repayment was prison! The same outcome as Samson. I'm saying that Joseph had a prison and Samson had a prison! Yes, both purity and sexual immorality had a prison. And I need you to understand that exercising your purity is hard but so is sexual immorality - We will have to choose our hard, we must "pick a struggle"- decide what challenge you want to focus your efforts and energies on, and which one will yield the best possible outcomes; bearing in mind that each bears an eternal consequence. I am reminded me of a poem that caught my attention:

Marriage is hard. Divorce is hard
Choose your hard.
Obesity is hard. Being fit is hard
Choose your hard.
Being in debt is hard. Financial discipline is hard
Choose your hard.
Communication is hard. Not communicating is hard.
Choose your hard.
Life will never be easy. It will always be hard.
But we can choose our hard.
Choose wisely.

Whatever we choose will be hard. If we choose to exercise our purity, we will also face difficulties and challenges. If we choose sexual immorality, we will face much of the same. We're living in a broken world, with broken people and quite frankly, there are times and seasons in our lives when we must face our own brokenness too. The difference is Joseph's prison had a purpose, but Samson's prison was a consequence.

Choose the "hards" that will enhance your life, rather than letting them choose you. The pain you choose eventually becomes your edge. Just remember that you have an incentive: you are responsible for the consequences of your disobedience, but God is responsible for the outcomes of your obedience. Choose your hard. Choose wisely.

chapter nine

Broken

"God uses broken things. It takes broken soil to produce a crop, broken clouds to give rain, broken grain to give bread, broken bread to give strength. It is the broken alabaster box that gives forth perfume. It is Peter, weeping bitterly, who returns to greater power than ever."
~ Vance Havner

Allison walked into my office and the first thing I noticed about her were her eyes. She had beautiful eyes - sad but beautiful - and through them I was able to peer into her soul. Her soul was broken. When I met Allison, she was only 23 years old, but you wouldn't say. Three failed suicide attempts left her cynical and wounded beyond her years. For the next few weeks, I had the sacred honour of sitting with Allison in her pain, holding space for truth and grace to fill her heart. Her family wanted to primarily address the suicide attempts, but we both knew it was only a symptom of a deeper issue and they weren't ready for that. Thankfully Allison was ready. She was ready to face her brokenness. Allison was raised by her grandmother because her own mother, who was unmarried, fell on hard times. Allison was the fourth child, and what compounded her narrative was that she was the child of a married man and so she was not only rejected by her father but by her siblings and extended family as well. Her maternal grandmother was a hard woman, but she loved the Lord and made sure that Allison attended Sunday school every Sunday. It was at Sunday school that Allison learnt that she had a Heavenly Father, but He seemed much like her absent father - cold and aloof, unbothered and unconcerned that poverty not only robbed her of what every child needed to thrive, but also blinded the eyes and shut the mouths of those who should have put an end to the sexual assault that robbed her of her innocence. When Allison did speak up about the sexual misconduct she was enduring, she was labelled as "ougat" (An Afrikaans term for somebody who is sexually mischievous). When one of her perpetrators was caught, literally with his pants down, she was given a five Rands (South African Currency) by her aunt in attempt to buy her silence, because that perpetrator also provided for the family.

Allison was molested by several men in her family from 6 years of age until her 15th birthday - which was also her first suicide attempt. That year Allison met a young man who loved her eyes and promised to never make them cry again. He lied. At 17 she fell pregnant but lost the baby due to his blind rage - a blow to her abdomen caused a placental abruption. The next pregnancy ended in abortion and the pregnancies after that just would not hold past the first trimester. At 19 Allison attempted suicide a second time. Allison woke up in a government hospital surrounded by mentally ill individuals because there was no room for her in the other ward, or so she was told by the nurse who attended to her. She cried out to the God she was taught to call Father, but He didn't answer. At 21 Allison married a man who she described as a toxic and dysfunctional individual. She worked three jobs while he stayed at home, sat on street corners and drank with friends. Sick with nausea and pregnant again Allison got permission to go home, only to find her toxic and dysfunctional husband in bed with her landlord. Allison and her husband lived in a modest back room, on her property.

Allison started bleeding.

Crouched up in a pool of blood, Allison gulped down a bottle of pain killers, 42 tablets she was told. Her landlord, riddled with guilt called an ambulance. This was Allison's third failed suicide attempt. This time it was different though, while in recovery Allison vaguely remembers a man who came to visit her every evening; he held her hand and read words she can only imagine were from the bible. She had no fear; instead, she felt a peace she'd never experienced before.

Instead of despair there was a sense of hope that seemed to increase with every crescendo he reached in worship, as he seemed to sing over her. She didn't recognize his voice, but she thought him to be an older gentleman, alone in her room, wanting nothing from her, but giving her a sense of worth, honour and dignity with every word, every song of worship and every prayer. Every time she recalled the experience, she told me how she wished this unknown man was her father. She believed with all her heart that her life would have turned out differently if he was. Allison is not alone. She shares parts of her narrative with 1 in every 3 girls in South Africa. Statistics show that about a third of girls in South Africa will experience some form of sexual abuse during their lifetime, and one in five children will be sexually assaulted. You and I know that Allison is more than just a statistic, she's a person and she is broken. Too often we meet the Allison's of our world or sphere of influence and ask why she doesn't do better, why she doesn't go study or get a better job or leave that toxic and dysfunctional liar. We fail to see how her past influences her here and now, chaining her to a cycle of bad decisions and consequences. People have sharply criticized me for sitting with and holding space for young people who seem reckless and beyond redemption - if there ever was such a thing! Let me tell you, no one is beyond redemption! If they're still breathing, they're worth saving - according to Jesus, and I am in full agreement with Him! This is why ministry to children is so important, whether in the home, at school or at church. Wherever children are, our ministry to them is essential, because what *walked* with the fathers, *runs* with the children. In a spiritual sense, if as parents, we're not slaying the giants in our own lives, those giants only become more formidable in the lives of our children. In a physical cultural sense what one generation tolerates the next generation will embrace. Broken children become broken adults. There's a reason why you make decisions and conduct relationships the way you do. We speak to children about consequences, which is important and has its place, but can we speak to them about culmination? You and I are not only the result of our mothers and fathers copulating, but we are also the result of generations of habits, good or bad, curses and blessings. You're walking around with some serious information in your DNA, and unless you face it and deal with it, you will always just be a culmination of the wrongs or rights of your parents; the cross will just be a symbol you hang around your neck or tattoo on your skin.

I remember having a similar conversation with a young man who firmly believed that he didn't need to know about his estranged father or address issues in his bloodline because Jesus came and did away with all of that. While I agree with what Jesus came to do, I cannot agree with not evaluating your level of brokenness, because appropriating what Jesus came to do for us, demands that we face ourselves. Like Peter Scazerro says, *"Jesus may be in your heart but you've got grandpa in your bones."* There are certain things in my bloodline line that are centuries old and I don't stand a chance against them. The bible is clear that iniquity in the bloodline was a judgment that could extend to the third and fourth generations of a family (Ex.34:6–7). Bloodline iniquity shows up in the form of generational behaviour and generational mindsets that develop under the relentless pressure of satanic influence and temptation.

This is the reason I don't drink alcohol; I didn't need a scripture for that decision - my bloodline decided that for me. There are certain things I stay away from because I'm predisposed to them. But this required me to face my own brokenness. We know Jesus is the answer but what is the question? The finished work of the cross, is not - for the lack of a better phrase - one size fits all; it's for everyone but it's definitely not a cookie cutter approach to the uniqueness of our brokenness. We will have to face our own brokenness, and seek healing like Allison did, whether it's in counseling, therapy, deliverance or responding to conviction. We will have to face it in our own lives and accept its reality in the lives of others because if you desire strong godly relationships, whether in romance or marriage, it is important to note that there is a level of brokenness that is unsustainable; yes, there is a level of brokenness that will not be able to produce a healthy romance or marriage.

"Everyone is broken, but some people are way too broken - before you make them a life partner evaluate how broken they are, some levels of brokenness cannot sustain marriage." **- Rick Warren Paraphrased**

Not everyone should enter marriage until their awareness of brokenness leads them to owning their brokenness and taking significant, however small, but significant steps to surrendering their brokenness to Christ and being accountable for their healing. While you may not be responsible for your brokenness you are responsible for your healing. We should also know and understand that healing and deliverance are two sides to same coin. Healing refers to physical or emotional healing - the binding up of the wound, stopping the bleeding, stopping the pain. Deliverance is referred to as the casting out of demons, suggesting that people be set free from demonic oppression. Both are needed. We must accept, that we are responsible for our own healing, and we should commit to our own deliverance. We are not responsible for the healing of others. Do not take on the responsibility to heal for someone else, because healing *for* them is simply not possible. You're setting yourself up for failure. They must become aware of it, own it, and be accountable for it. You are only responsible for your own healing. We're born broken because of sin, but we literally break further because of the actions of others and our own actions. Jesus came to restore our brokenness in a general sense but also in a very specific sense, when we humble ourselves to face our brokenness He does a very special thing - He uniquely heals and makes us whole.

UNBREAK MY HEART

If only it was possible to have your heart *unbroken*. The reality of life is that you will have your heart broken at least once in your lifetime and the other reality is that you will probably break someone's heart too. They say that hurt people, hurt people. Well, broken people break hearts. The truth is, we are all broken. It is when you are reckless with your brokenness, that you will break hearts recklessly. One of the main areas people reach out to me, is for break ups and how to get through it. Because truth be told, there's a stage in recovering from a breakup where you feel you're never going to get through it, you literally feel like dying. It's a sacred honour to walk with people through heart break - and how they walk through it is everything!

Each heartbreak is different. The personal level of brokenness is unique, and we must be so careful that we appropriate Jesus as the answer to the specific question on the table. Every heartbreak has a key question. *Why me? What did I do? Wasn't I good enough? Why? Why? Why?* Because of this, there are many variables, but there are two things that you need to solidify on the inside of you, when navigating heart break:

> **#1.** Your heart was broken before it broke.
> **#2.** The person who broke it is broken too.

When you're aligned to this truth it puts your pain into perspective. It levels not only the playing field, but the dealing field too. You must deal with this truth about brokenness before you're healed of brokenness. When you're able to see your heart for the fragile broken part of your humanity that it is, dealing with your brokenness will not intimidate you, but humble you. And here's the thing about humility, it will put you in the best possible position for your healing.

It is when we understand that we were broken before we broke and that the person or persons who further broke us, is broken too, we can debunk myths such as:

> **#1.** Time heals all wounds - This not entirely true. Time has a way of distancing us from the event, but time in and of itself, is not a healer. *Jesus is the one who heals all our wounds.*
> **#2.** You can avoid heartbreak. This is also not true. *Heartbreak must come.* I wish heartbreak was a preventable experience, but it's inevitable: relationships require vulnerability, and vulnerability leaves us open to harm and susceptible to getting hurt.

Another incomplete teaching of the purity culture is that purity will protect you from heartbreak. Heartbreak is one of those aspects of this imperfect life that we must face at some time and if you've been heartbroken or are even going through a heart break right now, take heart, you're in good company. The problem with how we're presenting the Christian faith is that we're showcasing only the "feel good", we don't talk about brokenness and the role it plays in the life of the believer. We've placed a "me-theology" on the pulpit and wonder why we have a generation trying to avoid difficult feelings and emotions, having complete melt downs at the first sign of strain or conviction. We're trying so hard to avoid messy feelings without realizing that, firstly, although it might not have been orchestrated by God, He definitely can put it to good use if we allow Him to, and secondly, that even Jesus Himself was acquainted with heartbreak. This is why He is the best possible Person to carry us through it.

> "He was looked down on and passed over, a man who suffered, who knew pain firsthand. One look at him and people turned away. We looked down on him, thought he was scum. But the fact is, it was our pains he carried - our disfigurements, all the things wrong with us." - **Isaiah 53:3 MSG**

This prophecy is about the most unbroken One to pass through this life; the One who became so broken, that He is able to sit with, and sympathize with the utterly broken! Jesus offers us real hope in the face of heart break (Heb.4:15). Jesus shows us that He also suffered. He is described as a Man of many sorrows, well acquainted with pain.

Here's some wisdom in navigating a breakup. Whether you're initiating the breakup or are on the receiving end, remember to speak the truth in love (Eph.4:15). The problem with break ups today is that it's filled with lies and deception, in an attempt to lay blame and to not take responsibility; to either not face the truth or to save face. Like my 10-year-old daughter often says, *"Stop the cap!"* Although the truth hurts, it's what the Holy Spirit can use to also heal. And love, well, we know that love covers a multitude of sins (1Pet.4:8).

#HeartBreaker

Whatever you do, do not ghost. Take ownership of the realisation that the relationship is not working. Show up for the breakup, not online but in person.

Be honest and direct. If you're dishonest the other person might try to find solutions to your "made up" problems.

Think before you speak. Do not use cliche's or play the blame game. Lines like, "it's not you but me" won't work and blaming the other person for the breakup is cowardice.

Do not offer hopes of reconciliation if you have no intention of getting back together with the other person.

Sincerely apologise for the pain that you're causing, depending on the seriousness of the relationship. Don't fool yourself into thinking that you're not causing pain - you are.

Go no-contact if you have no intention of reconciling. Do not check in or check up on the other person.

Pray for the person you're breaking up with and pray for yourself to be more discerning when choosing to date someone else. You have a lot of work to do - on you - so stay humble.

#HeartBroken

The breakup is in their hands not yours and that's ok. You can't control their desire to break up with you, but you can control your response. So be present, do not zone out.

Listen to understand not to respond. Because if we listen to respond we lose the bigger picture, the breakup.

If indeed it is a breakup. Don't plead, beg or negotiate but position your heart to accept the breakup. Acceptance will be your superpower in getting through this.

Do not try to manipulate or hi jack the breakup. Do not make threats or start an argument.

If you're given an opportunity to respond, take time to think and pray before saying and doing anything. If you also need to apologise do so.

Do not try to pander to people's desire to know the ins and outs of your breakup. Do not gossip.

If you've been wronged, forgive, and release the person. Unforgiveness, bitterness and resentment will make it impossible for you to get through the breakup.

If you've ever experienced a breakup, then you know that the after math is just as gut wrenching as the breakup itself. It's the long nights, the flash backs, the regret, and the indescribable pain. It's a matter of getting through the onslaught of emotions and regret one day at a time. Resist the temptation to suppress, ignore or run away from facing and dealing with your brokenness, and very importantly your broken heart. When we were children we ran, we didn't have the grey matter or language to confront and work through the difficult and messy themes of our humanity. We ran, and emotionally retreated to where no one could find us physically or emotionally. And sometimes, as was Allison's case, when it comes to our broken hearts, we are still *that* little boy or girl; our emotions have not grown past the age at which they were broken for the first time.

Or we fought! Blindly swinging often left us bruised and bleeding. Every time we were triggered, we'd fight again, bleeding on people who didn't cut us. When we were children, we didn't fully understand that our trigger was not our trauma, and just because we *felt* attacked didn't mean that we were *being* attacked. Whether we fought or ran, we were only children. The psychology of brokenness is this: We are wired for connection, but brokenness rewires us for protection, we then kick into self-preservation mode, and that is why healthy relationships are so difficult for broken people. They do not have the capacity to build, but only perpetuate their brokenness by self-preservation, self-sabotage, self-pity, and self-centeredness which is reinforced by a victim mentality. They don't want to perpetuate brokenness, but trauma rewired them, and they think that there's no other way.

However, this protection response in children is for their benefit, their brain does this to protect them from the emotions and pain they don't really understand, and in reality, are not equipped to handle. Children are in survival mode; their brain is trying to keep them alive. I didn't understand this when my own experience with childhood sexual molestation crippled me at 21. I thought I could suppress it, ignore and forget what I didn't understand at the time.

It was only until I allowed God into my brokenness that I learnt that I wasn't the problem, it had nothing to do with what I wore or my behavior. Those who crossed sacred lines carried the problem. When a child is abused sexually or otherwise their mind is not reasoning according to absolute truth, to the child, the abuse is not the primary problem, children see themselves as the problem.

A broken heart is tragic but can prove to be a vital opportunity to face our own brokenness, which is a process. Brokenness might have changed our brain, but healing can transform our minds. What I've learnt was that this process is not linear, it's not first A and then B and C, but rather a parallel reality often dealing with multiple pieces of your broken heart at the same time; your own brokenness and someone breaking your heart is often interlinked, connected in some way. Someone walking away from a relationship with you can cause childhood abandonment and rejection to resurface. There's nothing like heartbreak to position you to address personal brokenness.

Here's another lesson I learnt; never waste a heart break.

I know it's painful, I know it's excruciating, but what I learnt in the labour ward, is that when you're ready to give birth, you'll hit what they call the *transition*. The transition is the most intense part of labour, but it's also the shortest - thankfully. Transition occurs when the cervix moves from 7cm to 10cm. This prepares the woman's body for the baby's descent down the birth canal. But like the mid-wife assigned to me said, "Baby girl, it's only going to get worse!" She was not helpful at all.

While the pain is real during transition it's really the emotional mayhem that overwhelms the strongest of women. It's at this point that women tend to lose control, they don't know what to do, they get scared and because they're already beyond the point of exhaustion they want to give up. It was my doula that gripped my hand, squared her eyes with mine and called me to attention. She said, *"Dominique, don't waste your pain. Use your pain to push, don't let a contraction pass without you pushing through it. You need this pain, push through it."*

I tear up every time I remember her challenging me to summon my courage. She spoke to the mother God called me to be, she commanded me to face my pain. I instinctively knew I wasn't leaving that bed without birthing my baby - a teachable moment of note!

Don't leave that heartbreak without facing your brokenness; don't move on without the lesson. There is value, great value in your broken heart. When we run from heart break and our brokenness, we're like cows according to a Native American story. When cows see storm clouds gather, they know a storm is coming and so they start to run from it. The problem with this approach is that the storm follows them, and they remain under the storm clouds longer than necessary. Why? Because cows are slow, so by the time the storm catches up to them they're moving at the same pace as the storm, they're moving *with* the storm.

But Buffalo, are different. When they see the storm clouds forming, they run towards it - they face it. It's cold, wet, and uncomfortable but they run *through it,* minimizing their time under the rain and thunder. Some of us are heartbroken and broken longer than what's necessary because we've chosen to run from our brokenness. Here's a principle to apply when it comes to heart break and brokenness - when you see the storm clouds forming, face it and move towards it. Trust me, you're going to get through it.

Instead of running from God... run *to* God.

"Therefore let us [with privilege] approach the throne of grace [that is, the throne of God's gracious favor] with confidence and without fear, so that we may receive mercy [for our failures] and find [His amazing] grace to help in time of need [an appropriate blessing, coming just at the right moment]." -
Hebrews 4: 16 AMP

Instead of isolating... connect with godly friends.

> *"He who wilfully separates and estranges himself [from God and man] seeks his own desire and pretext to break out against all wise and sound judgment."* **- Proverbs 18:2**

Instead of overthinking... focus on your goals.
"Let your eyes look directly ahead [toward the path of moral courage] And let your gaze be fixed straight in front of you [toward the path of integrity]. Consider well and watch carefully the path of your feet, and all your ways will be steadfast and sure." **- Proverbs 4:25-26 AMP**

Instead of trying to forget... learn the lessons.
"Senseless people learn their lessons the hard way, but the wise are teachable. **- Proverbs 21:11 TPT**

Instead of doing it your way... do it *God's way*.
"Trust in and rely confidently on the Lord with all your heart and do not rely on your own insight or understanding. In all your ways know and acknowledge and recognize Him, and He will make your paths straight and smooth [removing obstacles that block your way]."
- Proverbs 3:5-6 AMP

MY BODY MY CHOICE

Is it really "your body, your choice"? As a born-again believer, you're not a human on a spiritual journey, no, you're a spirit on a human journey, and you've been given a human body to steward temporarily. We've already established that your body belongs to God. It is a temple, but it won't last forever. So, what does it matter, right? Contrary to popular belief what you do with and in your body matters for this life and for eternity.

Now, choice as you know is a very powerful thing, it can either work for you or against you. We are, what we call free moral agents; we have the God-given ability to understand right from wrong (our conscience) and therefore can be held responsible for our actions. Our conscience is not only a force of nature, but also a result of nurturing. It's intrinsic as well as acquired. God not only gave us the ability to understand the difference between right and wrong, but someone also taught us the difference between right and wrong, whether it was a parent, a teacher, a leader, or a government official. Where this gets convoluted is when brokenness, instead of morality, informs our decisions. Whether it be a broken understanding or a destructive action, it has the potential to perpetuate our brokenness. A classic example of this is the abortion agenda. I say agenda because while it seems to offer a solution to a "problem" it is actually part of a bigger plan for mere mortals to play God and therefore perpetuate brokenness for generations. This agenda is multifaceted; this agenda is political, and biological; it's medical warfare; it's deeply and profoundly spiritual and I've made no secret about the fact that I think it's diabolical, demonic.

Feminism has led us to believe the lie that because a baby is incubated in our bodies that we have the right to decide whether our baby lives or dies. This lie has been reinforced with speculations about when life in the womb *actually* starts, and when that speculation failed under scrutiny, the lie just became downright nasty, to the point where we, as global citizens, affirm late term abortions. How? you ask. With our silence! There are places in our world where abortion can take place as late as 26 weeks! As I write this, - according to The Stew Peters Show - Canada, who used to be one of the most Christian countries in the world, has reached a new level of depravity. Today, this once God-driven and God-fearing nation, is now identified as being a more liberal version of America, that means having legal abortions, for any reason, up to the very moment of birth! Not only that, but Canada also has some of the world's most expansive euthanasia laws, and recently expanded its "Medical Assistance In Dying" (MAID) program, so that those looking to kill themselves don't even need to be terminally ill to obtain lethal drugs. Canadians can just ask their doctors for suicide drugs, simply based in chronic pain. MAID has unfortunately expanded this to cover purely mental ailments as well. This means people can kill themselves with a doctor's assistance simply because they are feeling sad or depressed, and the government will help them along the way. This applies to children as well. "Mature minors"- that means 12 years old and up - will be allowed to choose to end their own lives, and right now health authorities are reviewing if euthanasia should be easier for children to get. The country has children's activity books, promoting MAID as a healthy and natural option. They are targeting children saying: "if you are upset about something, or if you don't feel quite right, here's a pill, go kill yourself!"

There was a case of a woman, whose son was suicidal. He went into the hospital and instead of being treated and counseled, they called his mom ten days later saying, "your son chose to do MAID." They "assisted" his suicide while he was there. Not only do they want to give 12-year-olds the option of ending their own lives, but they are also trying to extend it to babies. So, if a mom has a baby up to twelve months of age, and she "feels" that there is something wrong with him/her, she can bring the baby back to the hospital and they will "medically assist" that baby in dying. These are mere mortals playing God! Do not underestimate the destruction of brokenness, it has the power to distort our perception of God, downgrading the Creator King of both heaven and earth, the One who created the starry hosts and calls them by name (Is.40:26), the One who knew us before we were formed in the womb, Who set us apart and appointed us (Jer.1:5), the God who humbled Himself and became what we so easily discard of - a baby - conceived by the Holy Spirit. If ever there was an affirmation of life in the womb, then it was our Saviour's incarnation. But somewhere along the narrative of our brokenness we concluded that God has no say, and so we ascended the throne becoming like God in our own eyes. Sounds eerily familiar. When we assume God's domain, we come crashing down to earth, with destruction in our wake. I am not so ignorant that I am not aware of exceptions that our attempt at "planned parenthood" offers. But there are no exceptions, or suitable reasons or excuses as children of God. Rape is not an exception because it is God who gives life, not rapists. Yes, we find this ideology so difficult to swallow, so cruel to comprehend, but the truth is, God does not support, or condone abortion, even where rape is concerned, even the vilest acts of rape. We therefore cannot condone, nor aid and abet the murder of the innocent, for temporary comfort. Abortion doesn't undo the rape; it only causes more brokenness. Brokenness will not only have us view wickedness as desirable, but we'll also view murder as a solution to a "problem", and in consensual cases, we are active participants in creating the perceived problem. What did we think was going to happen? How easy it is to soothe our conscience by coining terms such as unwanted pregnancy, unplanned pregnancy, and the latest addition to the family - unintended pregnancy. And yes, apparently there are differences in these phrases. If we consented to illegitimate, consensual sexual intercourse and we become pregnant, we don't have a problem, we have a consequence. As children of God, consequences are not done away with, they are *dealt* with, in a way that honours God and does right by those we have done wrong, and in the case of pregnancy, those who are a result of the wrongdoing. As the saying goes: two wrongs don't make a right. God is God and we are not. Life and death are in His hands. Let's stay in our lane, shall we?

Abortion is playing God and that never ends well. Allow me to introduce you to a young man who survived an abortion attempt. The enemy tried to take him out in the womb, but God. Needless to say, the topic of abortion did not sit well with him. He sat in my office triggered. Long story short, without minimizing his trauma, he shared with me how he found out that his girlfriend had an abortion without him knowing. What hurt him more was that he thought that she would have done it even with his knowledge. Assumption is a dangerous place to dwell in and so we navigated our way out of that hole, but we still sat with unspeakable pain at the thought of his unborn baby being aborted. This was new territory for me, so I proceeded with caution, because most of my abortion counseling was administered before the possible abortion and was facilitated with women, not men. I silently repented because I too had assumptions. That day I realized that not all men are unwilling fathers, some have had that responsibility, and right, forcefully removed from them. Yes, most men consent to and even force the issue, but not all men.

And so, the broken man I'll refer to as "Matthew", sat in my office, wrecked, and fragmented. He was broken for his sin of sex outside of marriage, and the abortion that came as a result of it. To add insult to injury, his girlfriend was now going through what sounded to me like Post Abortion Stress (PAS). The flashbacks, the nightmares, her outbursts and fits of rage evoked fear in him. She cried all the time, and he didn't have the emotional capacity to comfort her. He didn't know what to say or what to do. She couldn't pray, and neither could he. She turned to alcohol and marijuana to help cope with her grief. He felt helpless.

What was evident is that the abortion not only affected him deeply, but her too. In my office sat a young man broken not only for his sin of sexual immorality, an aborted child but also hurting because his girlfriend was hurting too. He didn't know how to feel towards her because she was broken too. We held space for his brokenness and grief, and we held some more space for his battle between what he felt *for* his girlfriend and what he felt *towards* her.
What we don't realize is that the decision to abort a baby is often driven by our brokenness in our perception of God and who we perceive ourselves to be. The result? The illusion of power or "control over the situation".

The driving force behind our broken perception of God and ourselves, is *fear*. We fear what people will think of us, what they will say, and how they will treat us. We're afraid of guilt and shame, so we exercise our perceived power in dealing with the "problem". We abort.

There is a reason why God tells us not to fear. Because unhealthy fear makes us see things that are not there. Fear makes us irrational. Fear will cause you to try and cover up what you did. Fear will cause you to run from God instead of to Him. Fear will have you play God. Fear will have you fight God. Fear will mess you up.

Off topic but a good point to make about fear: One of the catalysts to the severity of the Covid virus was fear. Fear is so powerful that its reach goes beyond your nervous system and can even touch your immune system. The fear and anxiety invoked by Covid had the power to make an already compromised immune system open to the suggestion of death. I say this respectfully because the effects of Covid were real, and we are still grieving, but there is no denying that fear and anxiety not only influenced many of the decisions we made during the pandemic but also well after. Unhealthy fear makes us do things we wouldn't normally do. Healthy fear can save our lives- like running from a snake, not touching fire and staying away from the edge of a cliff - but unhealthy fear will have us try to undo one wrong with another.

If you've ever been in a position where abortion crossed your mind know that there are alternatives, but it starts with you facing the truth about who God is and who you are not. It starts with seeking to know God and understanding His will and purposes for all things, even purpose for what you see as a mistake or unwanted pregnancy. You may have had an abortion. It's important that you know there is healing and restoration after abortion. What about when it wasn't your choice? Yes, it was your body, but it wasn't your choice. What about when you didn't consent to sexual intercourse? If you were raped? Interpol has named South Africa the rape capital of the world and with good reason. In South Africa someone is raped every 25 seconds. It is estimated that a woman born in South Africa has a greater chance of being raped than learning to read. What?! A survey done in 1200 schools in South Africa discovered that 2 out of every 5 male learners have been raped. Remember, these stats are only based on *reported* cases. What about the rape crimes that go unreported? Rape has no prejudice; it can happen to anyone and by anyone. And yet we blame everyone except the rapist. We blame the victim; we blame the circumstances and sometimes we even blame God.

While there are dynamics that make a victim more vulnerable such as substance abuse, risky behaviour, ignorance, poverty, and unhealthy associations to name but a few, allow me to say, there is no excuse or justification for rape whatsoever. With that said, Gods word still stands. He still cannot willfully allow abortion, even in those cases. All we can do is run deeply into Him, and allow Him to take care of us, and the innocent child that has come as a result. There is no judgment for any woman who has or is considering abortion after a rape; there is only the hope that you allow Jesus to fully heal you and give you peace. Years ago, I was privy to the conversation of a young girl who walked home from school but left a little later than usual. She was followed by an unknown man and was raped just 2km from her home. After the rape the perpetrator told the victim that he was waiting for another girl, but she didn't show, sadly the victim concluded that somehow it was her fault, because she was at the wrong place at the wrong time; that had she left her usual time, she would have not been raped. No, the crime was not hers. It was not a consequence of actions on her part. The perpetrator committed a crime - whether she left school later or not, he was not supposed to rape her! Dear Reader if you were ever sexually molested or raped, hear me good: whether you were drunk out of your mind, regardless of what you were wearing, whether you were out clubbing or alone in an office, whether you were at the wrong place at the wrong time, your perpetrator was not supposed to rape you! They committed a crime; it was not your fault; the blame lies squarely on their shoulders. We must not allow ourselves to pin rape on the victim or anyone or anything else other than the rapist. I came across an author and book title that made me straighten up and shout yes! South African Author Leyonie Marais wrote a book titled, *Dethrone the Rapist*. While her story inspires the reader on how to take back your power and still pursue your purpose, I can't help but wonder what would happen if we held the rapist up to God's standard for accountability?

It is estimated that only 14% of perpetrators of rape are convicted in South Africa and 85% of child rapists are known by the victim. We ought to hang our heads in shame. Allison's family knew but because they were dependent on the perpetrator, they covered up brokenness.

Did you know that rape is one of the leading causes of the spread of HIV/Aids? Because rape is a crime of force, the mucosal tearing and bleeding that occurs as a result makes the transference of HIV to victims a done deal.

Yes, I might be quoting statistics but if you were ever raped, know this; you are not a statistic and you are not alone. I would be a fool to try and answer the question that I am faced with, in every rape recovery intervention I have had the sacred dread (and honour) to be a part of: *"If God loves me why did He allow this to happen?"*

This question is asked in many different ways, through tears and pain, anger and resentment. It manifests itself through bouts of depression and episodes of anxiety. I've even heard this question through the silent cries expressed through suicide attempts. And there are many variations to this question.

> "Why do bad things happen to good people?"
> "If God loves me why did He allow bad things to happen to me?"
> "Why me?!"

I wouldn't dare try to answer it in a counseling session and I won't dare try to answer it here. The only thing I can and must do is to point you to Jesus.

Years ago, I had a mentor who had the wisdom to foresee and forewarn my young faith of the harsh realities of life. He loved me enough to temper my faith with Truth. We sparred through tough teachings on pain and hardship, trials, and tribulations. We would one-two punch through admonitions on the righteous suffering. He exposed me to muscle tearing truths that informed my perception of God and removed any delusions and projections that distorted my understanding of the Sovereignty of God.

Under his mentorship I learnt that when bad things happen to good people, or rather, when bad things happen to God's children, it's not a reflection of God but an indication of a very real enemy. He charged me to never forget that we have a good God but also a very bad enemy, whose chief goal is to kill, steal & destroy (Jn.10:10).

I've discovered that a "bless me" gospel has inoculated a generation against the truth; although we have a good God, we're living in a fallen world that produces broken people. This has blinded us to the fact that we have an enemy of our souls who is not only a strategist but also an opportunist and will capitalize any given opportunity (Matt.13: 24-30, 36-43).

Does God want to bless us? Of course! But our Good News has become so lopsided with teachings on blessings, entitlement and what we can get *from* God that we have a generation unable to walk the straight and narrow *with* God; a road that we must understand is marked with suffering.

Job's life shows us how suffering is possible even in the life of a child of God. It is true that sometimes we are the cause of our suffering; I am guilty of this, you know, when we blame the devil but we're merely facing the consequences of their own actions? Well, that's not the kind of suffering I'm wanting to address here. There is the kind of suffering that is brought about because of someone else's brokenness. Victims of rape and Gender Based Violence (GBV) are suffering because someone else violated them. Their suffering is undue. On the flip side, when a victim reports the crime and the perpetrator is charged and sentenced to imprisonment, the perpetrators' suffering is deserved.

And this is why it pains me when victims are blamed by family members and even the perpetrator for their imprisonment. We must unlearn this toxic reasoning; it forms the bedrock of rape culture. If we deconstruct this kind of thinking, we will have a chance at overthrowing the chokehold of rape in Africa. The victim doesn't put the perpetrator in prison by reporting the crime, the perpetrator has committed a crime and is solely responsible for their incarceration. The victim did the right thing by reporting the crime.

Before we dig deep allow me to say; God does not have a dark side. God is not a semi sadist; He does not take pleasure in our suffering. He's not power hungry or trigger happy. God is capable of wrath, but it's not directed at us. Does God discipline His children? Yes, He does. But discipline is very different to wrath, discipline is motivated by love, but God's holiness demands wrath for sin. And there is a day set aside where God will release His pent-up wrath and all the enemies of God will be consumed by it.

Hard truth #1

While we are in this world we face the imminence of suffering; it can happen at any time. Job was minding his own business; He worshipped God, was faithful to his wife, interceded for his children, stewarded his wealth with integrity and generosity. Job was described as the greatest man among the people of the East (1:3b).

Then one day the unthinkable happened. Job experienced loss after loss; a series of unfortunate events starting with his children being carried off by an enemy and seemingly ending with Job sitting on an ash heap. Job was covered in painful sores from head to toe and his only relief was a broken piece of pottery. Job's friends didn't even recognize him, they tried to empathize with him by sitting with him in his pain and discomfort but didn't say a word for seven days and seven nights; the bible attributes their silence to the realization of how great Job's suffering was.

Hard truth #2

There is a realm we are not privy to; there is a reality that's spiritual and unseen, yet more real than the world we find ourselves in. The reality is that there's a bigger picture we might not see this side of eternity. In Job's case there were conversations he knew nothing of, a wager of sorts, that he had no say in. Undue suffering is not only imminent it is also generally out of our control; we often have no say. And this is the tension every child of God must hold space for; the reality of making choices about matters you had no choice *in*. A contradiction? I think not. We might not be able to choose the suffering we endure but we must choose how we will respond to it. Our power lies not in the choice but in our ability to choose even when we seemingly didn't have a choice.

Hard truth #3

We have a real enemy who can cause real damage. He is not just some figment of our imagination or a Series we enjoy on Netflix. Notice how the enemy is portrayed by media as endearing, almost likeable. Lil Nas X goes as far as seducing Satan with a lap dance in one of his music videos. We must not underestimate that ancient serpent. Not only does the enemy come to kill, steal and destroy, he also comes to question us and to get us to question God. Understand that God is not intimidated by our authentic and honest questions; in fact, I can't think of a better place to take our questions. Someone once told me, *"There's no such thing as a wrong answer, but it is very possible to ask the wrong question."* While I don't entirely agree with this statement, I get the sentiment.

The truth is that when we're in pain it's ok, even healthy, to ask honest, raw, and vulnerable questions. Many times, it's those difficult questions that lead us to asking the right question. The catalyst to making the right choices when we've been wronged is asking the right questions. Something shifts in your heart and mind when you ask the right questions.

Hard truth #4

In His Sovereignty, God does allow suffering in the lives of His children. This is not an easy truth to accept when we filter God through our pain. The truth is we're all looking at God through something. When we look at Him through anything other than what He's revealed about Himself in His word, we open ourselves to distortion at best and deception at worst. How we view God matters, because our perception of God will determine how we approach our relationship with Him.

For example, if I view God as fallible as me, I won't approach Him as King and Lord, I'll approach Him as an equal and that can prove to be detrimental for me; in that my faith *in* God is directly proportional to my view *of* God. If I perceive God to make mistakes, and break promises like I do. That's not much to put my faith in, now, is it? If I'm projecting my difficult experience with my earthly father or authority figure in my life onto God, we're in for a relationship marked by insecurity, suspiscion, disappointment, and self-preservation.

Hard truth #5

God can use all kinds of suffering, even the kind that we inflict on ourselves. We still may not know why God allows suffering, but He does. He allowed His Son to suffer (Heb.5:7-10) and what that teaches us about God is that God prioritizes *purpose* over protection. *Can* God protect us against suffering? Does God *want* to protect us against suffering? Yes, and yes. God can and wants to protect us against suffering, but only if it serves *His* purpose. Protecting Christ against suffering would not have served God's purpose; you and I would have forfeited a Saviour who is able to relate to our suffering. We would have forfeited the assurance of knowing that Jesus' suffering served a purpose. We would have forfeited redemption from sin, and we would have forfeited eternity with our Father in heaven.

God can use anything even suffering. God wastes nothing, not even your suffering and pain, God doesn't even waste our tears; He stores it in a bottle (Ps.56:8). When it comes to suffering it is so important that you're able to discern the real enemy. There is going to come a day when God will draw back the curtains of time and we'll see that there was a bigger picture, a higher purpose, and that God was good. We'll see and understand the why's to every trial, and the reasons why God allowed our personal suffering. We'll also see what God did not allow, those things He kept us from. We'll see that all the entirety of our lives was, what I call, "Father-filtered." Job's suffering was Father-filtered. Listen, the real enemy must ask God's permission to induce suffering on a righteous person. Once you've discerned the real enemy, ask God for the courage and patience to respond with trust and wisdom. I've come to know that trust in God and wisdom in the face of adversity always results in worship (Job 1:20). I think it gets a bit tricky when those closest to us respond to our suffering with foolishness. Job's wife got her question wrong (Job 2:9). Job on the other hand asked the right question (Job 2:10). If you've ever asked the question, *"If God loves me why does life keep hurting me?"* Or you may have asked, *"If God loves me why did He allow this to happen?"* You are not alone, this question is real, it is valid; know that I have also asked this question. Only when I accepted the fact that God is Sovereign and that there are some answers, I will never get this side of eternity was I able to see God for who He truly is and allow Him to be God in my life.

Let me say I don't use the word "sovereign" loosely; in fact, it should be used with the utmost sensitivity and compassion to all suffering especially in the lives of others. God's Sovereignty is not an excuse to silence the honest questions of those who are suffering. Sometimes we use God's sovereignty with the intention to comfort but it mutes the authentic cries and questions of the sufferer.

> *"God's sovereignty is first painful, then slowly powerful, and over much time seen to be profitable. It is to be studied with great sensitivity for the experiences of others and deep reverence for the One who controls the outcomes of every matter in the universe."* **- James MacDonald**

Let me say it again God is not offended or intimidated by our questions. What I have realized though is that the reason why the enemy uses suffering to get us to question the love God has for us, is because, by implication it puts a question mark on God Himself, because, God is what? God is Love.

There are three things that automatically come under interrogation when we question the love of God has for us and the enemy knows this.

The first is *security*. If God doesn't love us, it means that we have no security. And the thought of no security short circuits how we've been wired. We function optimally when we're secure in the Fathers' love. When we have no security, we function from a place of fear and fear brings bondage, but a sense of security in God's love brings liberty. Please don't ever forget that.

The second is *identity*. It's a question of *"who are we if God doesn't love us"*? The enemy knows that when we don't know *Whose* we are, and *who* we are, we'll easily give up what we have, much like Esau and the bowl of stew. If the enemy is going to succeed in disarming, overpowering, or stealing from us, he must dismantle our sense of identity.

And thirdly, *destiny*. I've heard people say that a loving God will not send people to hell. And they are 110% correct. God doesn't *send* people to hell. People *choose* to go there when they reject the way of salvation that God provided through the sacrificial and atoning death of Jesus Christ. When the enemy puts a question mark on our destiny, we become unsure of what we're moving towards and essentially living for. When we don't know what we're living for, *anything* goes. Much like where there is no vision people perish (Prov.29:18), the same is true for where there is no sense of destiny - people go their own way - and the enemy knows this.

I am a keen observer of believers who suffer because I know that I might possibly go through the same thing in my lifetime. This is not pessimism, it is preparation; this is just me building the capacity and resilience to face the harsh realities of life. I find that this approach keeps me humble and intentional about deconstructing any sense of entitlement I may have as a believer. Yes, it is possible to feel entitled, to feel like God owes us answered prayers for good behaviour.

It was my second pregnancy, first trimester. I was napping three times a day, craving mangoes, literally living my best life and just thankful that our family would finally be complete. I didn't tell anyone not even *Sound Guy* – who at this point, was my husband of 4 years already – just Tiffany, our first born and I knew. Tiffany just turned two years old – she was bright eyed and bushy tailed - when I peed on a stick to confirm what I had known for weeks.

It was around the 12th week when I started noticing the subsiding of cravings and morning sickness, which was weird, but I didn't pay much attention to it until I started bleeding. I was planning a cute, creative way to let *Sound Guy* (whose real name is Henrico, but everyone calls him Ricardo, and I call him Rick) know that we were expecting a baby. But my call that day wasn't cute, and it certainly wasn't creative. We made an emergency appointment with our gynecologist.

No heartbeat, just medication and a list of do's and don'ts for a home miscarriage. I was shattered. With each contraction my heart broke for women who must give birth to stillborn babies; I tried to put myself in their position so that I could pray for them earnestly. Then the enemy started ministering to me, asking if I was really going to squat, bloody and tired - *and* concern myself with the welfare of others, at a time like this? Was I really going to intercede and cover other women I don't even know, in prayer? What about *my* pain, what about *my* loss? I didn't deserve this. What about my years of sacrifice and service to God? What about the times I put God and His will for my life first? What about the abortions I intercepted in the lives of other women? What about the lives of babies I saved by being present and powerful in the lives of scared and broken women?

I was having a Father-filtered moment, and my question was, why me? It was through much prayer with honest and raw questions that I surrendered to the reality that God was showing me what was really in my heart. God exposed that age old serpentine paradigm that made its home in my heart without me knowing it; and no one says it better than the old serpent himself.

> *"Does Job fear God for nothing?" Satan replied. "Have you not put a hedge around him and his household and everything he has? You have blessed the work of his hands, so that his flocks and herds are spread throughout the land. But now stretch out your hand and strike everything he has, and he will surely curse you to your face."*
> **- Job 1:9-11 NIV**

Here's my confession, I secretly believed that God owed me what I asked Him for; that because I laid my life down for His name sake that He should have spared me from suffering, that He should have not allowed me to go through the pain of a miscarriage; I mean there are women out here throwing their babies away and here I was willing and able to bring a child into the world! It took a miscarriage to show me what was really in my heart.

It took suffering to bring me to the right question; why *not* me? And so, I have learnt to appreciate the various responses of believers to their suffering. One such believer is Bill Johnson, a fifth generation Pastor and senior leader of Bethel Church, a charismatic mega church in Redding, California. On the 13 July 2022 Pastor Bill Johnson lost his wife to a long battle with cancer, and it was his response to her passing that astounded me. Three days after her passing he preached a sermon titled, "God brings beauty out of ashes" and said the following:

> *"Worshiping in pain is only possible on this side of heaven, so this is a privilege."*

There will come a time when we will worship God with no trace of pain or suffering - on the other side of eternity. Pastor Bill Johnson asserted the reality that because we're only experiencing it this side of eternity, to worship in pain is a privilege. If God can trust us to worship in pain, He can trust us with the worship in joy for eternity. He then goes on to make a statement that hurts.

"The backslider in heart will always judge God by what He didn't do..."

Ouch! I don't think I would have used the word, "backslider" but Pastor Bill Johnson did and I've interpreted this to mean that those who lose sight of who God really is will forget what He's already done; and that what He didn't do will cancel everything He's done. He then continued to say...

"But those who run with tenderness for who He is will always define Him by what He has said, what He has promised and what He has done."

Where's the lie? When our definition of God is informed by what He has revealed about Himself and not what we have suffered, we will not run away from God but run to Him; knowing that He is good even when things are bad. Pastor Bill Johnson then comes to the quivering conclusion that liberates every chained heart.

> *"I just don't have the right to reevaluate what He is like because I've experienced loss. It doesn't work that way."*

Job wasn't afraid to ask the tough questions about God and suffering. Job felt his loss, endured his pain, refused to listen to his friends who basically coached him in "making right" with God for the sake of getting out of his suffering; because according to them surely, he was suffering because he sinned. His friends could not reconcile righteous living with suffering.

But Job looked to God for answers. Job wrestled with the tension of God's sovereignty despite the brokenness of his world. While Job had questions for God, we soon see that God also had questions for Job. And in the same way, in our suffering, there are questions God will ask us too.

Helen Rosevere was a British medical missionary to the Congo during the volatile uprising of the Mau Mau. She went to Congo to serve God and share the gospel but was met with violence and brutality. Helen experienced the most feared of undue suffering, she was humiliated and raped. While she was recovering from her ordeal, she discovered that trials will always push you; either away from God or closer to Him. Helen chose to have her trial push her closer to God.

It was during her time of recovery that Helen wrote a statement that sounds like a question that God asked her. It literally sends shivers down my spine every time I read it: *"Can you thank Me for trusting you with this experience even if I never tell you why?"* After a long discourse between Job and his friends God finally speaks. I encourage you to read it, it will humble you (Job 38:1 - 41:34).

Job tried to prove his innocence, his friends tried to prove his guilt, but when God spoke Job's response is astounding.

> *"Then Job replied to the Lord: I know that you can do all things; no purpose of yours can be thwarted. You asked, 'Who is this that obscures my plans without knowledge?' Surely I spoke of things I did not understand, things too wonderful for me to know. You said, 'Listen now, and I will speak; I will question you, and you shall answer me.' My ears had heard of you but now my eyes have seen you. Therefore I despise myself and repent in dust and ashes."* **- Job 41:1-6**

God honoured Job because He asked the right questions. He didn't try to get himself out of suffering but trusted God enough to wrestle with real issues, and tough questions, and held space for God to answer. He trusted in the goodness of God even when things were bad, very bad, even when he didn't have all the answers. Job 19 reveals how Job's unwavering trust in a good God, in a bad world caused him to know beyond a shadow of a doubt that his Redeemer lives (Job 19:25).

It reminds me of Shadrach, Meshach and Abednego who told king Nebuchadnezzar in no uncertain terms that even if God didn't come through for them by delivering them from the fire, they would still not serve Babylonian gods or bow down to the statue he erected (Dan.3:17-18).

We may not know the *why's* but here's what we do know: We have a good Father who has secured our eternal destiny and therefore has given us His truth and wisdom to navigate what is temporary. And not only that, but we also have a Promise that is Yes and Amen that we can hold onto when we face broken people who have broken our minds, hearts and sometimes bodies too.

When the rubber meets the road, we can trust God even when the suffering we face wasn't our choice. And so, because of what God has already done and promised we can exercise wisdom even when we are faced with the brokenness of others and their attempt to break us. I don't know who this is for but even though GBV and rape wasn't your choice, you still have a choice to make.

Choose to seek help; the sooner the better. Both legal and medical intervention is available. Don't shower. Tell a trusted person, report the crime and get to the clinic. Trust me when I say I've studied the data and followed the science when it comes to GBV, sexual assault, the legal and medical systems of South Africa. Yes, we have more challenges than I wish to make mention here, but we must take our power back and make the right choices even when we're suffering because we didn't have a choice.

Discern the real enemy; instead of running from God, run to God. Dethrone the rapist. Stop glorifying the rapist by blaming everything but the perpetrator. Rape wasn't God's idea; it was the enemy's plan all along. Bad things happening to us is not a reflection of God but a very real indication of a very real enemy, who will use the brokenness of humanity to get us to question the love of God.

Let God be God; just because you're suffering does not mean that you now get to play God in the decisions that you make. God is God and we are not; suffering doesn't give us a pass to take our lives or bodies into our own hands. We perpetuate brokenness when we use our suffering as a reason to go against the will and ways of God - vengeance, bitterness, rebellion, unforgiveness and sin, all fall into this category. When the suffering you're facing was not your choice, seek God and ask Him your honest questions, He is not offended and nor is He intimidated. No, He is faithful and will lead you to the right questions.

WILDFIRES AND THE FIREPLACE

We were broken before our hearts were ever broken, and even though we're children of God it is very possible to experience suffering when other broken people try to break us. So, what about the brokenness we perpetuate? One of the ways we perpetuate brokenness is by not dealing and healing, but also by following its lead; that's when our brokenness, sexual or relationally leads our thoughts, words, or actions.

It's like the difference between a fire in the wild and a fire in the fireplace. A fire in the wild is unpredictable, dangerous, and consumes without bias. When our brokenness leads us, it's like setting a dry and parched field alight - nothing is safe from its spread. Given the right set of circumstances a wildfire becomes unstoppable.

There are many ways our brokenness can lead us, but I want to point us to a *triple threat* that has left many, whether single, married or divorced consumed by their brokenness. When we don't deal with and heal from brokenness but allow our brokenness to lead us, we literally, figuratively, and spiritually play with fire. No one plays with fire without getting burnt (Prov. 6:27-28).

Pornography; I was nine years old when I first discovered a dirty magazine, and I can't think of a better way to describe the experience other than my eyes drank it in. The images made empty promises to my curiosity and created an unrealistic standard in my heart for sex and sexuality. What was hidden in a cupboard somewhere 31 years ago is now a click away. Today we have a generation of young people who can't sleep without it. As a 9-year-old, I was intrigued, my fascination with pornography didn't last long but the damage was done. I had a distorted perception of sex and sexuality. Unfortunately, pornography has no intention of leaving you without damaging you. It literally rewires your brain. It's like a drug. Drugs can change the brains' plasticity and desensitize the dopamine center of your brain; pornography does the same thing. Like addicts are always chasing a higher high, so too are porn watchers. This is why they would rather watch porn than engage in intimacy with a human being. They will try to imitate what porn celebrates, insatiable desire. Porn has the power to make marital intimacy a nightmare. I've counseled with women who were nothing more than a piece of meat to selfish, aggressive, and emotionally unavailable and unstable men. Pornography gave rise to "monster-like" qualities in the men they vowed to submit to. I couldn't begin to even imagine how scary that must have been for them. Some of these women knew about their spouses' pornographic habits before they married and figured "boys would be boys". Never did these women imagine that a computer screen would be preferred to their caressing. How do you compete with unrealistic images and x-rated videography on repeat?

If you're dating and pornography is a part of your significant others' self-care routine, I would not advise entering marriage. Someone addicted to crystal meth cannot sustain themselves, let alone a marriage. In the same way someone who is addicted to porn does not have the capacity to build a healthy, loving, and intimate relationship. If you are married and you or your spouse is addicted to pornography, get help ASAP. Pornography is like terminal cancer.

    It kills intimacy.
    It kills empathy.
    It kills compassion.

It kills honour.
It kills dignity.
It kills respect.
It kills relationships.
Pornography kills. Period.

Contrary to popular belief women also struggle with pornography, often the softer kind, with a little bit of music and a storyline, but its porn all the same. I had a young woman write to me about her addiction. Her guilt and shame would not allow her to come and see me personally, but I'm just glad she reached out. She'd been addicted since her tweens, and she didn't want to go through another decade at the mercy of her lust for more.

The effects pornography had on her were textbook - addiction, feelings of loneliness, depression, feeling disconnected, low self-esteem, sexually objectifying and dehumanizing others and being emotionally illiterate. This girl was tormented by her inability to function without binging on gratuitous sexual aggression. And it's not like she didn't love Jesus, she was just having a hard time obeying His word and since no one loved her enough to be honest with her, I had to break down the relational and eternal implications of disobedience in this area.

Pornography affects how we relate to others - in a very bad way - it affects us, not only for this life but for eternity. Pornography doesn't come to play, it is aligned and obedient to the kill, steal and destroy mandate of its master. It is relentless in its quest for complete domination and a formidable opponent; it is difficult to overcome. One can easily become discouraged by how long it often takes to overcome its death grip. What you need to know is that pornography is physical and is very biological and deeply spiritual. Pornography is wicked and produces iniquity in us. Pornography will transition from being something we watch, to something we do, to something we *become*.

The young lady who wrote to me was ready for freedom, but we needed to locate the brokenness that provided pornography the doorway for entry and the stronghold that gave it jurisdiction.

Masturbation; (yes, I'm going there.) The internet broke when an 11-year-old American boy addressed his local school governing body about a book he picked up on a stand at his school library. I pressed through an awkward 3 minutes of his address, in which he read an explicit sexual interaction between two children more or less his age. He then concluded his talk by informing the board that his librarian asked if he wanted "more books like that" and if he wanted the graphic novel version. Meanwhile back in South Africa, our Department of Education seems unaware of what is allegedly being taught in our primary school syllabus. An image demonstrating how mom's and dad's make love has gone viral, and, Mzansi (another name for South Africa) had no chill. Tweeters lost their minds as parents become aware and started circulating images from the alleged sex education book. The Department denied any knowledge of the book. I hoped no one would tag me, but then came a knock on my front door. In front of me stood a mom who could confirm exactly what I hoped was not true. She shared with me how her daughter, grade 6 at the time, was a part of an "assembly" turned sex workshop, where her grade was shown how to use a condom, administer birth control pills and made aware that she did not need to inform her parents about visits to the local women's clinic. I called the principal and he confirmed that such an assembly had taken place and that he was not obligated in any way, shape or form to inform the parents of such an information session - Strike one.

He went on to say that it was imperative that they educate their students as young as 9 years old to engage in safe sex - Strike two. And furthermore, he would continue to do so as he had the backing of the Department of Education - Strike three. We agreed to disagree and hung up the phone.

There is a huge push to get children sexualized, the younger the better. Now please don't misunderstand me. I am not against teaching our children about sex and sexuality. I am against teaching them propaganda. I am against turning them against their parents and against God's design for sex and sexuality. It should not surprise us that not just media, but that books and education systems will strategically make sexual content accessible to our children. I have counseled with people who have sex addictions because they were taught to masturbate at school.

The sexual revolution has given us a generation who don't understand the purpose and beauty of their God-given sexuality and when they come to know Jesus Christ as Lord most things get transformed except their heart and mind towards sex and sexuality. They learn how to pray, fast, worship, serve and tithe but no one is teaching them how to accept, honour and exercise their sexuality. And I get it, shouldn't it be natural? Trust me dear reader, there is nothing natural about how sex and sexuality is being rendered in our generation.

As I write this, our country is embroiled in the BELA Bill debate. The Basic Education Laws Amendment Bill, or Bela Bill as it is commonly referred to, has caused waves in the schooling communities. The controversy is still ongoing and currently the department is conducting public hearings in all the provinces to give people a chance to talk about the matter. Essentially the bill aims at taking parenting power away from parents and significantly reducing the power of educators by centralising control: This will include - but is not limited to - the introduction and furthering of CSE – Centralised Sexuality Education. This is vastly different from sex education, which is a biological explanation of what sex is. *Sexuality* education is teaching our children, from as young as the age of 4 years old, that they have "sexual rights" and teaching them how to masturbate.

It was only a matter of time before a believer would try to corner me about masturbation. Surprisingly the "someone" was a *she* and she tried to deal with her inner conflict on her addiction to masturbating by getting me to affirm her reasoning. She reasoned that because no one was getting hurt and she wasn't technically having sex, it was therefore okay, right? Well… not exactly.

We established that firstly, she was having inner conflict for a reason, and secondly, someone *was* getting hurt, and that someone was her and quite possibly her future spouse. The reason she was having inner conflict was the same reason why masturbation is considered a wildfire. I then asked her what she thought about when she masturbated and then the lights went on. Masturbation is a manifestation of lust.

This is a radical thought, especially to a generation who have been raised to believe that it's permissible because "no one is getting hurt". "Experts" even go as far to advise that it's a healthy expression of adolescent sexuality. But to those who have been groomed by sexual predators this thought is not too far off. Masturbation didn't enter their lives through the guise of education but the reality of lust and sexual exploitation. Grooming exposed them to the conflict of pain, shame, and dopamine before they had the emotional capacity to deal with the contradiction. We held some space for her struggle. We worked through the tension of her conviction. And we allowed the Holy Spirit to bring to the surface the inception of her wildfire. Her wildfire was started by arson; an intentional crime of fire against her to satisfy a base human desire which resulted in damage to her temple. We sobbed.

Fornication; now there's a word you don't hear every day. It is antiquated and outdated. The conscience soothing terminology we use today is "pre-marital" sex. Pre-marital refers to timing; it implies that the vow of marriage was preceded by the consummation of the marriage. In other words, you had sex before you said I do. And therein lies our problem, this generation is *not* making their vows to the people they're sleeping with.

The rebuttal is that marriage is just a piece of paper. Listen, money can also be described as just a piece of paper but here we are, getting up early every morning, working crazy hours, sacrificing our families, our health and overall wellbeing to get our hands on it. We understand that money is *not* just a piece of paper, it has value, and it requires work. And in principle marriage is much the same, but the act without the vow creates an emotional recession. You can have sex without the vow but that is not pre-marital sex, dear reader, that is fornication.

Fornication is so serious that it is listed among the offences that will disqualify one from entering God's Kingdom. Now I could faff around the technicalities but that would be me not loving you well, that would be me affirming a heart posture and a lifestyle that will get you separated from the presence of God for eternity (1Cor.6:9-10; Rev.21:8). God has non-negotiables, and the enemy knows this. The enemy can't keep us from salvation, but he can get us to disqualify ourselves, much like Balaam could not curse the children of God but knew how to get them to bring a curse upon themselves. Balaam was a prophet who was hired by the Balak, the king of Moab, and three times Balaam tried cursing the children of Israel, he failed at each and every attempt. Balak promised to reward Balaam handsomely but refused because he could not curse God's chosen people. Balaam asked the wicked king (Num.23:8), *"How can I curse those whom God has not cursed? How can I denounce those whom God has not denounced?"* Later we see how Israel, although blessed by God, brought a curse upon themselves; the Israelites opened themselves to a serious plague because of fornication. And as I suspected Balaam had something to do with it, Revelation 2:14 confirms that Balaam might not have been able to curse Israel, but he taught Balak their weakness, their tendency to push God's non-negotiables.

> *"And Israel dwelt in Settim and the people began to commit fornication with the daughters of Moab."*
> **- Number 25:1 Aramaic Bible in Plain English**

Like a plague, our indifference to fornication is sweeping through our lives, families, churches, and bloodlines. The reason fornication is a deal breaker, a non-negotiable, is because it perpetuates brokenness, in our own lives and everyone connected to us. It opens us up to self-inflicted curses and consequences - we then become a misrepresentation of blessing to a broken world. Through the life of a believer fornication distorts God's message to the world.

Do you remember purity rings? Well, it really took off with the Churches' attempt to establish purity in the lives of young believers. It served as a reminder to not have sex before marriage. It proved to be a profitable spin-off to the purity movement; ministries cashed in on this trend. But the trend soon became a breeding ground for the very danger it sought to avert. People started to target those who proclaimed their purity with a ring. People saw it as a boundary they wanted to move, and not a non-negotiable to be respected. Those who wore purity rings were hunted for fun. The challenge was further compounded by celebrity culture, with big names such as Britney Spears, Selena Gomez and the Jonas Brothers all wearing purity rings. These celebrities and others like them either succumbed to the hook up culture and took them off or became the butt of jokes. Unfortunately, the taking off of these rings or being made fun of because of them was a very public act. Denny Pattyn, the founder of the Silver Ring Thing said this about purity rings in the public arena, *"Celebrities can both help and hurt his group's quest to create a cultural shift in America where premarital abstinence becomes the rule rather than the exception."*

Interesting. He then went on to outline how, if celebrities are not educated and inspired about their commitment to the Silver Ring Thing, their misdemeanours would be a bad reflection on the ministry. Pattyn likened purity rings to wedding rings. We then took it a step further and introduced promise rings into the mix. I can't trace the concept back to its inception, but it's basically, when a couple are dating and promise to someday get engaged and marry. It's where dating becomes a quasi-courtship without the proposal for marriage - and since no one is going to say it, I will: This is where we soothe the conscience with a ring before the actual ring because we're engaging in pre-marital everything.

Please note that this is not true for everyone.
Please understand, I am not against the concept of purity rings.
Lastly note, I am not against the concept of promise rings.

My *concern* is our inability and often unwillingness to accept and deal with our sexual brokenness, causing us to numb and dumb ourselves down to the truth and power readily available and at our disposal. We create trends and buy into extra-marital efforts to mute conviction and legitimize our brokenness - we create wildfires instead of building fireplaces. We underestimate the enemy and overestimate our ability to contain fires. Some of us have 3rd degree burns, some of us smell like smoke. No matter where you are in the wildfire spectrum, it's time to call in reinforcements; it's time to stop perpetuating sexual brokenness, and time to accept and embrace the beauty of our brokenness in the hands of our Healer. As I'm writing this, I received a voice note calling for urgent assistance because a woman set herself alight and as a result burnt her house down. How uncanny. Her children, still very young, 12 and 7, have nothing; everything was destroyed in the fire. They lost their mother, their home and anything that could be used to restart their lives. The kids escaped with the clothes on their backs. My heart is heavy because this is what happens when fire goes wild both in the natural as well as the spiritual. In this case a woman not only lost her life, but her children now bear the brunt of her wildfire.

We can overcome any wildfire triple threat that perpetuates brokenness by accepting that we are broken, and that beauty can come from our brokenness. There is a humility that permeates the lives of those who have been broken and accept that only God can make all things beautiful in its time. I've observed two kinds of people that come to me for counseling in the area of their brokenness. The first kind are broken but perpetuate brokenness by living their lives outside of God's will and purpose for their lives and relationships. The second kind acknowledges the brokenness but chooses daily, to not transition from victim to perpetrator, by refusing to continue in the brokenness that broke them in the first place. There is a certain kind of humility that accompanies the second kind of person. They're the kind of person Isaiah 61 speaks about.

"To bestow on them a crown of beauty instead of ashes, the oil of joy instead of mourning, and a garment of praise instead of a spirit of despair."

They are also much like what the Japanese call Kintsugi; the art of putting broken pottery pieces back together with gold. And again, the pottery doesn't put itself back together. The Potter does. And the result is beauty despite brokenness. What a beautiful metaphor. The pottery we know refers to our lives, but the gold, well the gold we see can be likened to faith. It is when we live our lives by faith in God and His word that our lives truly reflect beauty in brokenness. Take it in. You're a beautiful mess!

Wildfires have potential for destruction, but fireplaces create an environment where the fire can warm and comfort those who come near for its enjoyment. I want to share with you how I built a fireplace for my broken sexuality. I didn't want destruction.

Accepting Brokenness

When I accepted that my brokenness was not only written into my DNA as a member of humanity, but that it was also a part of my unique story, I was able to hold space for the Sovereignty of God over my circumstances and over my brokenness. It was when I accepted that others are broken just as I am, that I was able to extend the same grace and forgiveness I had received. This made me a formidable protector of God's throne in my heart; no one could take His place in my heart, not even me. Accepting brokenness in the hands of our Healer is a superpower.

> *"He heals the brokenhearted and binds up their wounds.*
> **- Psalm 147: 3 NIV**

Taking Responsibility

It is true that we might not be responsible for our brokenness, but we are responsible for our healing. When we come to know Christ as Saviour, it is our responsibility to not only know Him as Saviour but as Healer and ultimately to make Him Lord of our lives. Taking responsibility for our healing could mean different things to different people. For someone it might mean repentance, for someone else it might mean obedience, some might need to forgive or ask for forgiveness. It might require us to seek counseling, therapy and deliverance, there are those who will need medical intervention. The point of taking responsibility is doing what He leads us to do.

"Make a careful exploration of who you are and the work you have been given, and then sink yourself into that. Don't be impressed with yourself. Don't compare yourself with others. Each of you must take responsibility for doing the creative best you can with your own life."
- Galatians 6:4-5 MSG

Surrender to God

Surrender is giving up on the notion that we know best. It's the debunking of the idea that our preferences, feelings, thoughts or ways are higher than God's. Surrender is the admission and confession that God knows best and that we will not fight Him, His will or ways. Surrender is affirming that He is God, and we are not. Surrender admits that while we may be competent and able, our efforts and attempts fail in comparison to God's capacity and ability to bring about His purposes regardless. Surrender is the only option when it comes down to your way or God's way.

"Going a little ahead, he fell on his face, praying, "My Father, if there is any way, get me out of this. But please, not what I want. You, what do you want?" **- Matthew 26:39 MSG**

I almost feel like I discovered the practice and power of building a fireplace for my sexuality too late. The other thing I discovered is that building *and* maintaining our fireplaces is not just for the season of singleness but for marriage as well. Because here's what no one talks about - marriage doesn't heal our brokenness, it exposes it. Marriage doesn't cure lust. Marriage is not the "Promised Land". Marriage is more than just our happily ever after; marriage is like a fireplace, it's a safe and intentional place for the fire of our sexuality. Marriage is where you learn to handle the heat. While wildfires distort God's message to the world, fireplaces reflect God's heart for our sexuality. Dating cannot hold our fires. Purity rings or promise rings have their place but make poor substitutes for fireplaces.

REDEEMING THE RAINBOW
Trigger warning***
I counseled with a young person who was distraught at the fact that same sex attraction might always be their struggle. Their heartfelt desire was to be delivered from homosexuality completely. I could not make such a promise and that was hard for this young person to hear. Can God heal and restore? Can God deliver completely? Of course, He can, but that's not my call to make. God decides how and when to heal and deliver us from brokenness. The truth of the matter is that on this side of eternity, sin although defeated, will always be crouching at our door and that although we are saved and being saved from sin, its presence, power, and punishment - the temptation to sin - will continue to pull at our flesh until the day we die. While the desire to sin decreases with sanctification, we must not be ignorant to think that we will never be tempted.

What this young person and I needed to establish was that even if God did not take away the desire for same sex relations, would this young person still honour Christ as Lord in their heart and life? It was heart breaking to see this young believer struggle with the tension of the Lordship of Christ and the proverbial thorn in the flesh.

I do believe that this struggle is so difficult because we wrongly associate sexuality with identity, we even use it interchangeably. We have a community, who have assigned their identity to their sexuality; for example, because someone experiences or engages in same sex attraction, they therefore conclude that they are homosexual. As a result, they get caught up in a lifestyle that fundamentally is a departure from the will and purposes of God for their sexuality; because they think that *is* who they are. They have taken on an identity defined by their sexuality; they are self-identified by their sexual desires and appetites.

If we're going to address sexual brokenness, we can't not address the appropriation of the rainbow by LGBTQ+ community to mean something that it's not. And more specifically, we must declare the power of redemption for those within the queer community who have received Jesus Christ as Lord. There is healing, restoration and redemption for every self-professed follower of Christ who struggles with sexual brokenness. I cannot speak about being unchained without calling our attention to this.

The rainbow does not mean pride, it means promise. For me personally, and unequivocally, the rainbow is a sign of Gods mercy, not a symbol for humanity's confusion. A covenant making and promise keeping God gave us the rainbow as a sign of His mercy, never to destroy the world again with a deluge. Today that very symbol has been placed on a flag to mean sex, life, healing, sunlight, nature, magic & art, serenity, and the spirit of the LGBTQ+ people.

A flag, dear reader, is a powerful thing because it's also a very spiritual thing. A flag is a symbol of presence, ownership, association, and relationship. Biblically a flag is symbolic of loyalty. Flags were also referred to as banners, standards, and emblems. When you raised a flag, it was a banner to which you pledged allegiance, a standard to which you submitted to and an emblem that showed your loyalty. As a Christ follower our allegiance is to God first, His Spirit-filled Word is what we submit to, and we our loyal to our identity in Christ.

Flags were not only symbolic, but they also identified people groups. Did you know that the tribes of Israel had different banners. It is interesting to note there are more than 20 different pride flags and recently the acronym for the queer community got extended to LGBTQIA+.

If you are like me, and don't quite know what all the letters stand for, then here's a breakdown as according to the National Runaway Safeline: *"The acronym LGBTQ represents: Lesbian, Gay, Bisexual, Transgender, Queer/Questioning as it relates to gender identity and sexual orientation. While LGBTQ+ is the GLAAD* (Gay & Lesbian Alliance Against Defamation) - *recommended acronym for this community of people, you may find other organizations use variations like LGBTQI (the "I" represents "Intersex") or LGBTQIA ("A" represents "Asexual,") In 2020, the National Runaway Safeline (NRS) began using LGBTQIA2S+ to recognize those who identify as "Two-Spirit." This phrase refers to people who identify as having both a masculine and feminine spirit"*.

The rainbow has been appropriated to mean pride, and pride is not only dangerous, but it also endangers; it is a danger to others and more fundamentally it is a danger to us. To lift a flag that means pride invites a few things, I'll mention only 3.

> #1 Disgrace (Prov. 11:2)
> #2 Punishment (Prov. 16:5)
> #3 Destruction (Prov.16:18)

We can try to justify pride linguistically and socially, because it's true we can be proud of our achievements, people, and things in a healthy way, however pride at its core is the shift of ultimate confidence in God to confidence of self. Pride is the lifting up of self and over and above God. How ironic? Lucifer fell because of pride. And now we know him as Satan. His name changed from meaning "Morning star" to "Adversary", because of pride.

He was disgraced; his punishment was eviction, and his destruction awaits him in a lake of fire. Just as a side note, hell wasn't created for people, hell was created for Satan and the fallen angels, and he has made it his mandate to take as many of God's image bearers as possible, with him to hell.

Now, am I vilifying the LGBTQIA+ community because of their flag? No. I'm merely *flagging* their flag and what it stands for. Why? Because what the pride flag stands for will be the *fall* of the child of God; he who pledges allegiance to a flag, pledges allegiance to all that that flag represents, and in this case, it is in direct opposition to God. Pride is not a virtue, it is not something God blesses or honours, in fact God opposes the proud.

> *"You're cheating on God. If all you want is your own way, flirting with the world every chance you get, you end up enemies of God and his way. And do you suppose God doesn't care? The proverb has it that "he's a fiercely jealous lover." And what he gives in love is far better than anything else you'll find. It's common knowledge that "God goes against the wilful proud; God gives grace to the willing humble."* **- James 4: 4-6 The Message**

Read that again. God goes against the willfully proud. Read it slowly. The NIV translation uses the word "oppose". Something I found interesting and terrifying at the same time, the Greek root word for oppose means *to draw battle lines against*. Dear Reader, God is at war against pride and those who elevate themselves above Him.

What about inclusivity? The LGBTQIA+ flag also represents inclusivity; Inclusivity based on what? Based on sexuality. And the pride flag representing sexual inclusivity is in every public-school class in America. The west is leading and countries like South Africa are not too far behind. The inclusivity is based on the premise of love is love. While love may be love for others, for the child of God, *love* is not love. Love is a Person; God is love and pride is inconsistent with His love. God's love is exclusive and sets us apart from a world system and view that elevates self and our own way of doing things. A self-proclaimed gay man named Frank Rodriguez, the Operations Executive Director for Gays against Groomers did and said the unthinkable against the LGBTQIA+ community by stating the following.

"Every teacher who has a pride flag in their classrooms should be fired and arrested. The pride flag is a sexual flag. It represents nothing other than sexual things."

He categorically stated that he was pushing back against the agenda that's happening in classrooms all over America. Now, him and I are very different in our belief systems and the values we've chosen to build our lives on, but we both can't help but to see the push by the LGBTQIA+ community to have all people accept and adopt their pride and gender ideology; which is being enforced through all spheres of influence, education, government, media, business, culture, medicine, politics; through every medium possible.

Sadly, we also see this push in the church - as in the institution- because not every church is the Church. I said what I said. But I digress.

Back to the agenda, I'm touching on this very sensitive topic not to school or challenge the LGBTQIA+ community, because look, they can live how they want, it's their choice - I have a focus. I'm only touching the tip of the iceberg when it comes to the LGBTQIA+ community to call out those in this community who profess Christ Jesus as Lord; I am calling believers who struggle with sexual brokenness *out* and calling them *to* the life they've been redeemed for.

So, we've flagged the pride flag, now to critically think through the gender ideology language. Have you heard of pronouns? Of course, you've heard of pronouns. I recently spoke with a parent whose daughter just hit high school and is fluent in pronouns as to validate and not disrespect members of the LGBTQIA+ community. Did you know that not calling a member of the LGBTQIA+ community by their preferred pronouns, is referred to as misgendering, and is seen as an act of violence? Yes, violence, because according to activists, violence is not only physical but also psychological.

Where misgendering got scary and real was when a transgender school shooter killed 3 adults and 3 children at The Covenant Christian Elementary School in Nashville in the US, and the LGBTQIA+ community were outraged because the shooter was misgendered. Instead of seeing the incident for what it was, the LGBTQIA+ community took to social media and protested, not against school shootings and murder, but against the fact that the shooter was "misgendered".

Then to add insult to injury, in a response to the shooting, the White House Press Secretary, Karine Jean-Pierre, stated that the Trans community was "under attack". Wait! What? Who was attacking the Trans community in the school shooting? To be clear, there were 6 victims in that shooting, if we *must* talk about identity, there were 6 Christians killed in that shooting. There was 1 murderer, and please forgive my "unwokeness" (just roll with it, pretend it's a word), but misgendering the murderer should be the least of our concerns as a society.

It would seem that there is a language we must learn and adopt if we are to show "respect" to the identity of the Trans and Non-binary communities, regardless of the fact that, that same "respect" is not garnered to the Christian and conservative communities. Just for your basic information, pronouns include but are not limited to;

> they/them/theirs,
> she/her/hers,
> he/him/his
> zie/zir/zirs

A quick search showed that zie/zir/zirs are neutral pronouns, but they/them/theirs? Forgive me but my first thought was the *"we are many"* response to Jesus' question to the demon possessed man (Mark 5:9). Am I saying that someone who wants to be referred to as they/them/theirs is demon possessed? I would say, "very likely". You have my permission to come for me.

What I will say is that it is grammatically incorrect. The rebuttal is that using plural pronouns for a single person has been used since the 14th century. This is true... for cases where gender was unknown or irrelevant. So, there's that.

It begs the question though; why is language and more specifically the use of preferred pronouns so important to Trans and Non-binary people? Most sources report the same findings; being intentionally misgendered makes Trans and Non-binary people feel dehumanized, it invalidates their identity, they feel disrespected, isolated, uncomfortable, even hated. It doesn't stop there. Riley J. Dennis believes that misgendering a Trans person causes real psychological violence and contributes to physical harm.

I fear that using this argument as a basis to enforce compliance to demands on language only shows that the only people who are a threat to the LGBTQIA+ community are themselves. The data shows that despite social reforms and medical affirmative care that the suicide rate in the LGBTQIA+ community has not dropped instead rises steadily each year. While transgender activists insist that this is because of how they are treated and stigmatized in society, the data on mental illness in this community suggests that there are issues within themselves that needs addressing.

Spiritually, I believe this "misgendering issue", and the push to get everyone to comply with it, is Satan's way to garner validity and acknowledgment of something that God has not ordained or agrees with. He may not get you to agree with the lifestyle, but if he can get you to compromise on this one language issue, where pronouns are concerned, he has won half the battle in getting Christians on board and placing their stamp of approval on it. He asks the question: what is the harm in calling them what they want to be called? The answer, it goes in direct violation of what God had originally said, and that is sin and compromise enough for him. Watching the transgender ideology unfold in real time over the past two years has opened my eyes to several concerns I have for believers who find themselves connected and aligned to the LGBTQIA+ community and agenda. I say agenda because you can't help but see the breakdown of masculinity, femininity, childhood innocence, family and community as designed by God.

Two students on an unknown college campus in the US were asked what they thought of the LGBT agenda being pushed on the youth. Their initial response was that they are the LGBT and there is no agenda but in the same breath one of them stated that, and I quote, *"I feel as though every child should be gay. I'm actually gay and I'm studying to be a teacher right now and I'm going to make every child in my class gay."*

Now we can argue about the integrity and validity of this statement, but you can't help but see that there is an agenda, because the same rhetoric is used when asked about the LGBT in relation to youth and children.

In South Africa we have what we call State Capture; found often but not always, in transition countries. State capture occurs when the ruling elite manipulate policy formation and influence the emerging rules, including laws and economic regulations, to their own advantage. The captured economy is trapped in a vicious circle in which the policy and institutional reforms necessary to improve governance are undermined by scheming between powerful firms and state officials who extract substantial private gains from the absence of clear rule of law.

I have reason to believe that the agenda of the LGBTQIA+ community whether they know it or not, whether they confirm or deny, can be described as Culture Capture. There is a ruling elite who are a minority, but who are manipulating policies and influencing all spheres of life to their own advantage. The culture is being trapped in a vicious cycle with the aim of accessing men, women, and children with the expressed purpose of normalizing confusion, delusion, and perversion. Am I coming on too strong? Certainly not!

It's time the Christian community gave as much strength and violence to the push back, as the LGBQT community gives in pushing its agenda. *Matthew 11:12 "And from the days of John the Baptist until now the kingdom of heaven suffereth violence, and the violent take it by force."* We need to take our communities, our families, our children, and our sexuality back by force.

In war there are many strategies one can employ, depending on your objective. Some armies take no prisoners, others settle in the land and colonize, and others take captives. Nebuchadnezzar was the head of such an army; he invaded Jerusalem and took captives back to Babylon. Daniel, Hananiah, Mishael and Azariah were among the captives that Nebuchadnezzar carried off to Babylon. I can't help but notice similarities between the modus operandi of Nebuchadnezzar and the Culture Capture we are witnessing today.

Similarity #1 - Name change. You must understand that when a Jewish Mama gave her baby a name it would be closely linked to their child's identity as a Jew but also to their *destiny*. They weren't like us today, we choose names because of how it sounds, Jewish mama's chose names because of what it meant. Every time they or someone else mentioned or called their child's name they would be calling out the meaning and their destiny. To a Jew a name was like a prophetic declaration of your identity and destiny. Nebuchadnezzar changed their names to mean something totally different to what their mothers named them. Their new names would help assimilate them into their new culture, but it was also an attempt to change the loyalty of the Hebrew boys from YHWH to the Babylonian gods. Notice that with the LGBTQIA+ community your sexuality, gender identification or sexual orientation *is* your identity. You are either lesbian, gay, bisexual, transgender, queer/questioning, intersex, asexual and more. Your label becomes your identity. Ever heard of dead naming? A dead name is the birth name of a transgender person who has changed their name as part of their gender transition.

Similarity #2 - New language. With their names now changed Daniel, Hananiah, Mishael and Azariah were taught the *language* and literature of the Babylonians. While I am all for education and learning new languages, notice how far the LGBTQIA+ community is going to satisfy their narrative for gender ideology. Not only are they changing words, but they are also enforcing these changes in all spheres. Failure to comply to their language results in outrage, name calling, violence and even the threat of a lawsuit, incarceration, or consequences for "hate speech". Here are some of the new words:

> *Cis Woman* means you were born a woman and identify as one.
> *Cis Man* means you were born a man and identify as one.
> *Trans Woman* means a man who is transitioning to a woman.
> *Trans Man* means a woman who is transitioning to a man.
> *Chest Feeder* means a person who breast feeds a baby.
> *Birthing Person* means a person who gives birth to a baby.
> *Childism* means prejudice against children.
> *Non-Binary* means a person that does not conform to gender.
> *Map* is a person who is attracted to minors...

These are but a few of the new words, this list grows every day for the sake of inclusivity, which we know is informed by gender ideology.

Similarity #3 - Different Diet. So, the Hebrew boys are named, trained and now they will be integrated into the culture by what they *consume*. Notice Daniel, Hananiah, Mishael and Azariah are ok with being called by another name and speaking another language for the sake of culture but when it comes to their diet, they pushed back. Why? Because now the culture was touching on their covenant with God. Their dietary laws were connected to their covenant relationship with God. You must understand that a Jewish man couldn't even go to the toilet without being confronted with his covenant, it was cut into his flesh. A Jew would sit down to a meal and be reminded of their covenant with God by what they consumed, even to this day. So, when you think of your relationship with God on these terms, it helps one better understand the concept of "you are what you eat." Now let's make the shift from physical consumption to spiritual. What we take in matters, and those who seek to capture the culture know that. The LGBTQIA+ community wants the culture to consume their transgender ideology, and they do this through pushing policies and reforms on education, medicine, media, and religion.

You may ask what's wrong with inclusivity? Is it so wrong to be tolerant? And what does Dominique's observations on the warfare tactics employed by Nebuchadnezzar have to do with what we're experiencing in the culture today?

We're in a war for the hearts of this generation and the warfare strategy is captivity for the purposes of cultural integration, to establish and perpetuate norms that depart from God's plan and design for our hearts and relationships. This strategy started with the emasculation of men, we're in the middle of erasing women, and they have made it no secret that they are coming for our children. I submit to you that this strategy has been in operation for decades, the reason we're seeing it unfold is because number 1, slowly but surely, we're waking up to what the enemy has been doing while we were in a spiritual slumber and number 2, the LGBTQIA+ community is not hiding it anymore. I prophetically declare that like Daniel, God is raising up a generation that will not compromise on their covenant relationship with God. They will push back with more than just words, but with lives that align with love, truth, and grace. Inclusivity doesn't mean compliance and tolerance doesn't mean acceptance.

We must redeem the rainbow for believers who struggle with sexual brokenness, their community is not pride, it is not the LGBTQIA+ community - we are their community, the community of faith, who will speak life, walk in love, and hold space for their healing, restoration, and sanctification. We must remind them that God tells them who they are and their identity in Christ determines the living out of their relationships and sexuality.

In our mission to redeem the rainbow we must touch on gender theory and where it comes from. We're about to enter the dark side. Strap up, it gets rough. Prepare to be triggered if you haven't been already.

Gender theory started with a man named Kinsey. When it came to sexuality, he believed that true happiness was found in a life of perverse sexual experimentation regardless of one's age. It was this belief that drove him to implement social reforms aimed at ridding society of Judeo-Christian values. He was seen as a social reformer, the godfather of gender theory.

What his contemporaries discovered was that his research was fraudulent. The data he collected for his gender theory claims were collected from convicted sex offenders and child molesters. His research was conducted in prisons, not among ordinary, moral, law-abiding people. He also performed awful sexual experiments on children and babies. His research is found in his book, *Sexual Behaviour In The Human Male*, and in this book, you will find a chart called Table 34. This table documents the orgasms of very young children, including babies as young as 5 months old. This man was not brought to book for his crimes against children, rather his perversion is celebrated by academia and Hollywood. His ideas form the foundation for sexual education in public schools in the US today. But he wasn't alone - enter another man, a psychologist and professor at John Hopkins University, named John Money. Gender ideology was his brainchild, he's the one who coined the terms gender identity and gender roles. According to Money, babies are gender neutral at birth, and one's environment determines whether you're a man or a woman. The world soon heard about his theory, that a boy could be raised as a girl and vice versa.

It gets worse, Money tried out his theory on twin boys. At 8 months the twins went to be circumcised, but the procedure went wrong, and the first twin's penis was burnt off. They then didn't do the second circumcision. The traumatized parents didn't know what to do and went to Money for help. He then convinced the distraught parents to transition him into a girl. Money also conducted sexually abusive experiments on the twins throughout their childhood, which included the simulation of sex acts on each other. Money reported that, up to the age of 10 this experiment was a complete success. This was a lie; the results were a disaster. The transitioned twin never fully accepted his female identity, and eventually his parents disclosed their dark secret; he then chose to transition back to a boy. His name was David, and as an adult he spoke up about the abuse and damage done to him by John Money. One of his attempts at disclosing his story was done on the Oprah Winfrey Show. The trauma that David, his twin and family went through left unimaginable wounds. His brother died of an overdose at 38 years old and David committed suicide.

There was never an apology or retraction by John Money, instead his delusions were adopted by mainstream psychology and these false claims form the basis of gender ideology today.

The reason you and I never knew the foundations of these ideologies is because there are powerful and influential people who don't want us to know and very importantly, we haven't done our due diligence in critically thinking through LGBTQIA+ claims about gender, identity, and sexuality. And we're out here wondering where all this is coming from. Suddenly there's this massive surge in gender dysphoria, and transgenderism seems to be at an all-time high.

In Britain for example, the number of young women being referred for gender treatment has exploded over 4000% in the last decade. Between 2016 and 2017 the number of females requesting gender surgery in the US quadrupled, the rates are exploding. Surveys show that the leading demographic asking for gender transition are teenage girls. The difference with the gender dysphoria reported is that it seems to be peer motivated and social media motivated. Gender dysphoria does not seem to be an organic problem; the girls seem to have developed dysphoria in adolescence as opposed to traditional gender dysphoria that surfaces in childhood.

Two words - Social contagion.

We are experiencing first-hand the effect of social contagion on the culture. Social Contagion is a ubiquitous process by which information, such as attitudes, emotions, or behaviours are rapidly spread throughout a group from one member to others *without* rational thought and reason. We have an entire generation that's accepting the transgender ideology without thinking it through.

In the US and where all social media can be found we have the youth culture caving in on itself because for every young person transitioning to the opposite gender, we have a young person de-transitioning. Young people are de-transitioning because they are the living proof that the transgender ideology is a lie. What's scary is that policies in psychology, medicine and education are designed to keep parents out of the decision-making process of sexual transition. From the school to the operating table, parents have little to no say, and South Africa is no exception.

Over the last decade there has been a huge push for parents to ensure gender affirming care. The age of consent for medicinal and surgical intervention in the US is 15, which means that you might not know that your child is on puberty blockers and will have no authority over any surgical mutilation that will take place in the name of gender affirmation. Medical professionals advised that if gender affirming care was not given to children, parents would put their children at risk of suicide. And many well-meaning parents gave their approval for surgical intervention with the children for the fear of losing their children.

The propagandistic sloganeering among fearful and accommodating parents promoting this is *"I'd rather a living son, than a dead daughter."*

But what we are seeing is young adults de-transitioning because they've discovered that what they needed wasn't surgery but therapy. Instead of mutilating their perfectly healthy bodies, they needed people who would sit with them in their dysphoria and hold space for their difficult questions and feelings and to help them come to terms with their gender.

We ask, how did we get here? Something tells me that we know exactly how we got here. We got here when we departed from God's design for our sexuality, when we started to self-identify instead of looking to God for our identity. You see when self is our highest authority nothing can truly satisfy, we will go from one thing to the next in the hope that we will find the utopia we've created in our minds. If you follow the narrative from the sexual revolution to date, you'd be blind if you cannot see where this is heading. I said it before and I'll say it again, the LGBTIQIA+ agenda is after our children. As you read this book the stage is being set for the decriminalization of pedophilia, as I have mentioned previously. I am sobbing. Activists are calling for Pedophiles to no longer be called by their perversion but to be called MAPS (Minor Attracted Persons) because as one Educator stated in a public school, "*they can't help being attracted to a 5-year-old.*" Australian Senator Malcolm Roberts exposed the UN and WHO for their current attempt at child grooming. They have put together a framework for Europe that demands that sex education begin at birth under the State's guidance and not the parents?! You just can't make this stuff up.

This is our problem; we are sacrificing our children in the name of inclusivity and tolerance. We have an entire youth subculture, mutilated, sterile and broken because we have failed to ask critical questions. Had we done our due diligence we would have found that the LGBTQIA+ claims on sexuality are unfounded. And the issue at hand is that their agenda leaves no room for anyone to disagree; if you do not affirm their ideologies, you're labelled a transphobe and found guilty of hate. But see, here's the thing God doesn't allow us either - we are not allowed to hate anyone but neither can we affirm their lifestyle. We are commanded to love the person, but my love cannot be devoid of truth.

The truth is there is no gay gene, you're not born gay, and there is no conclusive evidence to suggests this. We all were born this way which is why we must be born again. Everyone is born with the capacity to depart from God's design for sex and sexuality. Is same sex attraction real? Yes, it definitely is. It is a courageous thing to pause and identify why. Is homosexuality a sin? Yes, it is, it is rooted in our sinful nature, and it is a lifestyle God calls those who practicing it, out of. Is gender dysphoria real? Yes, it is, it is characterized by questions… and the transgender ideology is not the answer. Can you self-identify? No, you can't. That's not your lane, let God be God and let Him tell you who you are, who He has called you to be and who you're becoming. He hasn't called you to transition; He's called you to be transformed into the image of His Son, Jesus Christ our Lord. Were you assigned a gender at birth? No, before you were born God knew you and knit you together in your mother's womb, your gender is a part of your assignment on the earth.

chapter ten
Soulties

"People who cover their faults and excuse themselves do not have a repentant spirit."
~ Watchman Nee

Soul ties. Fact or fiction? Truth or myth? In my toxic dating era, I didn't question its validity. In fact, I accepted it as true. Why else would I feel connected and attached in this way? Why else would I be drawn to someone who obviously didn't love or care for me. Surely there must have been some tying of my soul because what believer actively seeks out what is not good, not healthy, toxic, and dysfunctional? Or who seeks out someone who has moved on? Who lies to themselves then believes the lie; that all the insanity is for the purpose of closure knowing full well that you would return to that dysfunctional relationship in a heartbeat?

Surely, I must have been soul tied? How else do you explain the madness and the obsession? Because "what you won't do... you'll do for love", right? Listen... I ticked all the boxes for being soul tied.

Unhealthy attachment to the person. Check.
Obsessed with the person. Check.
Taking on traits, mannerisms, addictions, and attitudes. Check.
Remaining in an abusive relationship and defending the person. Check.
Reoccurring dreams, thoughts, and fantasies of the person. Check.
Unable to throw away objects that reminded me of the person. Check.

Looking back now I see how very happy I was to accept my perception of being soul tied. And this was because I romanticized the notion that I couldn't help it; my soul was tied to the soul of another. It was a "reason" that seemed to make sense of the desires I felt I had no control over. It was only until I entered courtship with Ricardo that I started thinking critically about what I accepted as my reality for so long. Sure I had people who taught me prayers to break soul ties, we even did little prophetic actions to break the hold others had over my soul. One time, I even called back all the parts of me that was tied, my mind, my eyes, my hands, my heart... my body. But I was still checking the boxes?!

How would I break the ties because I couldn't take soul ties with me into marriage? I needed to deal with soul ties once and for all. When you're engaged in critical thinking it's important to ask critical questions. And I don't know why I didn't think of it before, but if I was going to deal with soul ties surely the Word of God would give me critical information, understanding and the method of dealing with soul ties decisively. But I had to stop and ask if soul ties were even biblical?

Soul ties; as in the noun, is not even mentioned in the bible. I checked various translations, but nothing, not even in the MSG version which tends to use more descriptive contemporary language. That disturbed me a little, but I soon got over that because there are important words such as "Trinity" and "Rapture" that are also not mentioned in the bible. The difference however is while those words are not found, the concepts for them are built on foundational truths that *are* found in the word of God.

So, here's where the alarm bells went off. Soul ties as a noun or even as a concept is not supported by the bible as a whole but rather by 2 specific verses that many well-meaning bible teachers build their entire teaching on. Let's review.

> *"Now when he had finished speaking to Saul, the soul of Jonathan was knit to the soul of David, and Jonathan loved him as his own soul."*
> **– 1 Samuel 18:1 NKJV**

> *"Do you not know that your bodies are members of Christ? Shall I then take the members of Christ and make them members of a harlot? Certainly not! Or do you not know that he who is joined to a harlot is one body with her? For "the two," He says, "shall become one flesh." But he who is joined to the Lord is one spirit with Him. Flee sexual immorality."*
> **– 1 Corinthians 6:16-19 NKJV**

The challenge with taking these two scriptures to prove the reality and validity of soul ties is that number one; to fit the soul ties narrative both scriptures would need to be used out of context. And number two; you would need to ignore every other scripture that teaches on the nature of the soul. President and Senior Writer at Christianity FAQ, Daniel Isaiah Joseph does not mince his words concerning the teachings around soul ties:

> *"Soul ties aren't illustrated, defined, or taught in the Bible. The concept is rooted in secular self-help trends and popular psychology. Furthermore, as conventionally understood, the idea of soul ties undermines the Bible's teaching about the soul as well as healthy and holy relationships."*

Could it be that by merely putting the word "soul" into a concept that we've actually tampered with the biblical definition of soul? Have we made our understanding of the soul something that it's not? Have we engaged in teachings that contradict what the bible teaches on the nature, ability, and function of the believers' soul?

I have reason to believe that the term *soul tie* is an imposter; that the concept of soul ties misidentifies the real problem. When we accept teachings that are unbiblical, we run the risk of bondage and being chained. Could this be the reason why I did special prayers but nothing special happened? Could this be the reason why I summoned back parts of me but never felt healed and whole? Could this be the reason I was in a season of courtship but felt like I was carrying invisible chains? Is this why I felt tormented by past relationships? Is this why I felt like the more I was trying to break free the more I was bound? Could it be that believing an imposter kept me chained? Lies can never unchain, only the Truth sets us free... because Truth is a

Person. I read an interesting confession that gives me the language to communicate this discovery on the teaching of soul ties. Read.

"The concept of "soul ties" is a new age, not Biblical, belief. Soul ties are not in the Bible! Jonathan and David's friendship and "shall become one flesh" are not about "soul ties." I should know, because when I was a new age teacher before I was saved, I taught and wrote extensively about soul ties, twin flames, cord connections, etc. I repent and apologize for these false teachings that have now seeped into the church."
- Doreen Virtue

The soul is that unseen part of us that is considered to consist of the mind, feelings, will, emotions, motivations, purpose, and capacity for relationships with God and others. We have enough evidence in the scripture to indicate that the soul and spirit are distinct but related and connected from the moment of salvation. The bible teaches that the soul is eternal and cannot be destroyed by man (Matt.10:28).

The soul can be strong or weak (2Pet.2:14), saved or lost (James 1:21). We know the soul was created by God (Jer.38:16). What we might need reminding of, is the fact that the human soul needs the protection, purification, and atonement of God (Lev.17:11; 1Pet.1:22). Thank God for Jesus. Here's what blows my mind time and time again; every person you have ever met and will ever meet is a soul living in a body, their soul will last forever. They will either reject Christ and face eternal death or accept Christ and glory in eternal life (Rom.6:23).

Now here's where the cookie crumbles, a soul tie cannot be the reality of two souls being tied but merely the unhealthy attachment one has to encounters, experiences, desires and sin. Yes, believers can nurse attachment to sin and feed it.

IF LOVING YOU IS WRONG, I DON'T WANT TO BE RIGHT
Denver had a serious case of bad girl syndrome. Did Denver love Jesus? Yes, with *most* of his heart, but there was a portion of his heart that would always belong to his ex-girlfriend Tammy. She'd moved

on years ago, leaving him tormented by unanswered questions and a flaming desire for closure. He was obsessed with wanting to know why she left him. He toyed with some reasons but not knowing *her* reason often left him wounded, feeling rejected and curled up in the fetal position.

He was triggered. His mother abandoned him when he was 4 years old and he didn't know why she had left either, so even if it meant the end of him, he would have closure with Tammy. He just wanted to know what about *him*, caused her to leave him, maybe that would give him some insight into why his mother left him. Tammy made him feel erratic and unstable, like a wild man. Together they were the definition of toxicity. Unsaved and ungodly, Denver put up with her abuse - though he also, often returned disrespect. The drinking, partying and trauma seemed to be their bond. They would "break-up-to-make-up" because in his mind, there was nothing quite like the make-up sex that followed. When he was with Tammy, he felt alive. She made him feel past the numbness of abandonment and rejection. When Tammy walked out the door for good, Jesus knocked on his door. Denver opened the door to Jesus at a tent crusade and had a genuine salvation experience. He soon joined a bible believing and Holy Spirit filled, faith community and seemed to grow in leaps and bounds. Denver met a beautiful Christian girl, and they started dating and were accountable to their leaders. Life seemed to be getting better for him. He was finally optimistic about his future - this new woman in his life, was quite possibly his future wife and a hope at a family of his own. But his walk with God was abruptly halted when Tammy made a reappearance and declared a hostile takeover. Denver was back in her bed and seemed to have come back from the dead, fully awake and alive to his reclaimed carnality. He tried to hold onto his newfound romance, with the person Tammy referred to as his 'church girl'- but she could never be Tammy to him. Tammy walked in and out the door of his life over the next 5 years and Denver watched his spiritual vitality waste away. He seemed to go through the motions of the Christian life, his spiritual regimen soon became Sunday services and the odd mid-week service, but like the church in Sardis (Rev.3:1) he had a reputation for being alive but was as good as dead. Even though he knew that Tammy was not good for him and subsequently his walk with Christ, Denver could not let go of her or his obsession with why she couldn't, or wouldn't, commit to him. Tammy sent Denver a WhatsApp message on the morning of her wedding. She was marrying one of his party buddies at court, and despite his objections, she signed on the dotted line. Denver was shattered, but still knowing what he knew - and being hurt the way he was - he still found himself back in her arms, every time she beckoned. Denver went from sexual immorality to adultery in a heartbeat. Two decades ago, it would have sounded like a soul tie to me, one that I would have convinced him must be broken if he is to move on and grow in his walk with God. Today, knowing what I now know, my advice to him would be very different.

IF LOVING YOU IS RIGHT I'D RATHER BE WRONG

Chelsea had been married for 10 years, and in that time grew weary of her husband's emotional detachment. Everything she envisioned for her marriage was nothing more than a daydream - far removed from the reality of his cold shoulder, borderline misogyny and the sex she felt obligated to give herself over to. What was once was a whirlwind romance was now a routine of school runs, debt consolidation and carefully fabricated happiness on social media accounts. She was tired of building a career, being married – but acting in the capacity of a single parent - and maintaining the home. She would end her day at work, only to be thrust into more work. Intimacy had become a burdensome chore. She loved her family, but she was exhausted. Her husband no longer pursued her, he had stopped opening doors and pulling out chairs in the first year of their marriage; he vacated the roles he had promised to fill and stopped making any effort to make their house a home. Soon they were just strangers co-existing in the same four walls. She learnt to function and cope without him, and he was happy to let her continue in that vein. They were both saved and so they kept up the smiles and graces because that's what good Christian couples do, right? As Christians, our toxic trait is that we think and act like we will never experience anything negative because we are saved. Unfortunately, this is not true, so when we do experience problems, even growing pains and healthy conflict within our marriages, instead of seeking the help we need, we mask it, we hide it, and we keep up appearances. To admit we are struggling is somehow equivalent to admitting the failure of the marriage, and that would mean that our salvation wasn't real to begin with. This is where Chelsea and her husband found themselves, so they abused one another in ways that didn't leave physical marks, but wounded their souls and crippled their children. The truth is Chelsea's husband didn't know how to love her in a way that she could understand and so he gave up trying a long time ago. Chelsea was emotionally exhausted and tired of begging to be loved, seen, and affirmed. This was not what she signed up for and wanted out.

Had Chelsea made a mistake to accept her husband's marriage proposal? Maybe her soul mate was somewhere out there, waiting for her. Surely this poor excuse for marriage could not be all there is to her life? Chelsea started reminiscing about old boyfriends who adored her. The one that came to mind consistently, and pulled at her heartstrings, was Clint. Could Clint have been her soul mate? Was he the "one that got away"? He worshipped the ground she walked on when they were dating and was heartbroken when she broke up with him. She started feeling like such a fool for letting him go, she might have had the happily-ever-after she always dreamed of. Chelsea gave into the temptation to stalk his social media accounts, and soon started to convince herself, that his wife was living the life that Chelsea was supposed have. She concluded that she married the wrong man, and that her soul mate was out there loving someone else. Chelsea was miserable. She filed for divorce. She could not and would not reconcile herself with staying with her husband, "for the sake of the kids'. Her exact words were, *"we don't belong together."*

The misunderstanding of concepts such as soul ties and soul mates will be the end of us. Soul mate as a biblical concept depends on how you use it. Many people use the term soul mate to describe a meaningful relationship. It is often used in the context of marriage but not always. For the most part it refers to two people who *should* be together because of a "special", almost spiritual connection. I've witnessed a man walking out of his marriage because he "met his soul mate".

The blatant lying and justification that came with that confession was audacious to say the least. He expected the church to accept his new wife just because he believed God "sent her to save him from a loveless marriage". Thankfully I was not the senior pastor, and I wasn't asked my opinion.

HE TOUCHED ME

Trauma bonding is a psychological response to abuse and happens when an abused person forms an unhealthy attachment with someone who has hurt or abused them. Mind you, not everyone who experiences abuse sympathizes with the abuser. This unhealthy attachment is reinforced where there is dependence, such as in the case of a child who is being abused by a parent or caregiver. Think of it this way, when someone's main source of support is also their abuser a trauma bond may develop.

What you will often find in children is that they will then associate love with abuse. I've counseled with women who believed that unless their husbands beat them, their husbands couldn't possibly love them. There are specific conditions that reinforce trauma bonds. I'll mention 3:

> **#1** The victim experiences harsh treatment or abuse with small intervals of kindness
> **#2** The victim is isolated from other people and their perspectives.
> **#3** The victim truly believes there is no way of escape.

The most convincing way to tell when someone has developed a trauma bond is when they try to justify or defend the abuse, and the abuser. There are other signs as well. I'll mention 2:

> **#1** The victim becomes defensive or hostile if someone intervenes and attempts to stop the abuse.
> **#2** The victim is reluctant or unwilling to leave the abuser or the hostile environment.

Years ago, Ricardo was walking home, probably from church, when he came across a man beating a woman who appeared to be his girlfriend. As is his nature, Ricardo jumped in to defend the young woman. His aim was to only immobilize the abuser, and not to harm him, but what he didn't see coming was that the beaten and bruised girlfriend turned on him and started fighting Ricardo in defense of her abuser.

But what happens when two victims of abuse form an attachment? What happens when two people who have experienced similar trauma form a bond? This kind of bond is like a trauma bond but *distinct* in that the person you're in relationship with didn't cause your trauma, but they might perpetuate it, or the shared trauma becomes the basis of the relationship. But truth is that anything built on trauma tends to collapse. Trauma is really a bad and very rocky foundation. Furthermore, trauma-based relationships over promise and under deliver on healing and happiness. Now, this is not always the case between two people dealing with trauma, because truth be told, we all have a measure of trauma. But it's when trauma is not dealt with, and wounds are not healed that we open ourselves to creating unhealthy bonds and attachments to others.

> *"Trauma can ignite a fire inside of you that makes you feel an attraction similar to a moth to a flame."* **- Jessica Baum**

Trauma bonds cause us to be strongly attracted to what caused the trauma in us in the first place, and it's *that* attraction that usually draws us into more trauma. I don't know if this is for you but please note that unresolved trauma can look like chemistry and that's very deceiving. As Cindy Cherie so aptly states *"When all you know is fight or flight, red flags and butterflies feel the same"*. Often, you will be attracted to someone who speaks to your childhood trauma and wounds. It's important to interrogate your baseline for attraction and chemistry because that determines the kind of person you attract or are attracted to.

I've seen this play out time and time again in the lives and relationships of believers who fail to address their childhood trauma.

Men seek out the black widow and women are drawn to the flame like a moth. We also underestimate Daddy wounds and Mommy trauma. A young man with daddy wounds caused by his father walking out may not walk out like his father did, but because of his conviction places very high value on being present. He, however, may still be emotionally and spiritually absent, which can cause dysfunction in a marriage and family. A young woman on the other hand with mommy trauma tends to overcompensate or neglect to discipline her children because her mother treated her harshly. The effects these types of traumas can have on the husband-wife relationship is grim. Generational trauma often causes us to swing from one extreme to another.

Unresolved trauma can display itself in psychosis, but unfortunately, will more often play out in all our relationships, especially romantic ones. When trauma is all someone knows that's all they will seek out. This why Truth is so important in the life of a believer because it heals the heart, transforms the mind, and sets the victim free! A toxic trait that is always evident in a relationship between people who try to build their relationship on shared trauma, is that wounded people always try to heal old wounds through new connections, especially romantic ones. The greatest temptation you will have to resist as a wounded person is the temptation to hand the power to heal your wounds, over to another person. You must resist the temptation to use others as an express ticket to healing and happiness.

BREAKING SOUL TIES

The nature of the believer's soul demands that we relook our view of soul ties. Let me shock you: not even marriage ties two souls together. Think about it; death ends the jurisdiction of marriage and Jesus clearly taught that there will be no marriage or sexual intimacy in heaven. The act of marriage in vow and intimacy connects the flesh (Matt.19:5), but *not* the soul. This is why even after you marry and are intimate, it's difficult becoming one especially when the honeymoon is over, because the question is which *one*, or a *new one*? Because your soul has autonomy, you must learn how to master it in relation to others. A classic example of this is a wife submitting her will to that of her husband. And where is the will found? In the soul. Submission needs her permission.

Now I understand that we can't rush through this because it's more complex than what I'm making it sound, but let's reason together on this. Your soul is that part of you that lasts forever, and if you're in Christ it has been saved and is undergoing sanctification. Saved from what? And why be sanctified? Well, I'm glad you asked. We know that Jesus is yesterday, today, and forever more the same (Heb.13:8). This is also true for salvation, it is past, present and future (Eph.2:8; 1Cor.1:18; Rom.5:9-10).

Salvation was laid out since the foundation of the world. When we come to believe it is a very present reality and there will come a day that if we endure to the end, we will be free from the presence of sin.

> We have been saved from the penalty of sin,
> We are being saved from the power of sin and
> We ultimately will be saved from the presence of sin.

I wish I could expound more on this, because this truth will fundamentally change how you view your soul, and when you change how you view your soul, you move from toxicity to wellness, from dysfunction to functional - it will empower you. Child of God your soul is pure gold... with some impurities. This is why sanctification is key to breaking chains and cleaning your soul. Sanctification is the forming of Christ in us through the indwelling Holy Spirit. The Holy Spirit will often work like fire and burn away the impurities we have in our soul due to sin and its effects.

Now as awesome as the soul is once you become born again, it is not in a vacuum. It is connected to other parts of you. You are body, soul and spirit and they're all connected. It is your spirit that became alive at salvation and made you alive to God, your soul is now undergoing sanctification and forming Christ in you and your body is the temple and home of the Holy Spirit, empowering you to live the life God called you to. These elements of who you are, are not separate from one another - they are closely linked. So close in fact that you can't touch one part of you without touching everything else. This is why what happens in your body effects your soul, and what happens in your soul effects your body, and your spirit holds the tension between your soul and body connecting you to God. In our human strength, wisdom and understanding we cannot separate our trichotomy. Only God can, through His Word.

> *"For the word of God is alive and active. Sharper than any double-edged sword, it penetrates even to dividing soul and spirit, joints and marrow; it judges the thoughts and attitudes of the heart."* - **Hebrews 4:12 NIV**

I submit to you the possibility that we have confused sin muscle memory in the flesh with the tension of the will in the soul. Like an athlete who has trained for years develops muscle memory, your flesh remembers sin and can engage it in without thought. And strictly speaking your soul remembers sin too, but the difference is that your flesh does not have a will, your soul does. Your flesh needs your soul's permission to act on the sin muscle memory. Let me ask you this: when you've ticked all the boxes for a possible soul tie, could it be that you don't have a soul tie issue, but that you're dealing with a flesh issue? And that your soul doesn't need ties broken but that your heart needs to be broken? Could it be that you don't need a special prayer, but you need to repent?

I say this because a human spirit who possesses a soul cannot tie itself to you. That is outside the human scope of operation. A soul tie can't make you do things - obsess, stay in an abusive relationship, or sabotage any attempt for you to move on. If your will has been compromised, then your soul has been compromised. What do I mean by that? If you no longer have autonomy over your soul then one of two things has happened; either you surrendered it to Christ - a battle which every child of God must engage, yielding and surrendering to Christ daily - Or you are possessed by a demon. Shocking, but true. The point is that a human soul cannot be tied to your soul. Only a spirit can.

"Soul ties" misidentifies the real problem. Special prayer to break a soul tie keeps us boxing with shadows instead of going to the source and walking in victory. When you feel like you're experiencing what pop psychology calls a soul tie, you're experiencing the pull on your carnality. If the pull is in your flesh, you need repentance and discipleship, if your will has been compromised by a demon you need repentance and deliverance. Why? Because you can't cast out the flesh and you can't disciple a demon. When we understand the true nature of our soul and the power of salvation over it, we can take *responsibility* for our decisions and actions. If we're going to be functional in the way we conduct romantic relationships we must understand that a past relationship, illegitimate and premature sexual encounters, heartbreak or need for closure cannot tie our souls to another person. As a believer we must repent and deal correctly with thoughts, feelings and desires that pull us toward past or ungodly relationships.

If Denver was taught, trained, and disciplined correctly he would have understood the soul in relation to salvation, and salvation in relation to sanctification. It would have still been his responsibility to keep in step with the Holy Spirit but at least he would have been taught the Truth that has the power to set him free.

Misconceptions around the soul in the life of the believer, is dangerous. It's like being armed with an AK47 but you choose to go into battle with a butterknife. Saints, please understand that he Word of God is not optional in our lives, it is the highest authority over our lives and relationships. The reason Christian marriages are not on the rock of Jesus Christ, but the rock of divorce is because we are governed by our carnality, ignorance and sometimes willful disobedience. This is not true for all divorce cases, which is why I must address this in a bit more detail.

If Chelsea and her husband had taken the time to seek God and come to a discerning spiritual leader before they succumbed to defeat and the "soul mate" deception, they would have been able to cancel the divorce culture in their lives.

God hates divorce, He's made it very clear on how He feels about it (Malachi 2:16). But He has also made provision for men and women who suffer at the hands of a spouse, because God knows how broken humanity is.

There are two concessions in scripture for bible-believing men and women who are suffering in marriage.

Disclaimer: These concessions have contexts and varying degrees of application. The purpose of sharing these is to provide a reference point for biblical guidelines for divorce in the life of a believer. Further engagement, study, counsel, and prayer is recommended when a believer is considering a divorce.

The *first* reason is adultery.

> *"It has been said, 'Anyone who divorces his wife must give her a certificate of divorce. But I tell you that anyone who divorces his wife, except for sexual immorality, makes her the victim of adultery, and anyone who marries a divorced woman commits adultery."*
> **- Matthew 5: 31-32**

And the *second* reason is abandonment.

> *"But if the unbeliever leaves, let it be so. The brother or the sister is not bound in such circumstances; God has called us to live in peace."*
> **– 1 Corinthians 7:15**

These are concessions. One of which Paul advises is not from the Lord but from him. He counsels that the believing spouse is released from their vow when an unbelieving spouse leaves or abandons them. I've had a mentor who chose the high road in the face of adultery. He chose to forgive and continue working on his marriage with his adulterous wife, who subjected him to years of betrayal, insecurity, and pain. He truly believed that God would touch her heart and heal their marriage. Even though he had a concession from the Lord, he made the decision to stay and work through it. His wife was a believer, in fact she was a street evangelist who worked extensively with the homeless, downtrodden, and marginalized. But she avoided dealing with her trauma and wounds.

She tried to be faithful but placed herself and her husband at risk with clandestine and illicit sexual encounters often with random, nameless strangers. My mentor engaged in long periods of fasting and praying, seeking out prayer warriors to assist in prayer and intercession for his marriage. Until one day his wife walked out and abandoned him. I saw him navigate the most excruciating season of his life, knowing that he had given his all and surrendered to the reality of divorce in his life. Was it God's will? What I do know is that God released him of any sense of obligation towards his vows and wife because she committed adultery. That was his story.

Many others have taken the concession first and God brought the healing and restoration later, where spouses remarried after intervention, therapy, and accountability. I've noticed that when God's will and word is made a priority God always works things out for our good and His glory. Then there are others who divorce for their own reasons.

My mentor later remarried but also within the biblical framework of remarriage. He is healing, growing, and thriving because he prioritized Truth over carnality and pop psychology. Continuing in our story, there's no denying that Chelsea was exhausted, frustrated and honestly believed that she married the wrong person. Her husband on the other hand lacked the emotional intelligence and obedience to the Truth, to love his wife as Christ loves the Church. They allowed their flesh to lead their souls and filed for divorce for reasons other than what God has conceded. The way we conduct relationships lends itself to divorce culture. Not feelings or lack thereof, not poverty, not sickness or disease, not infertility or a spouse earning more money than the other are good reasons for divorce. How about falling out of love? Let me remind you. Love is not a feeling, neither can you make it. Love is a choice. We choose to love when the feelings of love walk out the door.

Divorce in the life of a believer for any other reason other than what God permits is indicative of a deeper more sinister root, almost always found in the carnal nature. Why should the children suffer and endure the divorce of their parents, where there's no adultery or abandonment? It's nothing other than the elevation of self over another. I'll let that simmer.

Breaking soul ties is not about two souls, it's about your soul; understanding its power and purpose and walking in the humility required to live a repentant life, especially when it comes the pulls your flesh has on your soul.

The truth about repentance will unchain you!

Here's what repentance is not:
Repentance is not confession. They are two very different things. We think that because we confessed thoughts, desires and behaviours that connected and attached us to others that we are ok. Confession admits guilt. Confession can appease the conscience for a while. Confession is not enough. But repentance is the superpower in the life of a believer who is transitioning from toxic and dysfunctional to healthy and godly relationships.

Repentance is:
- The change of mind towards sin.
- The change of mind towards God.
- The change of mind that leads to a change of behaviour.
- The change of mind that leads to a change of direction.

Repentance is brought about by godly sorrow which in turn is brought about by the kindness of God (2 Cor. 7:10). Repentance occurs in response to God's kindness, where one comes to be sorry. Please note, not "sorry" because you got caught, but sorry that you chose yourself above God. It's coming to the point of regret, and regret is not always a bad thing. Regret becomes problematic when it doesn't lead to repentance, but is invasive and results in overthinking, rehashing and condemnation.

Repentance is the change of one's mind about sin and about God, which results in turning from sin and turning to God. We don't have a soul tie problem. Our problem is that we have developed an emotional connection to sin. We are sin sympathizers. We're hard on sin in the lives of others but soft on sin in our own lives. We entertain desires, thoughts and actions that will lead us to sin.

We attach a story line and melody to sin, so that it's not so sinful - if that were possible. Singles are singing, *"I'll make love to you if you want me to"*, we're watching porn - albeit soft - because it's part of a series; we're fornicating because we're wearing promise rings. We're doing our relationship like we're married because it's just a piece of paper, and we're going to get married anyway. We're married but chatting late into the night on social media with a colleague or someone other than our spouse. We're not soul tied, we're carnal.

When we justify and make excuses for our sin, it is safe to say that we have created a trauma bond with sin. Think about it. Sin is a harsh task master - an abuser that robs us, hurts, and exploits us, yet it feels good from time to time. It's the classic push 'n pull trauma dance of us - the victims - and sin - the abuser. But we're not really victims, are we? We cover up for sin and make excuses as to why we can't leave a life that is led by our feelings, desires and flesh. 15 years ago, I looked at Ricardo and then took a hard look at Jesus and realized that I was ready to face the truth about my soul and, in a manner of speaking, untie myself from ignorance, pop psychology and carnality. I repented, checking the boxes for soul ties and took responsibility for my flesh. I committed myself to not walk into trauma induced relationships or sympathize with sin or anything that hinders. I could hear chains falling.

PART FOUR

chapter eleven
Healed and Whole

"Christ is the Good Physician. There is no disease He cannot heal; no sin He cannot remove; no trouble He cannot help. He is the Balm of Gilead, the Great Physician, who has never yet failed to heal all the spiritual maladies of every soul that has come unto Him in faith and prayer."
~ James H. Aughey

Jesus *always* had His way with women. Not in the way that we associate with men, or in the ways that works like Jesus Superstar or like what Dan Brown's Da Vinci Code, would have us believe. He had the best way possible with them, a higher way; a way that brought honour, dignity, and liberty to the most vulnerable, overlooked, oppressed, and condemned. Whenever Jesus interacted or engaged women they were seen and heard, empowered, and capacitated. Now Jesus was no feminist, but He was *for* women and not against them. He elevated them, gave them a voice, a place, and a mission. He created space for their uniqueness and depended on them for ministry. Like it or not, Jesus is the standard for our attitude towards women in the marketplace, home and church. Jesus didn't touch a woman without healing, restoring, and honouring her body, soul and spirit.

One such woman was Mary Magdalene.

"After this, Jesus travelled about from one town and village to another, proclaiming the good news of the kingdom of God. The twelve were with Him, and also some women who had been cured of evil spirits and diseases:

> Mary (called Magdalene) from whom seven demons had come out; Joanna the wife of Chuza, the manager of Herod's household; Susanna; and many others. These women were helping to support them out of their own means."
> **- Luke 8:1-3**

What was your life like before you met Jesus? What was your life like before walking with, and serving Jesus and His mission in your life and the world? Where were you when He found you? What were you doing when He called your name? Were you a mess like I was? Did you also feel like you didn't deserve to be saved, healed, or delivered? Did you try to clean up your act before fully surrendering your life? Did you also run from Him instead of running to Him?

How about being possessed by seven demons? Let's just say that Mary Magdalene was the kind of woman that was often on the receiving end of bombastic side eyes. People might not have known what was wrong with her, but Jesus did. Jesus never misdiagnoses our condition. Others see red flags and symptoms, but Jesus sees the root and cause of every manifestation in our lives.

Now you may not be schooled in demonology, but what we must hold space for is the impact that demon possession must have had on her life. Of the plethora of effects of demon possession, there's only one objective any demon has when it enters your life - *torment*. Demons do not come to play.

I remember the first time I came face to face with a demon. I had seen others deal with demons and they made it look so easy, but for some or other reason this time the demon chose me. I had just moved back home from bible school; it was a Saturday morning, and I was spending some time in prayer and bible study when one of the girls in our youth knocked on our door. We'll call her Xena. Thinking nothing of her coming unannounced, I said she could chill with me and the Holy Spirit, which she seemed happy to do. She made herself comfortable. I was about 5mins into prayer and worship when the temperature in my room dropped - it became icy cold. I opened my eyes to check on the entry of the cool air when our eyes locked. Her eyes turned pitch black, she opened her mouth and started blaspheming. I rebuked the demon. *Rookie mistake number 1*. We don't rebuke demons, we cast them out. We can rebuke people, circumstances and situations influenced by personalities or high things, but demons? No, we cast them out! I know that now. I was concerned for my family and didn't want to alarm them, so I grabbed her by the arm and my keys and started walking briskly to the church which was a 5min walk from where I lived. *Rookie mistake number 2.* We don't go to secluded places alone with those possessed by demons, even if it's a church. We should rather call for back-up. Demons give humans supernatural strength. I realized that the demon was allowing me to pull her along. What was I getting myself into?

That demon mocked me all the way to the church. I started trash talking back. *Rookie mistake number 3.* While there are some instances where information from the demon could help with deliverance, the baseline for dealing with demons is identifying them and casting them out! Nothing could have prepared me for what I saw in that church. As soon as we entered the church, she ran from me and hid behind the pulpit. I approached prayerfully and asked the Holy Spirit to help me, because I had no idea what I was doing. I called her name, and her voice responded crying for help.

Then the demon roared, *"she's mine!"* I shouted back, *"let her go!"* We went back and forth for what seemed like an eternity. Finally, she came out from behind the pulpit. I blinked once and then she was standing on the floor in front of the pulpit bent over backwards with her head hanging behind her knees. She started to run- now had she run bent over forward, I think that could have been somewhat possible, but she was bent over backwards, and started running backwards!

After 3 hours of pleading, *(rookie mistake number 4)* and begging the demon to leave her we somehow found ourselves in the vestry. The demon, still very much in control of her body and in control of my feeble attempt at deliverance, provoked me to a shouting match. *Rookie mistake number 5.* We don't cast out demons by shouting, speaking authoritatively yes, but shouting for hours is not effective. I was exhausted. I tried one more time to shout louder than the demon and with that she fell to the ground, eyes closed she lied there so still. I sank back relieved that the demon was gone. Demons are master deceivers. She wet and soiled herself. I thought it was gone. We got her cleaned up, but we were back in the vestry the next day during the Sunday service. "Not again!" was my initial thought. This time our worship leader joined me, she knew exactly what to do. I watched our worship leader closely and made mental notes. Out of nowhere Xena's hands started contorting and as if in slow motion her hands started moving towards her neck. The demon started choking her using her own hands. Within 30 mins our worship leader had identified the powerful demon and cast it out with authority and power. I then became intentional about learning the difference between demon possession and demonization and how to minister deliverance in respect of that difference. I learnt about my authority as a believer and how important discernment and sensitivity to the Holy Spirit is, when dealing with people suffering because of demons. I also learnt that not everyone who comes to me for help with suffering is demon possessed but should there be foul play involved it's important to be well prepared and courageous. People's healing is at stake.

In the weeks that followed Xena shared with me her story of incest, sexual abuse, and excruciating torment. Xena experienced torment because of one demon. Now multiply that by 7. We're talking torment on another level. Torment speaks of extreme pain, anguish, the utmost degree of misery either of body or mind. Mary Magdalene was tormented in her mind, and it manifested in her body, she was in pain physically, emotionally, psychologically, no part of her person was unaffected or untouched by agony and suffering. She had no control over her will or emotions. She had no say in how she spent her time or money. Her body was not her own, it belonged to her tormentors. How did she get to this point?

The truth is we don't know. What we do know is that demons use doors to enter the lives of believers such as trauma, rejection, sin, cultic practices, bitterness and wait for it… *unforgiveness*.

FORGIVEN

Unforgiveness single handedly fills my counseling schedule with tormented souls. Not everyone is possessed, but many are subject to being man-handled and roughed up by thoughts, emotions, illnesses, and darkness that refuses to let them go. If there's one thing I almost always must teach on and counsel through with believers who find themselves chained... is forgiveness.

I've been asked through clenched teeth and desperate tears, *"how do you forgive what you can't forget."* I've been asked raw and authentic questions that I've often asked myself, questions like:

- *"How can I forgive someone who does the same thing over and over again?"*
- *"Why can I forgive everyone else except her?"*
- *"Why can't I forgive?"*

It's these statements that often get me on the back foot:

- *"I don't see why I should forgive."*
- *"I don't feel like forgiving."*
- *"It's not fair!"*

I'll tell you this, forgiveness is not easy, and it is not for the faint hearted. Here's what I realized in my own struggle with unforgiveness: True forgiveness is often misunderstood. Yes, false forgiveness is a thing. So, here's what forgiveness is *not:*

Forgiveness is not a team effort; we've been led to believe that unless someone asks for forgiveness we can't forgive. Don't get me wrong, reconciliation takes two willing parties, but forgiveness only requires one person. This is why you can forgive someone without being reconciled to them. When you forgive, you do not - I repeat - you do *not have to* build a relationship with a toxic, dysfunctional, narcissistic, or an abusive person.

Forgiveness is not acquitting the guilty; we think that when we forgive, the guilty don't have to answer for their actions. When a crime is committed the guilty must and should be charged in a court of law. I've seen many wrap the wounds of the victim with injustice by failing to report crimes in the name of forgiveness.

Forgiveness is not weakness; we often mistake meekness for weakness. Just because someone is the first to forgive or ask for forgiveness, we think that they are weak or in need of the other party. The person who forgives is anything but weak. As in the words of Alexander Pope, "to err is human; to forgive, divine."

Forgiveness is not a feeling; because we still feel the pain associated with the trauma inflicted on us, we think we cannot forgive. We wait until the hurt and humiliation has subsided before we attempt to forgive and then when the pain resurfaces, we enter a vicious cycle of guilt and shame. We condemn ourselves to walking in unforgiveness because we're in pain.

What is often a hard pill to swallow is that God *commands* us to forgive. So, it would be in our best interest to know what true forgiveness is. False forgiveness waits for an apology, covers up injustice, is seen as a weakness and is misconstrued as a feeling. When we walk in what forgiveness is *not*, we remain bound and in chains. June Hunt in her book, Counseling Through Your Bible Handbook defines forgiveness as:

> *"Forgiveness is dismissing a debt, dismissing your demand that other owe you something. Forgiveness is releasing your resentment, releasing your right to hear 'I'm sorry' or your right to get even. Forgiveness is as much about you as your offender. It removes from you the weight of resentment, freeing you to live a life of joy and peace."*

Here are two things that I discovered:

Number 1: *Forgiveness is a choice.* It's not that deep. Please excuse my bluntness. Your trauma is real, your feelings are valid, your truth is seen and heard but our problem is that we want the whistles and bells, the frills, and butterflies. We've romanticized apologies and while hearing *I'm sorry* gives one a sense of justice, the truth is that when it comes to true forgiveness an apology is simply not a requirement. You can forgive without an apology.

The problem often is that we need the validation. We require an apology so that the person knows how much they hurt us, as though that would change how much you are hurting. It really doesn't.

Author Najwa Zebian, makes a very valid point in our quest for seeking the apology before releasing forgiveness; she says:

"Do you really need the person who hurt you to say "I hurt you, and I am sorry, and I feel awful that I did it"? It's beautiful to get it, but do you need it? Do you not know how painful the pain was when you experienced it? Do you need them to tell you how painful it was, and give you permission to feel it? You don't need it; you want it. You want it because you believe that your relief is going to come when they acknowledge what they put you through. The one who broke you cannot heal you. You can't expect the person who broke you into pieces, to bring those pieces and say "I'm gonna put you back together". You can't do that... well you can, but why would you choose to do that? Someone who has the power to destroy you - and uses that power - why would you trust them with rebuilding you?"

Again, you can forgive without an apology. However, there is a flip side. When was the last time you accepted an apology, you never got from someone, you're in a relationship with? Well, you need to stop doing that, and although it sounds contradictory to what I just said, I need you to understand why.

When people wrong you in some way and they aren't willing to apologize or acknowledge what they put you through, you have every right to be angry, upset, hurt, to feel wronged by their actions. Just because they don't admit them or because they don't apologize, it does not mean that the harm was not done. You have every right to feel the pain of what they put you through. Do you need them to apologize to move on. No. But - and here's the kicker - if you thinking of keeping a relationship with them in some way, then yes, absolutely, the acknowledgement and apology is needed, because here's what you are telling yourself and them when you continue the relationship - when there was no acknowledgment of pain, that they caused you – you're telling them *"it's okay if you hurt me"*. What you are telling yourself, is that "what they put me through, even though it hurt so much, even though it's shaken my trust in them, and even though it's made me feel like I'm not respected or valued, it's something that I can live through." Sure, you can live through it, and sure you can survive it, but do you want a life where you feel the bare minimum of human decency towards yourself is not there. Is this truly the life that God has called you to? God is huge on accountability, and if we are to remain in relationships, we need the accountability of the acknowledgment of pain caused and the apology that speaks of love and a willingness to help us heal.

Number 2: *forgiveness is a process*. We must face the offence, feel the offence, and then forgive the offence; yes, in that order and as many times as it takes. You will not conquer what you will not face. Stop minimizing what happened to you. No, *it* wasn't okay and it's okay to face and admit that. Stop making excuses for the person that hurt you. It's not Christ-like to diminish the weight of an offence - sometimes you might have to exercise wisdom by overlooking offences that are small and insignificant, but we never make excuses for offences. Yes, love does cover a multitude of sins, but there are times that you will have to call out bad behaviour. Please, when those moments come, handle them with care.

You're not a robot so stop acting like what was said or done to you didn't hurt you. Feel what you feel and deal with it. Denying pain is not forgiveness.

Did it anger you? Good! It shows that you know you're worth more than their bad treatment. Stop avoiding difficult feelings. It doesn't make you less anointed to feel sad, mad, lonely, hurt or rejected. Our feelings are indicators, they show us where a line has been crossed. They're a reference point. To truly forgive an offence, you must *feel* it. While feelings are indicators, they are not leaders. We are not led by feelings to forgiving someone. Forgiveness is a command we obey, and it is a process we go through.

> *"Above all, have fervent and unfailing love for one another, because love covers a multitude of sins [it overlooks unkindness and unselfishly seeks the best for others]".* **- 1 Peter 4:8 Amplified Bible (AMP)**

This text details how we can move closer to forgiveness. We seek to find ways to forgive and display this fervent and unfailing love for one another. It may be hard to forgive, and especially in marriage, we need to forgive multiple times, often without the apology, and since these offences don't fall under Gods concessions or allowances for divorce, we, as the injured party might need to find ways to remain in the relationship in the absence of apology or acknowledgment. This is where this love comes in. It overlooks unkindness but uses kindness as a "weapon" to fight unforgiveness.

When we display the love of God - that is shed abroad in our hearts by the Holy Spirit - we are displaying kindness in response to unkindness. This kindness, this response comes from us having been sanctified, justified through faith, and having peace with God, giving us access, by faith, to grace; grace we can now extend to the person who we need to forgive, and who rightly also needs our forgiveness. Seeking to be a conduit to release this kind of divine forgiveness, builds our character, and fills us with hope, and more so, within marriage, it produces perseverance, as we need to consistently, over and over again, practice this (Rom.5: 1-5).

It is in this, practising Gods kind of kindness, that we can unknowingly, and without manipulation, lead our spouses to repentance; and repentance is 1000 times better than an apology, because repentance means being so sorry for what you have done, and that you will do whatever it takes to keep it from happening again. It doesn't necessarily mean that they won't ever hurt you again, in that way, but it does mean that they *intend* to never do it again. And that means they will be more careful in the future to consider you, and your heart when doing things that may hurt you.

> *"Or do you have no regard for the wealth of His kindness and tolerance and patience [in withholding His wrath]? Are you [actually] unaware or ignorant [of the fact] that God's kindness leads you to repentance [that is, to*

change your inner self, your old way of thinking – seek His purpose for your life"] - **Romans 2:4**

Here's the truth: The real reason it's sometimes so difficult for us to forgive others is because we often forget what we've been forgiven of. Say it isn't so? Unforgiveness is the obsession with the faults of others and the categorization of their sins and ours; somewhere in the back of our minds we believe that somehow, we're not as bad as them. We've come to the humanistic conclusion that our offenders deserve to be punished but us? Ah yes... *we* deserve our pardon. It happens to the best of us from time to time. Jesus taught on this and exposed our grandiosity with a parable.

I encourage you to read Matthew 18: 21 - 35. When we withhold forgiveness, we are like the servant who was forgiven but refused to forgive a fellow servant. The key to walking in forgiveness is, understanding that you've been forgiven. Listen, every sin you've committed, are busy committing and yet to commit was placed on Jesus when He died on the cross. Jesus paid in full the debt you and I owed and therefore we've have been released - not from consequences, remember that - but we've been released from punishment and the wrath of God if we have accepted Christ as Lord and are found *in* Him; and if, like David, we continue to confess and repent sin as soon we become aware of it.

When we withhold forgiveness, we run the risk of developing the heart of a Pharisee. One Pharisee comes to mind, Simon (Luke 7:36 - 50). It took the tears, hair, and perfume of a sinful woman to show Simon the error of his ways. Jesus, true to form addressed Simon's faulty thinking.

> *"Two people owed money to a certain moneylender. One owed him five hundred denarii, and the other fifty. Neither of them had the money to pay him back, so he forgave the debts of both. Now which of them will love him more?" Simon replied, "I suppose the one who had the bigger debt forgiven." "You have judged correctly," Jesus said. Then he turned toward the woman and said to Simon, "Do you see this woman? I came into your house. You did not give me any water for my feet, but she wet my feet with her tears and*

wiped them with her hair. You did not give me a kiss, but this woman, from the time I entered, has not stopped kissing my feet. You did not put oil on my head, but she has poured perfume on my feet. Therefore, I tell you, her many sins have been forgiven – as her great love has shown. But whoever has been forgiven little loves little." - **Luke 7: 41 - 47NIV**

Simon thought that the sin of the repentant woman was greater than his. Jesus showed that instead of that counting against her, it was working for her because receiving the forgiveness for her sin, created capacity within her to love her Master more.

I doubt Simon lived long enough to read Paul's letter to the church in Rome, in it the Apostle Paul declared (3: 23 - 24), *"for all have sinned and fall short of the glory of God, and all are justified freely by His grace through the redemption that came by Christ Jesus."*

Simon's problem was that he measured his sin in comparison to others. Am I saying sin more so that you can love God more? No, that is not what I'm saying. What I am saying is, recognize that you were also forgiven of sin, regardless of its shape or size, it was sin and you needed to be forgiven of it. I am saying, that because you have been forgiven and need and receive God's forgiveness every day, I want to ask, who are you to withhold forgiveness from others?

Only when we understand what and how much we've been forgiven, will we be willing to forgive others. If you're struggling to forgive others, understand your own need for forgiveness, this will give you a heart that will forgive as you have been forgiven. Remember what forgiveness is not. Remember that forgiveness is a choice and a process. When we withhold forgiveness, we are handed over to tormentors.

"His lord was angry, and delivered him to the tormentors until he should pay all that was due to him. So my heavenly Father will also do to you, if you don't each forgive your brother from your hearts for his misdeeds."
- Matthew 18: 32 - 35

Hold up!

Surely God will not hand us over to tormentors? Child of God, that is exactly what God will do if you withhold forgiveness. Whether in this life or the life to come, the torment for unforgiveness is real. Unforgiveness and torment are first cousins. Ever wonder why you're so sick in your body? The doctors can't tell you what's wrong with you? Ever wonder why you can't stop rehashing and over thinking; instead of processing trauma or an offence you're ruminating - actively engaging in a cycle of anxiety induced thinking.

When you have unforgiveness in your heart, a consistent prayer life becomes an enigma, building strong, healthy relationships is a pipe dream. Unforgiveness goes from your heart to your mind and then to your bones. It locks and bolts the prison that you'll share with your tormentors and throws away the key.

Not forgetting that unforgiveness births bitterness, and part of that torment is an absence of the presence of the Lord. Hebrew 12:14-15 states: *"Make every effort to live in peace with everyone and to be holy; without holiness no one will see the Lord. See to it that no one falls short of the grace of God and that no bitter root grows up to cause trouble and defile many."* (NIV)

Other translations state to *pursue peace*, or to *work at living in peace* with everyone. That includes actively seeking to forgive, even when it's hard; it's realizing that choosing unforgiveness places us with those who choose to be unholy, and in that state, we will never see our Lord. It's knowing that that bitterness is a root that will continue to grow, and it will bear fruit, causing trouble and *defiling many*, not just you.

Our responsibility in forgiveness is again cross refenced in the book of Romans 12: 18-19 *"Never repay anyone evil for evil. Take thought for what is right and gracious and proper in the sight of everyone. If possible, as far as it depends on you, live at peace with everyone. Beloved, never avenge yourselves, but leave the way open for God's wrath [and His judicial righteousness]; for it is written [in Scripture], "vengeance is mine, I will repay," says the Lord."*

This is choosing forgiveness over revenge or pay back. It's choosing forgiveness over our right to receive an apology. Its choosing forgiveness over their lack of acknowledgment or validation of the hurt. Its choosing forgiveness as your responsibility to reconcile the relationship - *as far as it depends on you* - to restore peace, to restore wholeness, to restore intimacy. You might say to me, "I can forgive others, but I can't forgive myself." Red flag. Nowhere in scripture are we taught to forgive ourselves. Saints, we can't pay our own debts, we are the reason we're in trouble in the first place. We must call a friend. And His name is Jesus. We don't have the capacity to forgive ourselves, others yes, but not so much ourselves. Our job is to accept and receive forgiveness. We don't get to take it upon ourselves. God is God and we are not. We ask for forgiveness. God forgives. We accept His forgiveness. We then extend forgiveness to others. Don't fumble this.

Not pain, circumstance or offence determines whether we forgive or not. Jesus was flogged, humiliated, and hanging on a cross, when he was praying that God forgives His perpetrators. This shows us that we can chose to obey God's command to forgive even in pain. Not even the fact that Jesus' face was marred beyond human likeness was grounds for unforgiveness. Even in intense physical pain Jesus made the choice to pray for the forgiveness of those who pierced, ridiculed, falsely accused, and wounded Him. People who have not experienced the forgiveness of God are crippled in trying to build relationships. People who are unable or unwilling to forgive should not get married. And here's why:

> You will be required to forgive on a daily basis.
> You will need to be forgiven on a daily basis.
> You are not perfect.
> And neither is your spouse.

Budget for their mistakes and double that budget on yours. At least once in your lifetime you will feel like you're unable to forgive someone, it's heartbreaking when it's your spouse.

Forgiveness is a command and is a requirement to walk in relationship with God and others. Unforgiveness opens us to torment. I believe it was Joyce Meyers who quoted Marianne Williamson, "Unforgiveness is like drinking poison yourself and waiting for the other person to die."

Yes, you harm yourself emotionally, mentally, spiritually and unforgiveness eventually manifests itself in your body. You will find that doctors can't figure out or explain what's wrong with you. You can't pray, worship, or sustain meaningful relationships, your mind is consumed with the apology they owe you. You bleed on people who didn't cut you. Unforgiveness is a doorway that gives tormentors access to you spiritually and otherwise.

At 18 years old, I knew I had to forgive my dad. I blamed him for everything. While there was validity in my victimhood, I made the error of walking around and filtering all of life through a victim mentality. But I needed him to forgive me too. I did and said things that hurt him and my family and then turned around and used his mistakes and weaknesses as justification for my choices and actions. Yes, my dad was wrong in many ways but that didn't cancel my mistakes. God does not overlook our wrong actions because they are in response to the wrong actions of others.

We tend to blame others for our dysfunction. Our problem is that we use our trauma as an excuse for our own toxicity. What others did might not have been our fault, but our healing is our responsibility. Walking in forgiveness means that we also recognize our faults and ask for forgiveness where necessary. Initially I strongly resisted the Holy Spirit's guidance in asking his forgiveness, because I magnified his offence to me and minimized my offence to God. In essence I was Simon the Pharisee. I repented, and asked God to forgive me for my bitterness, unforgiveness, rebellion and disrespect towards my father.

I couldn't stop the tears or the trembling while recounting to my dad all the ways in which I hurt him. My apology was not generic, vague or a reverse apology - we tend to do that when we don't take ownership of the role we played in the breakdown of a relationship. I intentionally did not mention how I felt when he hurt me.

Then something broke.

The hold over my mind and heart lifted. In that moment it didn't matter if my father returned my apology or not, because quite frankly it didn't matter. What mattered was me extending the same forgiveness to my dad that I had received from God my Father. We don't know how Mary Magdalene came to be possessed and I don't know how you came to be hurt, traumatized or offended but here's what I know; Jesus never misdiagnoses, and He will not only deliver you, but His desire is to make you healed and whole. He did it for Mary Magdalene, He did it for me and He is willing and able to do it for you.

FREEDOM

There's nothing like chains to show you the value of freedom. This is why a sinful woman was willing to debase herself, break her jar, wash Jesus' feet with her tears and dry them with her hair. Sin bows to forgiveness, despair magnifies joy, war illuminates' peace and bondage elevates liberty. God is a mastermind; He uses the brokenness of our world and lives to make His grace glorious. For Jesus, it was the promise of joy that enabled Him to endure the cross.

> "Keep your eyes on Jesus, who both began and finished this race we're in. Study how he did it. Because he never lost sight of where he was headed – that exhilarating finish in and with God – he could put up with anything along the way: Cross, shame, whatever. And now he's there, in the place of honour, right alongside God." **- Hebrews 12: 2 MSG**

When you're in chains, freedom is always the goal. And freedom Dear Reader, is no pie-in-the-sky-when-you-die, Mickey Mouse club house, wish upon a star sort of engagement. No, freedom is the spiritual reality that spills over into every aspect of the believer's life. Just as chains finds its way into every element of our lives, so freedom works itself out from in here to out there. It's not only our spiritual reality but also what we must take hold of.

"It is for freedom that Christ has set us free. Stand firm, then, and do not let yourselves be burdened again by a yoke of slavery."
- Galatians 5:1 NIV

Some translations say, *it's for liberty that you've been set free*. Hear me, it's one thing to be *set* free and quite another to *be* free. The reality of your freedom is contingent on your ability to continue in that freedom and not return to the things that once enslaved you. This is easier said than done. The Israelites wanted freedom but when faced with the terror of their past and the fear of the unknown, they wanted to go back to their chains, not once or twice but several times on the journey to God's promised land.

"They said to Moses, 'was it because there were no graces in Egypt that you brought us to the desert to die? What have you done to us by bringing us out of Egypt? Didn't we say to you in Egypt, ' leave us alone; let us serve the Egyptians?' It would have been better for us to serve the Egyptians than to die in the desert." **- Exodus 14: 11-12 NIV**

"In the desert the whole community grumbled against Moses and Aaron. The Israelites said to them, 'If only we had died by the Lord's hand in Egypt! There we sat around pots of meat and ate all the food we wanted, but you have brought us out into this desert to starve this entire community to death." **- Exodus 16: 2-3 NIV**

The Israelites have a safe space with us because I'm sure you and I can relate to their reasoning. Here we have a classic case of taking the victim out of bondage but being unable to take the bondage out of the victim. They were out of Egypt, but Egypt was still in them. In a manner of speaking Moses, Aaron, a pastor, a parent, a friend can possibly help bring you out of bondage but only Jesus can take the bondage out of you, but again, only with your permission and cooperation.

What you must understand is that freedom is the goal; being set free is what Jesus did to start you on that journey. And then secondly, being set free will take you out of your comfort zone but freedom will demand that you don't go back there. We tend to run back to what's familiar at the first sign of struggle, testing or adversity. This is why you'll return to a toxic relationship - don't allow loneliness to make you reconnect to chains. Walking in freedom with a bondage mentality will open you up to the temptation to run back to bondage at the first sign of having to die to your flesh. You'll literally think of all the ways you were happier as a slave. It was in my season of courtship that I had to come face to face with the reality of my own need for healing, deliverance, and restoration. Jesus set me free from bondage and I knew I wanted to walk in that freedom - and here's the thing with freedom - while being set free is something that happens outside of yourself - contrary to popular teachings - you can't set yourself free, Freedom requires your cooperation. Jesus won't *do* freedom for you. Mary Magdalene was set free by Jesus and then used her freedom to become a bondservant of Christ. A bondservant is a slave but with a difference. A slave is sold or bought, and the slave doesn't have a say in the transaction pertaining to them in any way shape or form. But a bondservant is someone who voluntarily bonds their life to someone. When Jesus set her free from slavery to demonic oppression, she used her freedom to be devoted to Christ. I had to choose what I would use my freedom for. I could either return to the old ways of doing things or I could follow Jesus into the new way of life He had for me. I could live my life by default, or I could live my life by design. I had to choose between my way or God's way, the new nature, or the old nature. You can't have both.

Insanity is doing the same thing over and over again and having the audacity to expect a different outcome. As free as I was in Christ, if I continued to filter my life through my pain and allowed my trauma to give me my sense of identity; if I persisted in dysfunction and self-preservation; if I walked in the chains of my past, I'd only sing about freedom on a Sunday morning but never walk in it. Sadly, this is the life that many believers choose, they use their freedom in Christ to lead them away from Christ, back to a life of bondage and chains, and this, more often than not, happens through relationships.

"You, my brothers and sisters, were called to be free. But do not use your freedom to indulge in the flesh; rather serve one another humbly in love."
- **Galatians 5:13 NIV**

> Our flesh is selfish.
> Our flesh is disobedient.
> Our flesh chooses its own way.
> Our flesh pushes its own agenda.
> Our flesh is impulsive, impatient, and insolent.
> Our flesh wants instant gratification.
> Our flesh exalts self above God

Xena was set free, but she did not continue in her freedom, she returned to a life of resentment and unforgiveness and so her tormentor returned and brought along 7 more tormentors; more powerful. Xena hung herself.

> I went numb.
> I blamed myself.

Through prayer, reflection and counseling I accepted the fact that we are the sum total of the choices we make. Death by suicide was Xena's choice. I would have wanted her story to end differently.

You and I? Our story *can* end differently. Instead of bondage we can be free, truly free (John 8:36). We don't have to return to the things that once enslaved us. We can be free to build lives and relationships that are free from generational curses, childhood trauma, spiritual foul play and the domination of our flesh. We can be free to not only be healed but also to be made whole.

In Luke 17:11-19, of the ten lepers healed, only the one leper returned to thank Jesus for his healing showing us the difference between being healed and being whole. Ten lepers recognized that their bodies were broken and diseased and so they cried out to Jesus. Only Jesus could set them free, but their freedom required their cooperation. Jesus instructed them to show themselves to the priests. Freedom from leprosy required them to put their faith in Jesus' word and to actually do what He told them to do. Jesus has given us a framework for our lives and relationships. Walking in freedom will require us to actually do what Jesus tells us to. For the lepers, it turns out that on their way to the priests they experienced healing in their bodies. One of them, when he saw he was healed, came back, praising God in a loud voice. Notice that he threw himself at Jesus' feet. Jesus misses nothing and asks rhetorically, *"Were not all cleansed? Where are the other nine? Has no one returned to give praise to God except this foreigner?"*

And then the scripture (Luke 17:19) that speaks to this chapter.

"Rise and go; your faith has made you well."

The nine lepers received healing but this one leper who returned to Jesus, Jesus declared was not only healed, but made well; the leper was made whole. His healing affected his skin but being made whole put his life back together again. Veronica Martin Thomas shows the distinction between healing and wholeness by comparison.

> *Nine had new dermatology – one had new theology.*
> *Nine had new careers – one had new conviction.*
> *Nine had new opportunity – one had a new hope.*
> *Nine had a new outlook – one had a new vision.*
> *Nine were restored – one was remade.*
> *Nine were released – one was liberated.*

Healing speaks to the *problem*, wholeness speaks to the *person*. Jesus cares about *what* happened to you, but He knows that in order to effectively deal with what happened He must deal with *who* it happened to. He will break the chains but wants the heart. He will heal and set free but wants you whole and walking in freedom.

Healing makes you look better but wholeness allows you to *be* better.

Healing makes you feel better but wholeness makes you *do* better.

Healing collects your tears but wholeness helps you *understand* tears.

Healing speaks to your pain but wholeness helps you *speak* to the pain of others.

Healing helps you find friends but wholeness *enables* you to be a friend.

FRIENDSHIP

Ever wondered why Jesus never married? Well, firstly, that would have been a theological catastrophe. And secondly, while I adore my husband and children and wouldn't exchange them for the world, I understand Paul's admonition to single people living in this dispensation.

> *"If anyone is worried that he might not be acting honourably toward the virgin he is engaged to, and if his passions are too strong and he feels he ought to marry, he should do as he wants. He is not sinning. They should get married. But the man who has settled the matter in his own mind, who is under no compulsion but has control over his own will, and who has made up his mind not to marry the virgin - this man also does the right thing. So then, he who marries the virgin does right, but he who does not marry her does better."*
> **– 1 Corinthians 7: 36-38 NIV**

Please read the entire chapter for context, but Jesus chose a better way. Firstly, God the Son having sexual intercourse with His creation is a line a good God will not cross. Secondly, marriage perpetuates our humanity, but it is not the height of our humanity; a beautiful thing - yes but not the only thing. Our problem is that we think marriage is the Promised Land. When in fact it's a reflection and not a destination; it's a vehicle for ministry not the engine that drives all of life.

Our problem is we've relegated it to a relationship goal to be achieved rather than the outcome it was designed to be. Our covenant with a spouse should flow out of our covenant with God. Our relationship with God is what makes marriage as a relationship and life station possible and sustainable. We refer to singles as half people when in fact basic math shows us that one is a whole number. They might need someone to complement them yes, but what they do not need is someone to complete them. Let's unlearn this harmful perception of singles please. Stop pushing them into attachments on the premise that they need to be completed. They don't need attachments they need connection. While I'm here let me touch on this quickly.

Please stop using scripture to shame young people into finding a partner. Yes, we know that it wasn't good for man to be alone, but he didn't know he was alone until God said so. Adam concerned himself with working the ground and attending the garden. It was only after he named the animals that he realized that there was something missing; that he could find no suitable helper. When singles know their God, know their identity, understand their purpose, work their environment, and patent a couple of things then let's talk about who and what they might need in their lives.   The enemy knew what he was doing when he awakened this generation too soon. We have young men and women who are divided in their devotion to the Lord even before they're married. Ouch!

Singleness is a gift and marriage is a gift. What we do with these gifts is our gift back to God and to the rest of the world. What gift might you be unwrapping now? Are you unwrapping the gift of singleness? According to Paul, given the time he wrote it in, this was a better way. Our world is lending itself to Paul's day more and more with the convergence of end time prophecies. Do you desire to be married? Here's a scripture that hits the spot.

> "But Jesus said, "Not everyone is mature enough to live a married life. It requires a certain aptitude and grace. Marriage isn't for everyone. Some, from birth seemingly, never give marriage a thought. Others never get asked – or accepted. And some decide not to get married for kingdom reasons. But if you're capable of growing into the largeness of marriage, do it." -
> **Matthew 19: 11-12 MSG**

Jesus didn't marry because He only had eyes for one woman, the Church; She had His heart and still does. Jesus showed us how men ought to treat and engage women who are not their wives, with all love, purity and honour. Some men propose on their knees, Jesus proposed on a tree. Jesus laid down His life for Her and rose again so that He could go to prepare a place for Her. And He'll be back to take Her to Himself. Jesus is the standard for marriage *and* singleness. Our problem is we want a lover in our season of singleness and then want a friend in marriage. We sabotage ourselves and relationships by making every heartthrob and series on Netflix the standard for our relationships and singleness. It just doesn't work. If you want to know how someone should treat you as a single person hold them up against Jesus. No, it's not unfair. Yes, I know we're not perfect. But our hearts became chained because there was no standard. When Jesus becomes the standard, purity becomes a non-negotiable. Start there. We see this with Timothy who was admonished to treat older women as mothers and younger women as sister with absolute purity (1 Tim.5:2).

But what about romance, what about feelings of attraction? What do we do with infatuation and sexual desire? If you're filtering these things through brokenness, trauma, and wounds like I did, then you're setting yourself up for chains. Let me shock you. Jesus holds space for both purity and sexual desire. We're all looking for a place to heal, and we want to be whole, but our problem is that we look for it in the wrong place. We can thank Julia Roberts for this thought-provoking quote.

> *"Women, you are not rehabilitation centers for badly raised men… it is not your job to fix him, change him, parent or raise him, you want a partner not a project."*

Allow me to add, this can be charged to men as well. Men you are not Daddy Day Care Centers for neglected women. We must stop looking for in relationships what can only be found in Jesus. When we find our healing and wholeness in Him only then can we bring it to the relationship we say yes to.

Here's the other thing; when Jesus is the standard, friendship is a litmus test. We're "friend-zoning" people, not knowing that friendship is the best possible way to make an informed decision about the person you would like to date or best-case scenario, spend the rest of your life with. Contrary to popular belief, not attraction, potential or chemistry can give you insight into whether or not you're compatible with bae, but friendship will.

This is your sign to relook your definition of friendship. Seriously. Friendship has lost its essence and meaning, it has been robbed of its power. All because we want what we want, and we want it now. Friendship takes time, it shares experiences and has the potential to grow love in all its forms. Friendship is one of the key components of building the fireplace that keeps the passionate fire of intimacy burning, and burning where it should be.

To be clear, friends-with-benefits is *not* a friendship, it's a "*situationship*", glorified fornication if you ask me. I'm trying to behave myself, but I'm going to say it… It's the twisting of true friendship for the selfish benefit of lust undercover. With a friend like that who needs an enemy? Because a friend-with-benefits is only in it for what benefits them in the moment; they want the "no strings attached" package with as little commitment, input and sacrifice as possible. They will sell you to your enemy, lust. Frenemy. Period.

And I get it, we often jump at the opportunity for relationship because we're afraid they might find someone else. The difficulty with this approach is that number 1, how we do relationships in this generation is counterproductive to the work of sanctification in the life of the believer and number 2, friendship will reveal if we're fit for purpose. I've been asked the question; can a man and a woman be "just friends?" We ask this question because we fail to understand the purpose and power of friendship. People who have been healed and whole understand the value and importance of friendship as a basis for relationship, romantic or otherwise. Friendship is more than *just*. Friendship and the ability to *be* a friend, builds capacity for healthy romantic love. Everyone wants friends, but few people are willing to be a friend, a real friend.

"A friend loves at all times." - **Proverbs 17:17**

Will you become romantically involved with everyone that's your friend? No. But romantic relationships require a strong foundation of friendship. And not just any kind of friendship but friendship based on the ultimate blueprint for friendship found in the Friend that sticks closer than a brother (Prov.18: 24).

> *"My command is this: Love each other as I have loved you. Greater love has no one than this: to lay down one's life for one's friends."*
> **- John 15: 12-13 NIV**

The kind of love Jesus speaks of here is a sacrificial love, a crucifixion type of love, this is the kind of love Jesus extended to the disciples as His friends, and nothing has changed, today you and I are lavished in His love. He calls us friends. It is in friendship that we learn and exercise the laying down of ourselves. not the good parts, but those parts of us that hinder community and fellowship and stifles growth and honour. In friendship we lay down obsession with self, narcissistic tendencies, toxicity, and dysfunction.

In friendship we learn how to create and honour healthy boundaries, we learn how to exercise our autonomy and to value the autonomy of others. We learn how to speak, to listen and handle conflict, all without the obligation of romantic expectations.

> *"I no longer call you servants, because a servant does not know his master's business. Instead, I have called you friends, for everything that I learned from my Father I have made known to you."*
> **- John 15: 15 NIV**

In friendship there will always be an exchange of information and revelation; information, as in the things you've not known before and revelation, the things you haven't seen before. It's in friendship that you see behind the "best foot forward" act that dating often encourages. Romantic feelings, infatuation and dating generally distorts our ability to see clearly. When we're focused on working on a relationship and not a friendship, we tend to ignore red flags, incompatibility, and mismatched values.

There's a discipline I've learnt to exercise in my friendships that has served me well in developing deep, authentic, and healthy relationships. Now granted, I don't have many friends, but I'm always striving to be a friend more than I'm yearning to have friends. Jesus is my ultimate friend, my husband is my best friend; my children know I am not their friend, but they know that I will be sometime in the future, for now I'm "mom". Because their perspective on friendship is largely influenced by their relationship with other little people, it is in their relationship with me that they will learn what biblical friendship is. I have a close group of friends who I call my "happy few" and although we are living our lives separately, when we do come together, we pick up where we left off, as as though we'd never been apart. Listen, your happy few needs to be low maintenance, I can't be functioning optimally with my closest friends needing reassurance of my love and support of them every time they don't get a call from me, or I forgot to check in.

Because of the many spheres and spaces I occupy, I am relationship with a significant amount of people, and the discipline that keeps my friendships and relationships healthy and functional is what Peter Scazzero calls *I-Thou* relationships, a term coined by Jewish theologian, Martin Buber in his book called "I and Thou."

Buber states that the healthiest relationship between any two human beings can only be described as an *I-Thou* relationship. What in the world is an *I-Thou* relationship? Ah it's the most beautiful thing.

> *"In such a relationship I recognize that I am made in the image of God and so is every other person on the face of the earth. This makes them a 'Thou' to me. Because of that reality, every person deserves respect – that is, I treat them with dignity and worth. I do not dehumanize or objectify them. I affirm them as having a unique and separate existence apart from me."* – **Peter Scazzero**

As opposed to *I-It* relationships, which are relationships that revolves around me and often manifests in my frustration at people not doing things my way, or when people don't fit into my plans. *I-It* Relationships see others as merely existing to accommodate me. *I-*

Thou friendships are built on love, autonomy, and mutual respect even when there are differences in backgrounds, perspectives or opinions. When friends walk in the love of God, you can expect God to fill that relationship with His presence, and the differences between us become sacred space, where we allow God to mediate on our differences. Let me say that there's a level of brokenness that a *I-Thou* relationship cannot sustain, as in the case of a believer and an unbeliever or a believer and an abuser.

In the case of a believer and a narcissist, I would strongly advise that you do not engage in any relationship with someone who demonstrates narcissistic tendencies, they do not have the capacity to love you, they only love their need for you. Narcissists can't maintain a healthy friendship; this is why engaging in friendship first will expose what you need to know and see before you make any sort of romantic commitment.

There are 4 ways friendships can go.

Friendships that head for disaster are the kind of friendships that have been initiated with an ulterior motive or started out on the right track but somewhere along the line got convoluted with premature and or illegitimate intimacy. These are the kind of friendships that don't uphold Jesus as the standard for how they treat others or the standard for how they allow others to treat them. It's the go-to narrative for friendships that follow romantic tropes. It's the friends to lovers' "situationship" and as with all relationships that cater for the flesh, it's very difficult to go back to being friends when things don't work out. The friendship, in most cases, was just a means to an end; an opportunity to satisfy the flesh.

I think this is what breaks my heart the most in the church culture and specifically youth ministry, when young people defraud one other in the name of friendship. Young men and women get close to one another, develop feelings – which one can decide to not act on, mind you - but do anyway and end up with their hearts in their hands and their heads hanging in shame. Don't get me started on older men in the church who approach the younger women under the guise of friendship and instead of praying for them, they try to devour them. I have made it my mission to become their worst nightmare.

I've taught the young people under my watch to either not respond or disengage when the conversation goes south, and to make sure they have evidence. If predators continue to badger, they send me the screen shot and I mediate. I take no prisoners. I once received a screen shot from a young woman who was being approached by a married man known to be a believer. He's modus operandi was friendship – he just wanted to be friends. Harmless right?

Saints please! A married man has no business being "friends" with single younger women in the church. Mind you he didn't belong to our local church but had connections with our assembly on a national level. Well, I gave her a good scolding because her eyes only opened when her married friend wanted naked pictures of her. We looked at all the red flags leading up to the absurd request and she realized her error and repented.

I'm on a mission to train up young women and men in godliness and propriety. I make sure they know that the reason these older men target them is not because they're more beautiful than the spouses but it's because the older men think the younger women are dumber than their spouses. I don't know where this generation started to think that attention from a married man or woman means you're something on a stick. No honey, it's an insult – treat the married person who approached you as someone who has just insulted you. Their interest in you is not cute.

Boy, was I taken to task by Mr. *Married-Wanna-Be-Your-Friend*. He denied everything despite me having evidence of his grooming. He then got his leader to call me, and I could hear him throwing tantrums in the background. I was having none of it, not from him or his leader. Driven by holy indignation I rebuked both of them; their entitlement, arrogance and misogyny manifested. A year later I was gutted to find out that they both had been caught in adultery – both of them had filed for divorce from their wives. Friendship has taken a beating at the hands of this generation.

Then there's friendship as a backup plan; this is an attempt at damage control. This usually happens when things started out as a romantic relationship but failed. They came in hot, the butterflies, late night chats, video calls, smoldering looks and lingering kisses. You know the early morning voice notes and late-night check-ins. The gifts were extravagant and made up for the fights and insults. One thing led to another, and they were doing dating like they were married but soon realized that it just wasn't working.

You know, the "love-lives-here" couples who post every hug and kiss, the power couples who self-identify as relationship goals. These are the couples whose entrance into the relationship was based on chemistry and energy. If there was a friendship it was very short lived, it was a matter of "touch is a move." They then find themselves high and dry with the novelty worn off, the classic "falling" out of love saga. And so now they *try* to build a friendship. It can go either way; they build a "friendship" that they run back to every time they need some tender love and care, if you know what I mean. Or they conclude, that they "can't be friends if they can't be lovers" – so they settle for blocking, ghosting – frenemies. They tend to act as though the relationship never happened. This attempt at friendship is a little too late.

This is difficult to navigate especially within the faith framework. I maintain – you don't have to enter a romantic relationship with everyone you're attracted to.

I've had to do some serious interventions with young people who tried friendship as an attempt at damage control. One such intervention was with a couple who I had forewarned of the dangers of dating right off the bat. They didn't even know one another; the young lady had just given her heart to the Lord. The young man had a track record of going from one relationship to another, but they were so twitterpated that everything I said was seen as an attack on their young "love".

The problem with these sorts of relationships is the pace; it's a matter of love bombing, over promising and under delivering at neck breaking speed. A few weeks later I was doing the dirty work of counseling and picking up the broken pieces. The young man moved onto the next relationship and the young woman left the church. Friendship is not a backup plan and doesn't function well as damage control. There was no friendship to begin with, so what do you do with something you didn't have in the first place? I will never forget my grandmother's words, *"you don't have to make a mistake to learn from one."* She wanted me to learn from the mistakes of others, she would say, *"a fool learns from their mistakes, an intelligent person learns from the mistakes of others, but a wise person learns by instruction. Dominique don't make the mistakes I made, make your own."* The thing is that you will have to be willing to listen and learn from others if we are to not repeat their mistakes. We have a generation not willing to sit still long enough to learn about love and life from people who have gone before them, they don't want instruction and so they invite destruction.

Then there's biblical friendship. I am yet to see friends who have Jesus as their standard for friendship, go wrong. I had one such friend in particular - not Ricardo, someone else. We shared the same values, love for God and people. We had awesome arguments and amazing conversations; we would engage on a mind level that I enjoyed very much. He was a critical thinker and challenged me to think from different perspectives. He made me laugh, and I thoroughly enjoyed our private jokes, the side eyes and the brotherly affection I received from him. Our mutual friendship circle had us engaging regularly and so to answer the question can men and women be *just* friends as some would say? Totally platonic? The answer is yes, our relationship was platonic.

This begs the question; can men and women be friends without developing feelings for one another? Now, that depends. What kind of feelings are we talking about here? Empathy, compassion, respect, care, and concern? These emotions are a natural response to spending time and sharing experiences between any two people, but how about attraction, desire, infatuation, and sexual chemistry? Well, that's another story. Because our friendship moved from spending time among friends and public spaces to alone and private interactions, conversations, and experiences, I opened myself up to feelings of *like*. Strong like.

I developed romantic feelings for my friend, and at the time I was duped by the illusion of falling in love, so, I had a choice to make. I asked myself if I was going to act on my feelings for him by presenting myself to him, you know, to make it known, by subtle but intentional words and deeds? Or was I going to starve these feelings? But that would mean an intentional change in the friendship dynamics and direction. I would have to "redirect" the friendship love boat.

He was attracted romantically to someone else, so that helped. I didn't know her but I knew him and so I helped him process his feelings for her. I listened to his endless scenarios of how to get close to her and to get her to like him. Then they finally started dating. Phew!

I was relieved but the relief was short lived, because their rules of engagement included me - his best friend. He got her to somehow date him with the understanding that I am his best friend and that him and I would also spend time together, and that sometimes I would spend time with them too. Apparently, that was a thing back then. She agreed, and I was like, what in the world?! So much for changing the dynamics and direction for our friendship? I then toyed with the idea of telling him, and then what? Be *that* friend?

Not too long before that I was dating a guy and in that situation I was the girlfriend, who had her boyfriend snatched by his best friend. I can laugh now but I was not impressed at the time. It really hurt. I was so disappointed. I decided not to be *that* friend. I decided not to present myself to my friend. I have no regrets.

Lessons were learnt, changes were made, capacity for platonic friendship was built and I was exercising my healing and walking in a measure of the wholeness that Jesus died for.

Now, for friendship that leads to Holy matrimony. Granted, friendship is not always the natural progression to romance that leads to the altar. But if you're going to make it to until death do us part, I've been told, that friendship will have to be a factor. Only in marriage, as God designed it, can friends be lovers and lovers, friends. With Ricardo I had the gift of a platonic friendship leading to a romantic courtship which culminated in a loving marriage. This year Ricardo and I celebrate 19 years of friendship, 13 years of which are within marriage. I am married to my best friend and lover. I consider myself blessed because not everyone has this experience.

It's hard to imagine that there was a time when men and women entered into marriage not for love but for a mission bigger than themselves - for family, companionship, longevity and legacy. They believed that love was more than just a feeling; it was a commitment to choosing to love every day despite one's circumstances. Over time the paradigm for marriage changed and the feeling of love became a determining factor in choosing a life partner.

That's the problem with us, like a pendulum we always swinging between two extremes, in one century we're marrying total strangers, in the next we're putting babies before the vows. In one paradigm we're seeing the big picture but in the next we can't see past our own sense of momentary happiness and fulfillment. Am I saying marry a complete stranger? Certainly not! Am I saying that we shouldn't marry because of or for love? I'm not saying that either.

Here's what I am saying. Singleness is a gift. Marriage is a gift. All of life is an opportunity to create within us the capacity to steward both gifts well. It is when we are healed and made whole by Jesus that we can bring all of who we are to our relationships and hold ourselves and others to His standard for our relationships. Relationships matter to God, in fact it matters so much that there is a relationship that determines our eternity, yes that's right, our relationship with Jesus. And in a manner of speaking, as His bride, we are His friends. Having a friend in Jesus teaches us how to be a friend to others, whether in singleness or in marriage.

IT'S A GENRÈ

People who are healed and whole, and who walk in this spiritual reality are in a class of their own. Allow me to clarify, being healed and whole is not perfection. As you know, perfection is not possible this side of eternity. So, you'll find that people who are healed and whole are the kind of people who accept their trauma, wounds, and brokenness for what they are but do not allow themselves to filter their lives through it or project it onto others.

Rather, their suffering is seen through the eyes of Jesus and put into His hands to be used as a healing balm for others. They've committed themselves to the process of forgiveness in their own lives and have extended the same grace, mercy, and forgiveness to others. People who are healed and whole, although they were victims, no longer function through a victim mentality. There's a difference between being a victim and having a victim mentality. Let's take a moment on this. Being a victim admits that something bad has happened to you. They do not deny this reality but rather explore and process the pain, hurt, and shame that being a victim brings. On the other hand, the victim mentality suggests that people, circumstances and even God, is out to get you. It is the filter through which one perceives all of life. It promotes an abdication from all responsibility, blames others and simply put, is narcissistic in nature.

Being in relationship with Christ requires that we transition from having a victim mentality to becoming a victor. Every victim turned victor through Christ, must live out the tension of walking through trauma, crisis, and challenges as more than a conqueror. This is a process that declares, *"It happened to me, it does not define me."*

Being healed and whole by Jesus is what makes you powerful. When Jesus declares you healed and whole you become qualified to speak to the pain and victimhood of others. And we do this by aligning our experiences, beliefs and convictions to His Word and Spirit. Hear me good: our experience doesn't qualify us, only when our experiences are aligned to Jesus will we truly be able to be in relationship with Him and reach others. I've seen people try to use their experiences as the standard for right relationship with Christ, even correcting people using themselves as the example and it only pushed people further from them.

I've also seen people try to use their trauma and shame tactics to try and get people who are in relationship with them to do what they want. What they do not realize is that their need to control is a trauma response and their attempt to control others with their trauma and shame dishonours Christ and only creates a relationship built on triggers, manipulation, and punishment. Unhealed mothers do this with their children, wounded husbands do this with their wives, and people do this to one another and create dysfunctional relationships. Families become enmeshed; not having clear and healthy boundaries and crippling the autonomy of its members. Romantic relationships become toxic and as Christians we are not immune to the threat of being unhealed and in relationship.

Let me say it again but maybe in a different way; there is a degree of brokenness that cannot be sustained within the context of relationship and as a result the relationship becomes unsustainable. It would be in your best interest to evaluate your brokenness and that of others with whom you are in relationship with. While we are not responsible for the choices of those we are in relationship with as a result of our bloodline; we must accept the responsibility we have to ensure that those we *chose* to be in relationship with - as friends or a spouse - gets our commitment to walking in the healing and wholeness that is ours in Christ Jesus, and that we get theirs.

While being healed and whole is not a once-off event, it does have a starting point. It starts with surrendering to Jesus. It is then considered a journey, and a decision we make daily or every time the pain of our past surfaces. It's what we refer to as keeping in step with the Holy Spirit so that we don't walk in pain-filters and trauma responses but rather in love and by the power of the Holy Spirit. When friendship is done correctly there are a few things that will happen in relationship and especially marriage.

Marriage is beautiful, awesome, and amazing but it can be a bulldozer or a pressure cooker depending on your commitment to being healed and whole. Marriage has a way of exposing us. While dating and courtship tend to bring out the best in us, marriage will expose deep rooted issues. For me it exposed my *insecurity*. As a child I didn't know where I stood. I remember always trying to figure out if I was loved or not, wanted, or unwanted, accepted or rejected and I tried to project that onto my husband. I thought marriage would solve the problem - it did not. It only exposed it. It exposed me.

Marriage exposed my need to control others, especially my husband - a trauma response to emotional pain and suffering. People who try to control others are in self-preservation mode; by controlling others they think that they will be able to control outcomes and avoid getting hurt. There's a difference between being in control and being controlling. When you're healed and whole there are things you must unlearn. I discovered that exposure is not necessarily a bad thing; it is a needed part of the process of walking in healing and wholeness. When you've committed your life to someone, the close proximity will cause faults and faulty thinking to be magnified. Notice how your spouse's faults get magnified in marriage? All of a sudden, my husband breathed too loud, ate too much, spent too much time at work, I mean, I would find fault for the sake of fault finding. What I didn't realize was that marriage was exposing him too; he was seeing things in himself that needed addressing and I wasn't helping. I wasn't being the friend he needed me to be, I wasn't walking in the reality of being healed and whole. Something the Holy Spirit taught me early on in marriage is that when my husband's faults seem big to me, I remind myself that he is not my enemy. My husband is my friend, and I am his - and a friend loves at all times - two are better than one. My job is to help him up, keep him warm and play my role together with him and the Holy Spirit, because together we are a three-strand cord that is not easily broken. It is not my job to control or try to fix him, that's God's job. Can I call him out? Can I communicate my concerns with him? Can I tell him how I feel? Of course I can, but it will require the healed and whole version of me, which is my commitment, that is my role and that is my lane.

One more thing marriage will do, it will amplify what gets said. Notice how anyone can say something but when your spouse says it, good or bad, it's loud! Our words can heal and encourage or cut and break down. Healed and whole people watch their words (Matt.12:36). Period. We're in an opinion era and we must resist the temptation to speak just because we can. When we say the right thing at the right time we bring clarity, understanding and beauty to the most difficult of situations.

> *"A word fitly spoken and in due season is like apples of gold in settings of silver."* **- Proverbs 25: 11 AMPC**

Being healed and whole and making the decision to walk in that daily, will affect your life and relationships on all levels. Your relationships will thank you for it.

chapter twelve
Unashamed

"A key to becoming shame-free is choosing to change your perspective, because when you do, you can begin to change your posture. When you choose to focus more on what Jesus has done for you, you will have the faith to stand up and start moving forward."
~ **Christine Caine**

Some days I stand in awe of my children, especially my son at bath time. It's like he gets some sort of superpower and runs naked through the house, and more often than not we have guests over. This superpower also somehow gives him the ability to look people square in the eye and giggle with sheer delight to see the look of shock or amusement on their faces. Not once does he blush or lower his eyes in embarrassment. He stands or dances there in all his glory, so comfortable in his skin and with who he is; that right there in that moment, I envy him.

Listen, I don't envy the fact that he's naked in front of strangers, that would be just wrong. What I envy is his innocence. He's totally ok with the fact that he's naked and oblivious to the social norm to cover up. We all were like that once, weren't we? But something happened, and we changed. We became aware and ashamed. We share this transition of awareness to shame with our parents, Adam, and Eve. Much like my son, they too were naked and knew no shame, (Gen.2:25) in fact the Aramaic reads, *"They did not know what shame was."* They certainly were not created with it; it was foreign and came as the result of disobedience and ultimately sin. It breaks my heart, but I will have to accept the fact that very soon my son will make the transition from awareness to shame. It's the way of every human being since the fall. Will he run and hide? What will he use to cover up his nakedness?

WHAT IS SHAME REALLY?

And if we may ask, what is shame really? I've always used the words "guilt" and "shame" interchangeably until recently I discovered that they are in fact different and significantly so. While guilt touches on what I've done and how it affects me and others, shame on the other hand, touches on who I am and what I might look like to others. In other words, I'm guilty because of what I've done to myself or others, but I'm ashamed of me and what I may look like to you - if that makes sense?

Dr. Joseph Burge highlights another aspect of shame we must consider, and notes that, "shame is a painful feeling caused by something dishonourable, improper, ridiculous etc. done by oneself or another." Shame is painful. It is over powering. It has the potential to imprison and bring you into bondage. Shame will cause you to run from God instead of to Him. It will distort your view of God, and blind you to the fact that you cannot hide from Him, and yet you will try.

This is also true for our relationship with others - because of shame we'll run, build walls, disengage, fake it, sabotage who we truly are. When we are taken captive by shame, we are punished by the fear that if someone should see us for who we truly are we will be rejected and seen as unworthy. Shame causes us to cower and hide. Shame will go as far as to try to cancel what Christ did for you and me on the cross of Calvary. Shame is real. There are several ways shame will enter your life, but the cause is always the same, sin. Whether committed against you or by you, it is the doorway through which shame enters. And when shame enters it has no intention of leaving. In my experience with counseling, I have found that shame is always the hardest to work through. While sin can be identified, confessed, repented of and of and forgiven, shame is like cancer - unseen until too late, sometimes. I've seen how shame continues to bring young people into bondage even after they've confessed and accepted the forgiveness available in Christ and His finished work on the cross

THE ENEMY'S BEST KEPT SECRET

What I've learnt on my "Unchain my heart journey" is that shame in and of itself is key and a very "necessary evil" if you will, in the process of repentance. Shame awakens us to the need for covering, the need for some sort of intervention. What the enemy meant for our destruction, in that shame makes us feel unworthy of God and therefore we hide from Him, cutting us off from relationship with Him. God in His divine plan of salvation uses the very discomfort and pain of shame, to point us to our need for God, creating the perfect conditions for a U-turn, a redirection back towards God.

Paul wasn't lying when he said, *"And we know that in all things God works for the good of those who love Him, who have been called according to His purpose"* - Romans 8: 28. Shame was meant to cause us to run and hide, but God uses shame to highlight our need for Him, so that instead of running from God, we can run to Him and be clothed with Christ.

Truth be told, we will not move towards something until we recognize our need for it, and it's in the recognition of our need for God, that a turning occurs. When we have sinned, the turning to God is called repentance. When someone has sinned against us causing us to feel ashamed, turning to God is called restoration - and God calls us out of both causes of shame! When we repent, there is a change in our minds about sin and as a result a change in our direction, and God is faithful to forgive us of our sin.

> *"If we confess our sins, He is faithful and just and will forgive us of our sins and purify us from all unrighteousness."* **– 1 John 1:9**

Now for the Enemy's best kept secret: The Enemy has a weapon of mass destruction. This weapon has the power and potential to keep you in bondage even after you've repented or been restored. I know this weapon exists because it's been used against me for many seasons and chapters, and in many relationships in my life - not just romantic. This weapon has the potential to cause you to be dysfunctional on all fronts rendering you toxic and a magnet for toxicity. This weapon is called *"displaced shame"*.

While shame opens our eyes to what was done and what effect it has on us and others, displaced shame is the placing of shame on you that's already been dealt with.

When we're ashamed and see our need for God's divine intervention and we turn to God for Him to save and restore us, we know, this action is called repentance. This puts us back into relationship with God, and because of what Jesus did for us on the cross, our guilt and shame has been dealt with. However, walking in that reality is like cutting the head of a venomous snake. Did you know that a severed snake head can still bite? Ridiculous! I know, right!? It sounds wild but according to snake experts, a decapitated snake can still kill you. It turns out snakes do this frequently. Even in the throes of death they're still in survival mode. It's been reported that in Southern China a spitting cobra bit and killed a man 20 minutes after its head had been chopped off.

Even though the snake is dead, the venom in the head must not be underestimated. The potential to bite and kill as a knee jerk reaction to being decapitated is still very real. And it's the same way with the enemy and shame. Even though the enemy no longer has power over the child of God, he can still do serious damage if we're not aware of displaced shame. Displaced shame is the reliving of what was done to you or through you and keeps you from experiencing the fullness of God's presence and love. Displaced shame keeps the child of God:

- Ashamed
- Imprisoned
- In Bondage
- Running from God instead of running to Him
- Distorts our view of God
- Blinds us to the Truth

- Puts shame back on us when it's already been dealt with
- And tries to cancel Jesus

Look at how Adam and Eve's view of God was distorted. They thought they could hide from God; they were blinded to the Truth. This in turn set in motion, their running and hiding - they were ashamed, imprisoned and in bondage.

What do you do when you become aware of sin? Yours and that of others? Do you try to cover it up? Do you try to hide from God and others?

When displaced shame enters our lives, we have the unique opportunity to identify it and respond to God's grace by coming out of hiding and reinforce His forgiveness, healing, and restoration in our lives. When we surrender to God and allow Him to clothe us with Christ, we no longer need to hang our heads in shame or displaced shame.

"Listen to my testimony. I cried to God in my distress and He answered me. He freed me from all my fears! Gaze upon Him, join your life with His, and joy will come. Your faces will glisten with glory. You'll never wear that shame-face again." **Psalm 34: 4-5 The Passion Translation**

WHO TOLD YOU THAT?

Let's backtrack a bit.

"Then the man and his wife heard the sound of the Lord God as He was walking in the garden in the cool of the day, and they hid from the Lord God among the trees of the garden. But the Lord God called to the man, 'Where are you?' He answered, 'I heard you in the garden, and I was afraid because I was naked; so I hid.' And He said, 'Who told you that you were naked? Have you eaten from the tree that I commanded you not to eat from?' **- Genesis 3: 8-11**

Would you agree that it's interesting to note that sin did not make Adam and Even naked? No, they were created naked, and gloriously so. What sin did was make them aware of their nakedness and ushered in shame. Their nakedness wasn't the issue – sin, and the awareness that it brought was the burning issue. When sin entered the world, so did guilt and shame, and so did their need to cover themselves and hide. God did not create guilt and shame, sin did.

God asks a question, not for His sake but for theirs, and thankfully ours too, *"Who told you that you were naked?"* God didn't tell them that they were naked, but here's what God did tell them.

God **blessed** them.

"God blessed them and said to them, 'Be fruitful and increase in number; fill the earth and subdue it. Rule over the fish in the sea and the birds in the sky and over every living creature that moves on the ground."
*- **Genesis** 1: 28*

What does it mean to be blessed by God? First, let's talk about what the blessing of God is *not*: The blessing of God is not the same as having the Midas touch and it's certainly not found in a good luck charm. It is not in a special prayer we pray over a meal or for success and happiness. The blessing of God is so much more than that. God doesn't bless things, He blesses people.

The blessing of God is *spoken - a public declaration of favoured status with God*. But it doesn't stop there - the blessing is the endowment of power to achieve prosperity and success. The blessing is both spiritual as well as an outward manifestation. In other words, when God blesses you, you will not only hear and know that you're blessed, you will also see it manifested in your life. When God blessed Adam and Eve, He spoke favour over them, and the capacity to accomplish His purpose for their lives.

God *gave* them:

"Then God said, 'I give you every seed-bearing plant on the face of the whole earth and every tree that has fruit with seed in it. They will be yours for food. And to all the beasts of the earth and all the birds of the sky and all the

creatures that move on the ground - everything that has the breath of life in it - I give every green plant for food. And it was so." **- Genesis 1: 29-30**

God knew what they would need, and He did not withhold anything good from them. He gave them everything they would need for their life in Eden and not for only them, but for every living creature under their care. Isn't God good? In that, He not only blessed them, but He also provided for them. Their needs were fully met; they wouldn't have to worry about what they would eat or worry about being eaten; every creature had the same eating plan.

When God provides, we thrive, but survival mode says, *"Eat or be eaten."* Adam and Eve could rest in God's providence and generosity because God gave them what they needed.

God *commanded* Adam:

"And the Lord God commanded the man, 'You are free to eat from any tree in the garden; but you must not eat from the tree of the knowledge of good and evil, for when you eat of it you will surely die."
- Genesis 1: 15-17

Do not underestimate the power of a command or instruction. It enables us to function or use something optimally. In order for Adam and Eve to function optimally in their environment and assignment they would need to know where the boundary lines were. Our problem is that we view instructions and commands in a negative light.

Notice the blessing and providence of God came before the command. Understand that God has a way of setting us up for success, because whenever God commands you to do something, you better believe that He has already given His blessing and capacity for you to carry out the command.

God told them who they were and what He created them for. His words brought blessing, revelation, and instruction, and this has not changed because God does not change. Today we understand that words are powerful and carry the power of life and death (Prov. 18:21). The Word of God is Life! God will bless you for your purpose and give you instruction, and commands you need to fulfill your calling, just like He did for our first parents. When we allow His word to inform our identity, our calling and purpose we will be and do what He has called us to.

But the enemy on the other hand speaks a different language - his native tongue is lies - he's been a liar from the beginning. In fact, Jesus calls him the father of lies and a master of deception (John 8:44). He's such a liar that even when he's quoting the truth he's lying (Matthew 4:5-6).

The enemy *questions* God's Word
"Did God really say…?"

The enemy *twists* God's Word
"… You can't eat from any tree in the garden?"

The enemy *opposes* God's Word
"'No! You will not die,' the serpent said to the woman."

The enemy tells *lies* about God
"In fact, God knows that when you eat it your eyes will be opened and you will be like God, knowing good and evil."

His modus operandi has not changed. He questions, twists, opposes, and tells lies about God and His children. Remember that even when the Enemy quotes the truth he's still lying.

What do you do when you become aware of sin? Whether it's yours or that of others? Do you also try to cover it up? Do you try to hide from God and others? Or do you go to God to hear what He has to say? When we run away from God and His Word, we're positioning ourselves for lies and deception from an opportunistic enemy. You might have heard:

"You're unloved"

"You're unwanted"
"You don't belong"
"You're a failure"
"You asked for it"
"You were born this way"
"You'll never change"

Who told you that? I can guarantee you it wasn't God.

A few years ago, I was introduced to the power of words. I counseled with a young woman who struggled with gender dysphoria and same sex attraction. She felt like an alien in her body, and to compound matters, she had a battle reconciling her sexuality struggles with her faith - she was a Christian. We sat down to plot her story and looked for flags to her brokenness. I made the mistake of assuming that somewhere or somehow, she must have been sexually abused or exposed to gender ideology.

She was never touched inappropriately. In fact, she was raised in a healthy, functional - and for the most part - loving Christian home. Her parents did an excellent job of filtering her online and media intake. All movies, even the music she listened to were all age appropriate. While I knew where same sex attraction stems from, I couldn't make sense of the cause of her gender dysphoria. But I prayerfully continued to hold space for her struggle.

One day I attended one of their family gatherings and the penny dropped. In her father's speech he disclosed that when her mother was pregnant with her, that they had thought she would be a boy; they bought boys clothes, toys and even had her room painted blue. The room erupted with laughter, it was the first time I heard it but when I glanced over to her, I could see by the pain in her eyes, that she had heard it many times before. She wiped away a tear and didn't skip a beat in laughing with everyone else. Her father went on to say that they were so disappointed to find that she was a girl. They then decided to give her a unisex name, and, by his own admission, treated her like a boy. When her brother was born 4 years later, needless to say they were elated they finally had a *"real boy"*, yes in those words.

For years she believed the lie that she should have been a boy and that only a boy was worthy of affirmation, acceptance, and love. Thankfully the penny didn't only drop for me but for her too. She identified the lie and went to God and finally, truly heard and believed what He had to say about who He created her to be.

NAILED IT!!!

The Cross changes everything, not because of what it was but because of who hung on it. The Cross totally flipped the script on everything we've done and ever will do wrong. It totally turned the tables on every curse and wrong done to us in our lifetime. The Cross transformed us from victim to more than a conqueror.

Jesus shed His blood so that you and I can bring our guilt and shame in its many forms to God and have Him nail it to the Cross, never to have the power to torment us again.

It's important to understand that we all have a narrative, a story of who we are and how we came to be. David had a revelation of our story and in Psalm 139: 16 he speaks to God and says, *"You saw me before I was born. Every day of my life was recorded in your book. Every moment was laid out before a single day had passed."*

In God's foresight He writes our story in His book. Think of the chapters you've been through, the pages you've turned, at some point it seemed like the enemy had the upper hand. There were times when it appeared as though there was no hope, no reason to push through. Everything we've ever done and ever will do is recorded in our story and that is nothing to be ashamed of.

chapter thirteen
Unapologetic

"Our identity is not in our feelings. Our identity is in Christ. Period."
~ **Jackie Hill Perry**

In bible school I came access course content dealing with the issue of identity, and because I have a passion for youth ministry it made me sit up and pay attention. If you love working with young people like I do, you will know that topics like purpose, worship and identity really resonates with them. Behind their selfies, playlists, and social media accounts they are asking the fundamental question, "Who am I?" The second question is: "What does that mean to the world?" or "what's my purpose Pastor D?" I'm usually smiling at this point, offering them a cup of something to drink, depending on the weather, inviting them to make themselves comfortable. I love listening to young people think out loud about who they are or who they are not and being a catalyst on their journey through self-discovery.

Back to the course content, I forget the author's name, but his train of thought started a revolution in my heart that totally transformed my understanding of who we are. He asked a simple, but seemingly rhetorical question to random people and their answers pointed to our natural inclination to associate identity with what we do or have. He asked, *"who are you?"* some gave their name, and he stated, *"no, that's your name, not who you are."* Some gave answers relating to their gifting, culture, race, and others made reference to their net worth and sexuality. And still his answer remained the same, concluding that your true self - or as we so eloquently say these days - your authentic self, is not a singer, lawyer, priest or millionaire and it is definitely not your sexuality. At this point I was wondering where he was going with this. Well, he didn't say it in so many words but much later I concluded that for the child of God, identity is more than a matter of who you are, but *whose* you are, and that whose you are determines and gives value to everything else in your life.

TO FEEL OR NOT TO FEEL

Few things challenge our true identity quite like our feelings. And this becomes problematic when we find ourselves having to choose between a culture that bows down to worship feelings or a misguided Christian narrative that demonizes them. There's a reason why Solomon warns us to avoid all extremes. The Message translation puts it this way.

> *"It's best to stay in touch with both sides of an issue. A person who fears God deals responsibly with all of reality, not just a piece of it.*
> **- Ecclesiastes 7:18**

Peter Scazzero says, *"To feel is to be human. To minimize or deny what we feel is a distortion of what it means to be image bearers of our personal God."* And I want to agree with him and encourage you to validate your feelings - feelings are important - but also recognize that your feelings do not determine who you are. We are not what happened to us, and we certainly are not what we feel about what happened to us either. We are not what we feel. Our feelings are important as indicators but pathetic as leaders. We cannot be led by what we feel about ourselves and our identity, we must be led by the Spirit of God (Rom. 8:14). Instead of trying to magnify or suppress our feelings we must put them into proper perspective by bringing them under the Lordship of Christ. And listen, I get it, identity is a big thing, identity matters, but it cannot be determined by my feelings, desires, gifting, or titles, because, when those things fall away and they will, where does that leave us? This is why I make it my mission to model for those I mentor and lead that our identity does not lie in what I feel or what I do, because my feelings change, and titles and roles come and go. I also strongly caution those who attach their sense of identity to what happened to them, that by doing so they sabotage their healing, because their sense of identity is so strongly attached to their trauma, they can't let go. What has happened to them has become their identity. This is why some people can't forgive because they've become so used to being the victim in their narrative that they remain in bitterness and resentment. Take away their trauma, struggle or pain and you take away their identity.

IT'S NOT ABOUT WHO YOU ARE BUT WHOSE YOU ARE

When we recognize God for who He truly is, we see ourselves for who we really are. Who He is determines who you truly are. If God is King, it means you're royalty (1Pet.2:9). If He's your Father, it means you're His child (Jn.1:13). If He's your Redeemer, it means you're redeemed (Is.43:1). This blows my mind every time. God is Spirit and if He's your Father then so are you! Contrary to popular belief you are not a body possessing a spirit. You are a spirit possessing a body, and that right there is your game changer.

Simon got his identity changed - in a manner of speaking - when He recognized Christ for who He truly is. When we see Jesus for who He truly is, we not only see ourselves for who we truly are, but Jesus also tells us who we are. I cannot emphasize this enough.

Like Simon we must consider who Jesus is, not just what people are saying about Him, because like the disciples confessed, people will always have an opinion of Jesus. Some said He was John the Baptist, others said Elijah, Jeremiah or one of the prophets (Matt.6:13-14). When we listen to what others think they know about Jesus, Jesus will be misrepresented, no matter how noble or worthy the opinions.

Jesus didn't care for the opinions of others. He wanted to know what those who were in closest relationship with Him thought of Him. Highlight this in your bible.

Jesus: *"But what about you? Who do you say I am?"*

Simon: *"You are the Messiah, the Son of the living God."*

Jesus: *"Blessed are you, Simon son of Jonah, for this was not revealed to you by flesh and blood, but by my Father in heaven. And I tell you that you are*

Peter, and on this rock I will build my church, and the gates of death will not overcome it." - **Matthew 16:13-18**

- You are not your trauma.
- You are not your drama.
- You are not your feelings.
- You are not your sexuality.
- You are not your suffering.
- You are not what happened to you.
- You are not that label.
- You are not that question mark.

You are who God says you are, and because God has zero identity issues, you can trust His revelation and proclamation of your identity.

> *"But now, this is what the Lord says -*
> *He who created you, Jacob,*
> *He who formed you, Israel:*
> *Do not fear, for I have redeemed you;*
> *I have summoned you by name; you*
> *are mine."* - **Isaiah 43:1**

God and name changes. No wonder we can look forward to a new name (Rev.2:17; 3:12). and He calls us His own, belonging to God. Therein lies our identity.

SORRY, NOT SORRY

There's a saying that goes, *"If I knew then, what I know now..."*

I didn't always walk in my true identity. I found myself apologizing for being a child of God, for being gifted, anointed, called, loved. I often played small, too afraid to live out my potential, to be and do what God called me to. And in the same breath I would cover up my feelings of hurt, anger, and frustration, I was afraid that others would see me as less than worthy to be called a child of God. I sugar coated lust and sin, which left a bitter after taste. I didn't always feel like a child of God, so I faked it. I just got so sick of saying sorry all the time!

Instead of walking in my true identity I self-identified (that's when you take on the the identity of something you relate to or feel that you are). I read the other day about a husband and father of seven- a 52-year-old man, who left his wife and kids to live as a transgender six-year-old girl named Stefonknee (pronounced Stef-on-knee). We raise our eyebrows - as we should - but we somehow think we're better off because our self-identification is not "as bad". The truth is that regardless of how we evaluate self-identification, it is inherently dangerous because it robs us of the honour of having our Father reveal and declare who we are. Self-identification is a trap and an indication that you've placed "self" on the throne of your heart.

The ugly truth is I followed how I felt about myself and what I related to, instead of what God said about me. I felt rejected, unloved, and ashamed and I self-identified as such. Remember the story of the ugly duckling? Well, he was hatched in the same nest as all the other ducklings, but he looked and walked differently, and as a result he faced rejection, shame, and ridicule from those who did not understand *whose* he was. He was not like them, but at that season of his life it felt more like a curse than the blessing it actually was. When we, as children of God conduct our relationships out of sync with our identity in Christ, we look crazy. Like beautiful swans trying to be ducks. We exhaust ourselves trying to fit the mold that culture created for relationships. We chain our hearts with dating and relationship methods and practices inconsistent with who God called us to be and do. And instead of embracing that we are in this world but not of this world, we try to convince others that we're one of them, when we are clearly not.

We have a God given identity which is utterly dependent on who God is and who He says we are! And He speaks to our identity through His word. Grab a pen, write this down, allow it to transform your mind and change the way you see God and yourself. It's high time that we God-identify and are unapologetic about it!

- I AM chosen (Eph. 1:4)
- I AM adopted (Eph. 1:4-5)
- I AM a child of God (Jn. 1:12)
- I AM born again (1Pet. 1:23)
- I AM a new creation (2Cor. 5:17)
- I AM clothed with Christ (Gal. 3:27)
- I AM baptized into Christ (Rom. 6:4)
- I AM hidden in Christ (Col. 3:3)
- I AM sealed with the Spirit of Christ (1:13-14)
- I AM redeemed (Eph. 1:7)
- I AM purified (1Jn. 1:7)
- I AM washed (1Cor. 6:11)
- I AM justified (Rom. 5:1)
- I AM sanctified (1Cor. 6:11)
- I AM accepted by Christ (Rom. 15:7)
- I AM blameless before Christ (Col. 1:22)
- I AM righteous in Christ (2Cor. 5:21)
- I AM complete in Christ (Col. 2:9-10)
- I AM free (Col. 1:22)
- I AM an heir (Gal. 4:7)
- I AM unapologetic (Gal. 1:16)

I have some homework for you that I believe will really make a difference in your life. I suggest that you take the next 21 days to focus on who God is and who He says you are. You can do this through prayer, meditation, or bible study, and for the sake of accountability, why not ask a friend to join you on your journey to God-identify. You might not always feel like who God says you are, but we walk by faith not by sight (2Cor. 5:7) and I'll add - not by our feelings either.

GRASSHOPPERS DON'T EAT GRAPES

I made the mistake of taking on the identity of something other than what God had created and called me to be. The Israelites made that mistake too; they did not see themselves as who God created and called them to be. God delivered them from Pharaoh, generational bondage, and slavery; He took them through the red sea, kept them through the desert wanderings for 40 years - where their clothes didn't wear out and neither did the scandals on their feet (Deut. 29) and now they were of the edge of their promise but they chose to feed into what they identified with, instead of who God said they were, and by implication what He would give them.

> *"But the men who had gone up with him said, 'we can't attack those people; they are stronger than we are.' And they spread among the Israelites a bad report about the land they had explored. They said, 'the land we explored devours those living in it. All the people we saw there are of great size. We saw the Nephilim there (the descendents of Anak come from the Nephilim). We seemed like grasshoppers in our own eyes, and we looked the same to them."* - **Numbers 13: 31-33**

Even though their report was realistic it wasn't what God saw or said. In fact, they also assumed that the people of the land saw them the way they saw themselves. Sadly, none of those who saw themselves as grasshoppers entered the Promised Land. They identified themselves with grasshoppers and as a result lost their inheritance. How many promises, opportunities and relationships have we forfeited because we lost sight of *Whose* and who we are? It was Moses, who then interceded for the Israelites and God, true to who He is, forgives them, but in no uncertain terms acts in accordance with how they saw themselves.

> *"The Lord replied, 'I have forgiven them, as you asked. Nevertheless, as surely as I live and as surely as the glory of God wills the whole earth, not one of those who saw my glory and the signs I performed in Egypt and in the wilderness but who disobeyed me and tested me ten times - not one of them Will ever see the land I promised on oath to their ancestors. No one who has treated me with contempt will ever see it."*
> **- Numbers 14: 20-23**

The important thing to note is that we don't walk in the fullness of what God has for us because we don't walk in the fullness of *Whose* we are. The grapes in the promised land were so big and so well developed that they had to have two men carry it on a pole between them (Num. 13:23). This is what God wants for our relationships; to be so abundant, so well developed that we need each other to carry the weight of the beauty, honour, abundance, and love. But if we see ourselves as grasshoppers - small and seemingly insignificant - then we won't have the capacity to enter the promises of God for our lives and relationships. We will always be afraid and settle for feeding on "just enough" when God's desire is to give us all He has for us.

THE GRACE EFFECT

There was a time in the Apostle Paul's life, when he thought he knew who he was - and in many ways I can relate – but not until he was knocked off his high horse and saw Jesus for who He truly is, did He grasp his own identity (Acts 9:3-19).

Years after his encounter with Jesus, Paul makes an interesting statement. He says:

> *"For I am least of the apostles and so not even deserve to be called an apostle, because I persecuted the church of God. But by the grace of God I am what I am, and His grace to me was not without effect."*
> **- 1 Corinthians 15: 9-10**

Grace is more than just a hymn we sing about. Grace in its various forms, is the power of God at work in the life of a believer. It's the empowerment to be and live up to our identity in Christ. Grace has an effect on who we are and what we do, how we live and how we conduct relationships. God gives us the grace to enter the fullness of his promises for us in every area of our lives. Grace isn't just for a Sunday morning or the mid-week bible study; grace is for the mess, chaos, the late-night scrolling and resisting the hook up culture.

The grace effect is real.
I was in my first year of bible school and interestingly enough, in my first year of what we will call my single season. I was 21 years old and for the first time since I was 11 years old, I did not have a "significant other". I had just broken up with who I thought was the "love of my life", my "soul mate" - I thought I was going to marry that boy. I kind

of felt that way with most of the relationships I was in. Truth be told, I was inlove with love? I spent an entire decade going from one relationship to another, and the result was a hurt, broken and wounded young woman.

One afternoon after lectures I decided to follow up on some young people under my spiritual leadership and care and was introduced to a very attractive young man. The attraction was instant, and, as this generation would say, we were definitely vibing. I was receiving all the right signals, from eye contact to attentiveness, from engaging body language to stimulating conversation, even the way he said my name! He seemed to have a way with words; he was flirty, funny, and sexy. I played cool, kept my distance, played hard to get. My instincts were fighting my conviction of singleness - I knew my heart needed healing and restoration, but I started toying with the idea that maybe I could get the healing and restoration I needed... *with* him.

I'll never forget the Holy Spirit's conviction, and the words that came to me, "*If it looks like Egypt, and it smells like Egypt, then it's probably Egypt.*" It was like the Holy Spirit's way of telling me it's a *NO!* from Him. I laugh now, but back then I knew that God was giving me a clear warning to stay away, and if I disobeyed, I was heading for bondage - again. Who I was and *whose* I was, was not going to allow me to step out of the will of God for my life. So, I committed my heart to obedience.

The following week I fell on my knees thanking the Holy Spirit for His conviction and divine intervention. The boy was given to drunkenness, had two baby mamas, cursed like a sailor and was something of a ladies' man - this is not to say that God didn't have a plan for his life, I just wasn't a part of that plan. The grace effect will empower and enable you to walk in the fullness of who and *Whose* you are, giving you access to the promises of God for your life and relationships.

MERCY SAID NO

I've heard it said that grace is freely giving you what you don't deserve, and mercy is withholding what you do deserve. You and I cannot work hard enough to earn grace - we don't deserve it, we are not entitled to it - a Good Father has decided to freely give it, not because of anything we've done. The gospel teaches us that we all have sinned and fall short of the glory of God - every single one of us (Rom. 3:23). Apart from Christ we deserve punishment, but in Christ, the mercy of God withholds that punishment. A woman is caught in the act of adultery (Jn.8: 1-11), making her an adulterer and by the law of the time, condemned to die by stoning (Deut. 22:22). This woman is brought to Jesus - but it's a test - if Jesus calls for the woman to be released, He could be accused of disregarding the law of Moses, but if He calls for her stoning in obedience to the Law of Moses, He will break the law of the Romans. Jesus seems to be in a catch 22 situation. Further studies show that the Scribes and Pharisees should have also brought the man she was caught with, but they didn't, and this only exposed the true intent of their hearts.

They didn't want justice; they wanted to trap Jesus and labeled an adulterous woman as condemned in the process. We don't know her name, we have no evidence of her identity, but every finger pointed to her condemnation - and according to God's holy law, condemnation is what she deserved. *But God.* Found between a rock and a hard place, the Rock that is higher than us (Ps.61: 1) stoops down and writes in the sand. The religious leaders thought it was going to be a good day for a funeral, but with a Master stroke, Jesus calls for those who were without sin to cast the first stone. Ironically, Jesus was the only one among them that qualified to do so; He was without sin (1Jn. 3:5), but the Rock of all ages didn't come to condemn - instead of exercising His right, He stooped down once more and wrote in the sand.

One by one her accusers went away, the older ones first until only Jesus and the woman remained. This was big. She was already condemned by the Pharisees, and deserved to die, but Jesus refused to condemn her. He withheld the punishment that was due to her. Mercy said *"No!"*

"Jesus straightened up and asked her, 'woman, where are they? Has no one condemned you?' No one sir, she said. Then neither do I condemn you, Jesus declared. Go now and leave your life of sin." **- John 8: 10-11**

This is why we can be unapologetic about *Whose* we are and who we are. Jesus could have, and should have condemned us, but He didn't. Instead, He came to save us, to save us from sin, death, the wrath of God and very often ourselves. It's time to stop saying sorry for receiving the grace and mercy of God that enables us to live.

Jesus knew *Whose* He was and came for everything the enemy said he couldn't have. Jesus came for you and me. He was unapologetic. Religious leaders, doubtful followers and unbelieving people groups were infuriated, offended, and often confused by the identity of Jesus, but not Jesus, no case of mistaken identity here.

- The Bread of Life (Jn. 6:35-48)
- The Light of the world (Jn. 8:12; 9:5)
- The Gate (Jn. 10:7)
- The Resurrection and the Life (Jn. 11:25)
- The Good Shepherd (Jn. 10:11-18)
- He is the Way, the Truth and the Life (Jn 14:6)
- The True Vine (Jn.15:1-5)

Jesus is the true vine. That big cluster of grapes in the Old Testament has nothing on Jesus. The cluster of grapes was the shadow, but Jesus is the substance. He is the fullness, and the fulfillment of every promise God has made, and when our relationships carry Him, we step into the promises God has for us and the relationships entrusted to us.

"For no matter how many promises God has made, they are "Yes" in Christ. And so through him the "Amen" is spoken by us to the glory of God." **– 2 Corinthians 1:20**

Child of God, when we walk in who God created and called us to be; when our identity is determined by *Whose* we are, when our identity lines up with what God has said about us and not what we feel or identify with, then our lives and relationships become a declaration that renders us unapologetic.

When we know *Whose* and who we are, we stop apologizing for:

- Who God has revealed Himself to be.
- Our identity in Christ.
- The work of sanctification of the Holy Spirit in our lives.
- God's standard for relationships and marriage.
- The life God has called us to.
- Our healing from past wounds.
- Restoration and becoming whole.
- Setting boundaries.
- God's grace.
- And His infinite mercy.
- Doing God's Will God's Way.

What do you need to stop apologizing for? One thing we need to do is to stop apologizing for, is how our trauma and pain makes others feel uncomfortable. Can we stop apologizing for what happened to us? Can we stop apologizing for being healed? Can we stop apologizing for being sold out to Christ, living according to His Word and by the power of His Spirit? Can we stop apologizing for being unchained?

I remember when I was about 9 years old, my friends and I were playing marbles on a dirt patch down our road when my friends started laughing. I looked up to see what they were laughing at. My ears went hot when I realized it wasn't what but who - it was my dad, and he couldn't find his feet. He was paralytic; completely and utterly drunk. I felt tears sting my eyes and then my cheeks, I was tempted to look away, to run away, but I couldn't. I dug my heels into the ground. This was my AHA moment, when light entered my young heart.

He was my dad, paralytic or not, he was mine!

I walked towards him not really sure what to say or do. He tripped over his feet trying to find his balance. When he saw me, he smiled and said "hello", instinctively I knew what to do, I took his arms placed it over my shoulders and step by step we made it home. I still heard giggles, but I didn't care. He wasn't heavy, he was my dad.

That wasn't the first or last time he would be drunk. Alcoholism is a recurring theme in my bloodline - that's why I don't drink - it's bigger than me and it's robbed me and my family of so much. I remember waking up one morning to sounds of screaming and fighting, I didn't know who to help or attend to first.

My 6-year-old sister was screaming, and visibly afraid and in need of comfort; my parents were engaged in a physical fight - at that moment I felt helpless. I remember many moments like that. I remember running for our lives, hiding behind a door in the home of an extended family member, telling myself not to breathe so that he wouldn't find my mom and me.

I ran a lot.

I ran away from home often. Once I ran over gang territory in the early hours of the morning praying that I got to my aunt's home alive. Another time I ran to the police station begging them to do something, to help. And somewhere between the many moments of feeling helpless, I sensed God telling me to run to Him. He told me that His name was a strong tower and that when I ran into Him, I would be safe. And it was there in the safety of God's refuge that I realized that all the pain, all the trauma, all the running was my journey, my testimony. The rejection, the mistakes, my mom, my dad, brokenness, alcoholism – everything - was mine! It was a part of me, and it was mine, and I needed to decide to give to Jesus. No more shame, no more apologies.

And when I least expected it, God did the impossible.

My dad did a 180-degree turn. He was headed towards destruction, but God intercepted his eternal destiny. While I can't give you the whole story - because that's his story to tell - looking back, we realize that my father was supposed to die because of alcoholism. *But God.*

Today my father is alive and well - but more alive than he's ever been - he's surrendered his life to Christ! Let me tell you, God restores. What alcoholism stole from us God gave back - from relationships to resources - God gave it all back. I now have what I've always longed for, a relationship with my father, a sense of family, connection, and love. Are we perfect? By no means, but we are family. We were once lost, but now we're found, we were blind but now we see. I was once broken, pitiful and sorry - now I'm unapologetic.

chapter fourteen
Unchained

"Your chains are who you were. They're not who you are supposed to be. Because of Jesus we can live free. We can live unchained."
~ **Hosanna Wong**

Did you know there are 46 million slaves in the world today? How is it even possible in the 21st century? With all our technological advancements, breakthroughs, scientific discoveries, for goodness' sake, man has been to the moon, like 6 times - or we *think* we've been to the moon 6 times - and yet we cannot rid our planet of this ancient evil. As the human race we have come so far, but according to research more people are in slavery today than any other time in history.

Yes, apparently slavery is a lucrative business. There are people in our world today that make serious money from selling other people and in particular, women and children! It is a $150 billion industry - one in 200 people is a slave.

A slave is defined as someone who is forced to work against their will; he or she is owned or controlled by an exploiter or "employer", and they have limited freedom of movement, are dehumanized, and bought and sold as property for sex or forced labour. The obvious question that springs to mind is, how does one person enslave another? And yes, one of the many ways is through human trafficking; there are not enough books in our world to record the horrors experienced by humans who become enslaved in this way.

Recently I read a story of a young woman who was trafficked at 12 years old and estimated that she had been raped 43 200 times. Read that again. Now do the math. That's 30 times every day for 4 years. Used and abused, exploited, and degraded - chained. As I tried to empathize with her situation, I found it almost impossible to imagine what she and countless others go through on a daily basis. Needless to say, this reality is heartbreaking but there is another reality I would like you to consider.

There is another kind of slave among us - and for a long time that slave was me. This is the kind of person who is free to go and do as they please, or so it seems, but they are held captive in their hearts. Their wounds, assaults and chains are unseen. There is no census or list that can show their number; they are everywhere, often in the mirror. I've heard it said that we never truly appreciate freedom until we've been imprisoned. I concur; we often take liberty for granted when we've never been chained. Chains should never be our choice, but they do often deepen our appreciation for liberation.

Have you ever wondered how a handler gets the majestic elephant - a creature so powerful and intelligent - to do exactly what they want? How does such a small handler keep such a big, powerful, and intelligent creature captive? Elephants are known to push down trees; in some countries festivals are held in their honour, where they perform choreographed dances, surely the elephant could escape from the handler if they wanted to? With its size and brute strength, who would be able to stop it? But as all elephant handlers know, with the right amount of conditioning, that elephant will stop trying to escape. When the elephant is still a baby, it is separated from its mother and chained to a large tree. For weeks, the young elephant tries to break free by straining and pulling. As a result, the chain would cut deep into its leg. At the end the elephant gives up on freedom and accepts that it can't go anywhere when something is tied around its right hind leg. At this point the handler can replace the chain with a piece of rope. A weak, pathetic piece of rope could be all lies between the elephant and freedom. There might be only a piece of rope around its leg but heavy, skin cutting chains are around its *mind*.

In many ways you and I are like that elephant - created fearfully and wonderfully, gifted and beloved - but somewhere in our past we were shackled to a person, an experience, a disappointment or mistake and we accepted that our minds and hearts are and will always be chained.

Jesus came so that weak, pathetic ropes and handlers would no longer have power over us. Like an abolitionist Jesus' mission on the earth was to bind up the broken hearted, proclaim freedom for the captives and release from darkness for the prisoners. Like the King He is, to bestow on us a crown instead of ashes, oil of gladness instead of grieving, praise instead of despair! His mission was complete when He hung on the cross and died, only to rise again one the third day and render us unchained.

THAT'S MY STORY AND I'M STICKING TO IT
I remember going through a very difficult season of transition in about the fourth year of my marriage. I was triggered, and I was magnifying all Ricardo's faults. I was very vocal and loud about it, my words were being amplified. Instead of drawing him towards me, which was my intention - my accusatory and controlling attitude was pushing him away from me. What I didn't realize was that I was actually being exposed. I wasn't walking in being healed and whole.

Another thing I failed to realize was that this was a part of a cycle; I would fall into escapism, I would conjure up fantasies of how different my life would be if I wasn't molested, or how different my life would be if I was actually wanted, appreciated, if I didn't make stupid mistakes. I would fantasize about having money, having a bigger house, my own car, someone who loved me the way I needed to be loved.

In stressful situations people often create escapist strategies that are positive and productive such as reading a book, exercising, listening to music, gardening - these exercises help people cope and the goal should always be to return to face and deal with the stress or disappointment they're facing. Other more negative and dangerous escapist methods are substance abuse, gambling, risky behavior, and we know that everything that goes up high must come down low. I was somewhere in the middle, not productive but definitely an attempt at self-sabotage, a mental creation of my own doing. I was living in a counterfeit world and did not confront or address the issues that were being exposed in me. What I thought was a coping mechanism was actually detrimental to me and my relationships, especially with my husband. One day during that time we had what others call an argument - we call it *energetic conversations* - the problem is that I'm usually the only one conversing energetically. I'm all over the place, climbing walls, coming in like a wrecking ball. And he would just stand there looking at me. I used to feel like pulling my hair out when he did that, and when I would ask him what he had to say for himself, he would respond, "What do you want me to say?" Shriek!

We've come a long way since then.

To keep everyone safe I locked myself in the bathroom because I was nanoseconds away from scratching his beautiful brown eyes out. I started wrestling with God, I was highly agitated in prayer.

My prayers hit the ceiling and crashed back down.

> Why can't he see his faults?
> Why doesn't he make the necessary changes?
> Why doesn't he see what I'm seeing?
> Why must I always be the one to humble myself?
> Why must I always be accommodating?
> Why must I always be the mature one?

I wasn't getting any answers, so I escaped; at least I was in control in my imagination. Then conviction set in. I looked up and caught my eyes looking back at me in the mirror. Our faithful Counselor, Teacher, and Advocate - the Holy Spirit - took hold of me in that teachable moment. And I realized 3 things.

1. I don't get to pass off my own version of events as the truth. Yes, there are always two sides to a story. We don't get to have our own narrative as the ultimate authority on what went down. As a child of God, our stories matter yes, we all have our truth - the way we saw things - we all have our narrative, but there's a big picture, an ultimate narrative, His story… we must never lose sight of that. For all intents and purposes there are three sides to our story. Your side, my side and the Truth.

"Every time I make an assumption about someone who has hurt or disappointed me without confirming it, I believe a lie about this person in my head. This assumption is a misrepresentation of reality. Because I have not checked it out with the other person, it is possible that I am believing something untrue. It is also likely that I will pass that false assumption around to others. When we leave reality for a mental creation of our own doing (hidden assumptions), we create a counterfeit world. When we do this, it can properly be said that we exclude God from our lives because God does not exist outside of reality and truth." – **Peter Scazzero**

It is my job to *interrogate* my narrative, *explore* your version of events and *align* our stories to God's Big Picture. There I was interrogating my husband when I should have been asking myself the hard questions. I should have asked myself why I overreacted to him not answering me when I asked him a question? Had I taken the time to rather explore his version of events, and not accuse, I would have been able to bring our stories into alignment with the Truth.

Here's a more accurate version of what happened that day. I asked my husband a question; I don't quite remember what that question was, all I know is that I asked him something. He didn't answer and so I assumed that he either ignored me or didn't *want* to answer me. I then *felt* unloved and unwanted. I started highlighting his faults with words like "always" and "never" and we all know where those type of words lead to. When you're in conflict with a spouse or loved one refrain from using those two words. What you want to do is deal with the issue at hand. How I got to the conclusion that I was unloved and unwanted just because he didn't answer me is what the Holy Spirit wanted me to see. Had I interrogated my conclusion I would have discovered that in that moment I had been triggered. You see, when I was younger, I used to be too afraid to speak to my dad or God-forbid ask anything of him. I would spend what felt like hours, building up the courage to approach him. Once I finally got to ask him for something, he would either ignore me or make me wait for the answer. I remember I would stand and feel ignored until he'd finally answer me. With tears stinging my face I'd walk away wondering if I was loved. Instead of interrogating myself I allowed a trigger to dictate my reality and didn't take the time to explore Ricardo's version of events. Had I done that, I would have discovered that he in fact did not hear me and therefore did not answer. Look, our feelings are real, but we must open ourselves to the reality that they are not necessarily the truth. Our feelings are valid, but they are not necessarily the baseline for our reality.

Just because you feel attacked doesn't mean that you're being attacked; just because you feel disrespected doesn't mean that you are being disrespected; and in my case, just because I felt unloved and unwanted didn't mean that I was unloved and unwanted.

If we're going to be unchained in our relationships, it's going to mean that we will need to interrogate the way we see things and explore the possibility that our perspective is not the only one we must take into account. Things don't end with our narratives; there is an overarching narrative that includes both versions of events. Being unchained means we look at our narratives from God's perspective. Allow me to say that God's perspective is not our trauma, pain, our opinion, or our interpretation of the bible- God's perspective is found in the Spirit-filled Word of God.

2. Comparison is the thief of joy. In a world filled with picture perfect lives we have never been more medicated, fearful, unhappy, and depressed. We're comparing our losing season with someone else's winning season. We're comparing our first chapter with someone's last chapter; our weakness with someone else's strength. A narcissistic trait we must unlearn if we're ever going to live unchained is comparison; the

measuring of ourselves against others, and measuring others against others, it chains us and kills relationships.

I was comparing my husband to a version of him I had put together in my mind. That version of him was informed by media, my trauma and what I felt I deserved and was entitled to. This made me very unhappy, and I brought that comparison-induced unhappiness into our relationship. Not only did I compare him to a version of him that I created in my mind, but I also compared myself to him. I compared his weaknesses to my strengths. I felt like I would do a better job at leading - He let me lead and needless to say it made me miserable. God's design and intent was for us to complement one another, not compete with or compare ourselves to one another or others. I very soon learnt that what was a burden to me was a mantle to my husband; while I might be a leader and even have the gift for leadership, that was not my role in relation to my husband. When it comes to our relationship, family, and home, he is God's ordained leader. I handed the reins back and I could breathe again.

"Make a careful exploration of who you are and the work you have been given, and then sink yourself into that. Don't be impressed with yourself. Don't compare yourself with others. Each of you must take responsibility for doing the creative best you can with your own life.
- Galatians 6:4-5 MSG

This is also true for every other relationship you will enter. I've learnt that just because you're good or gifted at something, it doesn't mean you must do it; you'll end up doing everything, exhausted, bitter, and resentful. It is in our best interest to make careful exploration of who we are - the sum total - let nothing escape your thoughtful and prayerful examination of your essence. Start with God, in knowing Him you will know yourself, let Him tell and show you who you are. Who God has created you to be is fit for purpose. Don't get so tied up in what you don't know about your purpose, get locked into what you do know. What God has already revealed about your purpose will lead you to what you don't know. So do what you know and what you don't know will be revealed. Stay humble and take responsibility for you, your lane and your calling. Don't compare.

Don't compete. It's you against you. Take responsibility for your life, your healing, your relationships, your marriage, your family, your time, your treasure, your talents, your future. This doesn't mean we can't be there for others; this just means in our *being* we are responsible for our lives and hearts.

3. Your story is yours to accept... so own it. While my story might not necessarily be the ultimate story, the point is that it's *my* story. The power to live my life for God's glory is in accepting my story; the good, the bad, the scandalous and the ugly. My blood line is mine, my inception is mine, my birth and childhood is mine, my trauma is mine, my story is mine. To be clear it's not me, it's not my identity, but it belongs to me and forms a part of me and so if God allowed it, it means I can accept it.

Here's what I've learnt - God wastes nothing! Not trauma, not drama, not a mistake, not a bad decision. God is able to take all things and turn it around for His glory and my good. *But* the unchained life is impossible without acceptance.

"You couldn't relive your life, skipping the awful parts, without losing what made it worthwhile. You had to accept it as a whole--like the world, or the person you loved." — **Stewart O'Nan**

Acceptance doesn't mean we like what happened or we agree with being wronged. Accepting someone has nothing to do with what I feel about that person or what I believe to be true. There are two things that bring us to the point of accepting someone or something. The first is *understanding* and the second is *trust*. We have an understanding that comes about by the human process of growth. So, as I grow older, the more I understand about myself, others, and the world around me. This level of understanding is very limited, because we are limited. This level of understanding can also be distorted depending on how we process our lives, experiences, and relationships. This level of understanding is subject to change. Then there is a level of understanding that is deeply spiritual, rooted in

God. To have this kind of understanding means that you stand under; submit to a standard established by God. Those who have humbled themselves, their relationships and lives to God are the ideal candidates for this level of understanding. It is available to us, and we must get it (Prov.4: 7).

When we have godly understanding it's like the next thing is *trust*. Not sure how that works but it's like when we have understanding, no matter what we're facing or how we're feeling, it's like the only logical thing to do is to trust God. When we understand that God is God and we are not, we are invited to trust Him to be God and to do God things - if that makes sense? When we understand that He is good and that He has a good plan, we can trust Him even when people are bad, and things don't make sense. When we understand that there are some things that are out of our control, we can trust Him to answer the door when feelings of depression and anxiety come knocking.

The combination of understanding and trust is key to accepting ourselves and others. Without acceptance, being unchained will only be something you read about in this book. I'm not satisfied - and I certainly know you're not either - to just read about being unchained. You want to *be* unchained!

Here's a truth that we don't preach or teach on often enough; Because of Jesus you are unchained! It's a matter of manifesting that reality. Every relationship in your life right now will only benefit from you walking in the freedom Jesus secured for you. *You* will benefit from the unchaining of your heart and living in that reality.

GREAT SEXPECTATIONS

I cannot say for sure, who first came up with the terminology, *"sexpectations"*, but I get it. There are expectations around sex that we'll get into in a minute, and it's really important that we do; but first, a few years ago my husband received a final payment demand from a major tech outlet. He was shocked because firstly, he didn't buy anything from this outlet and secondly the final payment amount was ridiculous, let's just say he didn't have that kind of money to pay for something he didn't buy. Long story short, it took us a minute to figure out that someone stole his identity, committed fraud, bought equipment on hire purchase and it was payment time. Fun! The tech outlet had no concern for the fact that Ricardo was defrauded, they wanted their money. In fact, Ricardo had to go to major lengths to prove that he was who he said he was and that he was not the person who purchased the equipment. We had our suspicions about exactly how things went down, because in order for the plan of action to work the perpetrator needed someone on the inside who would bypass certain anti-fraud policies.

But to bring it home, we have an enemy who stole the true definition and purpose of sex and defrauded generations... and now it's payback time, and it's a debt we cannot pay. It's going to take the intentional effort of those who know God's heart for life, love, and relationships to bring back the true meaning, beauty, and purpose for sex. When we believe the lies of the enemy and align ourselves to his distortion and destruction of the gift of relationships and by implication romantic ones, we aid and abet the enemy in fraudulently buying and selling a *deep-fake* sex that this generation cannot afford to have.

Let's deal with expectations, shall we?

When it comes to relationships everything rises or falls on expectations, and because things have fallen so badly for us in how we conduct relationships in this generation, we've concluded that expectations lead to disappointments, heartbreak, and pain, so what do we tell ourselves and others? The prevailing narrative is, *"Have no expectations. It's better that way, you can avoid all the hurt, sadness and regret that comes with having expectations."* This may work for a while, until you realize that something is terribly wrong. You see, you and I were designed for expectation. Expectation is a faith dialect. It's a language peculiar to us as a people of faith. When we go into any relationship or situation without expectations, we go against the very core of our being. We are not living in Nirvana saints! We are living in the real world, dealing with real stuff; we want real and authentic experiences, real significance, real outcomes - for real - and that means that sometimes we will have to deal with unmet expectations. Deal with it.

Expectations are important. People can only rise to our level of expectation.

Case in point - **The Pygmalion Effect**: Two groups of teachers were engaged in an experiment; the first group of teachers were deceived and led to believe that their students were the best of the best when in fact they were randomly selected and were classified as academically mediocre. The second group - the control group - were told that their students were mediocre and were poor academic performers but were in fact strong academic students. By the time the experiment was complete the first group of students showed enhancement and seemed to bloom under the motivation and tutelage of their teachers, as opposed to the control group whose academic progress seemed to either stall or drop. Why? Because they were *viewed* as mediocre. Can you imagine the response of the teachers when they were informed of the experiment?

Our expectations impact those that we're in relationship with. But what happens when our expectations are too high? Are they really though? We've created a coddled and entitled generation because we've set our expectations too low, and the result? Doing the bare minimum, doing just enough to get by, has left us complacent. Complacency is the smug feeling of satisfaction with who we are and what you've done. We love that feeling, don't we? You know why? Because it's devoid of self-inspection, reflection, growth, and transformation. We complain and make excuses when life gets too hard, and we get offended or defensive when people have high expectations of us. I don't know if you've noticed, but God has ridiculously high expectations of us. I believe He does this so that we don't make the mistake of aiming too low. Expectations are self-fulfilling prophecies - you get what you expect - if they're valid, because you best believe that expectations can be invalid. Allow me to explain.

There are 3 things you would need to make sure your expectations are, for them to be valid.

#1 *Realistic;* as opposed to unrealistic. Unrealistic expectations come from illusions we may have of ourselves or others. Here's an unrealistic expectation I had of my husband especially in the early days of marriage. I expected him to read my mind. I laugh now, but then I genuinely expected my "soul mate" - you know, "the one"- to know what I was thinking. Wasn't he supposed to finish my sentences and know what I needed when I needed it?

#2 *Communicated* **vs. not communicated.** You cannot have an expectation you are not willing to communicate. You're setting others up for failure. How can they meet an expectation they don't know about? We do this so often, then have the audacity to get upset when our expectations are not met. Listen, I'm preaching to myself here, but think about it; how many times did we not exercise invalid expectations because we failed to validate them by communicating them? Sometimes I think the reason we don't communicate them is because we don't even know what we expect, so we continually shift the goal posts, because we like getting dramatic about unmet expectations. Sometimes we're so used to dysfunction that we set others up to fail when it comes to our expectations.

#3 *Agreement* **- as in one accord.** This is when two or more people act single-mindedly, unanimously, in harmony, in unity, and without dissent; they are operating in one accord. In order for expectations to be valid there must be agreement to work together towards meeting the communicated expectations. Expectations are really a team effort.

Great *sexpectations* are no different. In order to be valid, they must be realistic, communicated and agreed upon. Our expectations of sex are unrealistic.

- It is unrealistic for us to expect illegitimate sex to satisfy, in wholeness and Holiness, Gods intention for what He created legitimate sex to do and be.

- It is unrealistic to have sex the goal when it's only the tip of the iceberg in marital relations.
- It is unrealistic to expect great sex without great effort.

To be clear, illegitimate sex can be defined as any sexual activity exercised outside of a healthy, loving marriage between a husband and a wife, who are biologically male and female, respectively. To be honest I don't think we've done a good job of teaching on the legitimacy of sexual desire. And when I say we, I mean the faith community, the body of Christ, the Church and by extension our local churches, who find themselves on the forefront of sexual warfare in media, medicine, business, education, and our interpersonal relationships.

The biggest mistake we've made was to abdicate our responsibility to teach and model sexuality by God's design. We've left it in the hands of secular society and robbed the church - and more specifically the God-fearing family unit - of the honour and beauty of exploring God's heart on the gift that is our sexuality. What did we think was going to happen? We sit with a generation who have unrealistic expectations of their sexual desires; misinformed and deformed by media and ideologies that are designed for the demise of God's design for sexuality and family. Houston, we have a problem.

Here's what no one is talking about; as phenomenal as sex is, it is not the goal. If it is the goal within its proper context, i.e., marriage, best believe there's dysfunction or abuse of some kind. Generally speaking - and there are exceptions - sexual intercourse only makes up 5% of your married life. It's an awesome thing, but it's not the only thing. It's an important thing, but it's not everything. It's vital to get the balance right with sex because if you don't, you can enter idolatry even in marriage. Sex is not a solution. It's not a band aid, it doesn't solve problems. Getting married for sex as a "cure" for lust is foolish. If sex was the antidote for lust, why are people still having affairs? Sex is not the goal, it's more like the half time, important, much needed, refreshing, a time to regroup and revitalize, not the goal. Sex alone cannot sustain or maintain a marriage - it's sex and a combination of many other things - things like commitment, trust, intimacy, purity, wisdom, grace, creativity, vision, forgiveness, patience, resources, teamwork, leadership, service, sacrifice, changing nappies, maintaining the home, paying the bills, self-care, school runs, meetings, ministry etc.

I see you back tracking and wondering about purity, and no, it's not a contradiction. Purity is as much for marriage as it is for singleness. Abstinence and purity are connected yes, but very different. Earlier, I explained the difference between abstinence vs. purity. Even in marriage, purity is a requirement for my sexuality, and too many of us are left to figure this out on my own.

We're not talking about it and teaching on it as we should.

Great sex is the result of great effort. Does this offend you? Contrary to popular belief, it doesn't *just* happen. You want to talk about unrealistic expectations? Let's talk about the movies, series and romantic tropes that have shaped our expectations on intimacy? There are 150 romance tropes that writers and directors use to dupe us into believing a 90min expression on love, sex, and intimacy, but here are just 10.

- Alpha Hero
- Beauty And The Beast
- Coming of Age
- Dating Game
- Enemies to Lovers
- Forbidden Love
- Girl Next Door
- Holiday Romance
- Learning to Love
- Love Triangle

What they won't tell you is that there are 4 pillars they uphold to ensure that you're hooked and falling in love with just the one expression of love - *Eros*.

Pillar #1 - The Couple: Lover and Beloved: they're usually attractive, and generally have some sort of trauma or drama that creates a degree of *empathy* within us. We now know that this is to get us to form an emotional bond with whichever route to love gets glorified in the storyline.

Pillar #2 - The Obstacles, Rivals, Taboos and Loved Ones: Without these there wouldn't be a story, and so to create a winning narrative you will need *opposition* to the love story. It helps create the "all or nothing," you know the "us against the world" narrative that crowns eros love as lord over our lives.

Pillar #3 - The Romantic Arc: Winning and Losing and winning back again. It's all about *winning* against the odds, and who doesn't want to win right? Who doesn't want to get what they've always wanted and dreamed of? But at what cost?

Pillar #4 - The Lover's Sacrifice: Ah yes, the grand finale, the final act that *secures* the happily ever after.

The truth is that these tropes and pillars cannot sustain healthy relationships - romantic or otherwise. It creates unrealistic *"sexpectations"* and totally disregards the time, patience, trust, forgiveness, prayer, love, respect, communication, and effort it takes to experience great sex. Whenever we take God out of the equation, love will not love. I never thought I'd say this, but there's no great sex without the greatness of God. But think about it. The greatest trope involved God Himself; it's what makes love possible. The Creator of the "lover" and the "beloved" also created great sex but the problem with our pillars of romance is that it refuses to pay royalties to Him who holds the patent. The pillars - without the patent holder - produces a counterfeit romance which cannot produce great sex. The thing with all things counterfeit is that it's a low-quality product, and you actually end up spending more money in the long run. Counterfeit sex is expensive; it will cost you your life, vitality, and relationship with God.

NEVER GOING BACK

Ever wonder why people sometimes return to the thing they prayed their way out of? Why do we return to the toxicity in others or in us? We judge the Israelites for wanting to return to their slave masters and bondage, but don't we do the same thing when we return to the person or thing that broke us? The disciples weren't squeaky clean either, they returned to fishing after Jesus said He would make them fishers of men. Sometimes difficulty, loneliness and faulty thinking can seduce us into reconnecting with old ways and flames. Never let a temporary inconvenience drive you back to people who inflicted permanent damage. I offer the same caution about things, habits and mindsets that got keep you chained. Just because you're lonely doesn't mean you must reconnect with toxicity or dysfunction. We don't drink poison just because we're thirsty. Don't do it. Don't go back. The unchained life demands that we leave our chains where they belong. Let's talk about the practicality of not going back. Among other things, trauma and wounds get us chained but trauma responses, wound induced mindsets, actions, habits, cycles, and patterns is what *keeps* us chained. Trauma and wounds need healing, but those thoughts, cycles, and patterns that you've developed as a result needs *unlearning*.

At the point of your trauma, you believed a lie and as a result you developed a thinking pattern which invokes certain difficult feelings, which in turn activates the responses you have to all of life and relationships.

Your trauma enforces your thoughts, your thoughts effects what you feel and what you feel influences what you do. This becomes a pattern and when this gets done over and over it becomes a cycle. And what is a chain? It is the continuous pattern or cycle linked together by repetition. When your trauma impacts what you consistently think, feel and do you, find yourself in chains. You might not be able to undo the trauma, but you can unlearn the thinking that impacts your feelings and actions. This is why we are to be transformed by the renewing of our minds and here's what we often don't get - nothing renews the mind but the Spirit-filled Word of God, there's just no transformation without it.

Never go back to *toxic*. Let me say this; your mood, attitude, or drama does not get to decide who or what is toxic. Defining toxicity is not assuming that one truth applies to the vast set of possibilities and manifestations of how it is displayed or experienced. I want to address the trend of diagnosing others as toxic. We must stop using our perceived toxicity of others as an excuse not to face and deal with difficult situations, conversations, and consequences. Just because someone doesn't agree with you, affirm, or validate you doesn't mean that they're toxic.

We've been taught to block, delete or ghost people because they're "disturbing" our peace. If their lives, words, or actions are calling you out on your stuff then what you're dealing with is conviction not their toxicity. If they've called you out on double standards, what you said or an attitude you have, then what you're dealing with is accountability and not toxicity - Learn to discern the difference.

Jillian Turecki, a certified relationship coach, teacher and writer who for 20 years has taught others how to transform their relationships with themselves and others, defines a *toxic relationship* by unpacking the term "toxic". *The word Toxic can be defined as something that is "poisonous", "imbued with poison" or "very harmful or unpleasant in a pervasive or insidious way"*, therefore a toxic relationship, has these elements prevalent - "*it is any relationship that is harmful and leaves you feeling drained.*"

God's Spirit-filled Word is the final standard we measure toxicity by, but it starts with us. Don't return to your own toxicity and don't return to the toxicity of others.

Never go back to *dysfunctional;* but the truth is, in order to know when something is dysfunctional, you will need to know what functional looks like. Start with functional so that you can identify dysfunction. All of life is identifying dysfunction and making sure that you deal with it and correct it. But isn't it true that things are convoluted of late? We find ourselves navigating relationships in a generation where what we know to be true, good and right, is now labeled outdated, bigoted and offensive. What we knew to be wrong is now right, what we accepted as normal is now abnormal, what was regarded as dysfunctional or delusional must now be affirmed and enforced. It's scary how quickly things are changing, the lines have been blurred. But as Children of God, we had been forewarned that these things must take place. In Isaiah 5:20-21 the great prophet illuminates the heart condition of those who have become corrupt in their thinking. He states: *"Woe to those who call evil good, and good evil; who put darkness for light, and light for darkness: Who put bitter for sweet, and sweet for bitter. Woe to those who are wise and shrewd in their own eyes!"*

Now more than ever before we must know the Truth, that it is absolute, it is the standard and our handle on all of life.
Never go back to *selfish*. A few minutes on any social media platform and you'll soon discover that there is a strong push to elevate self. You see it everywhere, ever so subtly, the nudge to start putting yourself first, to love yourself more than others, to be selfish. The enemy would love to get you to worship him, but it's easier to get you to worship yourself. Even children of God are getting caught in this deception and not seeing it for the idolatry it is. While it is true that we ought to love ourselves, we ought not build an altar or memorial around that. It is a command from God to love ourselves. In fact, in the book of Mark chapter 12, when Jesus is asked what the greatest commandment is, he says this:

> *"The most important one," answered Jesus, "is this: 'Hear, O Israel: The Lord our God, the Lord is one. Love the Lord your God with all your heart and with all your soul and with all your mind and with all your strength.' The second is this: 'Love your neighbour as yourself.' There is no commandment greater than these."* - **Mark 12:30-31**

Clearly loving yourself is the second greatest commandment, because without self-love, there can be no love for our neighbours. We can only love others to the measure we love ourselves - love your neighbour, *as* [you love] yourself. My concern is not for self-care or self-love, because how can we take care of others if we're not taking care of ourselves and how can we love others as ourselves if we don't love ourselves. This is not the problem; the issue is self *at the expense of* others. I know we get tired sometimes always putting others first, but that's the problem, God never asked us to put others first per se, we are supposed to put God first and in doing so we will have the capacity to love others well.

When self is placed above others, the very thing we're pursuing will always elude us. Jesus taught extensively on this, in Matthew 16:25 He said, *"whoever wants to save his life will lose it and whoever loses it for His sake will save it."* Being selfish is like trying to hold onto beach sand, the tighter you squeeze the more it falls out of your grip. The more you put self first, the more you seek yourself above all else, the more you lose yourself. It is when you seek God first and put Him first that yourself and others are put into their proper perspective and place in your life.

Never go back to *lesser loves*. It's tempting, I know. But it just won't satisfy. Every other love devoid of Agapè cannot love you.

> It cannot commit to you.
> It cannot choose you.
> It cannot serve you.
> I repeat… It cannot love you.

Every lesser love is conditional and is only committed to self. When backed into a corner it will choose self; it serves self and only loves as far as self is benefited. Lesser loves love you, for how you benefit them. Lesser loves are governed by feelings - needless to say this is why lesser loves are conditional. It cannot commit because commitment is doing what you said you would do even when the feeling you said it with, has left you. When the feelings leave a lesser love, it will choose someone else. A lesser love will no longer serve when its interests are not served, and its demands are not met. Never ever go back.

HOLY EVER AFTER

Shouldn't it be *happily* ever after? Well, that's what I thought, and I'm not alone. So many people want to live happily for the rest of their lives. If they can just get that college degree, that ideal job, that opportunity, start that business, if they can just travel, find the right person, just get pregnant, just find the family, and career balance, if they can just, just, just...

Is being happy wrong?

No, definitely not. Our problem is we've pinned it down to a destination, a place to arrive at. There is also a paradigm that sees happiness as a pursuit and an undeniable human right, something we're entitled to. The way I see it, if we see happiness as a destination, we'll never arrive. If we view it as a pursuit, we'll always be chasing it, and if we believe it to be a human right, we'll always feel robbed. Have you ever heard or uttered the following like I have?

"I just want to be happy?"
"Why can I never be happy?"
"When is it my turn to be happy?"
"If I can just _____ I'll be happy."
"I'll only be happy if _____."

Happiness is not a destination, or a pursuit and it's certainly not a right. Aristotle gave us a bit of insight into the psychology of happiness by categorizing it by *levels*; there are levels:

#Level 1: Laetus or happiness from material objects; simply stated a sensual gratification based on something external. It's intense but short lived. The challenge is that if this is the only level of happiness you live for, when crisis hits, life will seem shallow and meaningless.

#Level 2: Felix or happiness from comparison. This level all about the ego. It's about how good you look in comparison with someone else. It's a rewarding feeling but unstable because in life, there will always be someone better looking, someone smarter, someone taller, someone richer, someone wiser. No one can maintain that level of optimality, where they are always winning or looking better than everyone else - all of the time. When failure comes, a sense of worthlessness accompanies it.

#Level 3: Beautitudo or the happiness of doing good, for others. The basis for this level of happiness is the human desire for connection and the wellbeing of others. It's when the happiness of self is closely linked to and even dependent on the happiness of others. This level of happiness is longer lasting but also has limitations, because no one is perfect, and we are prone to hurting and disappointing one another. This also sounds awfully like having a people pleaser mentality, and that as you know is unsustainable. We cannot make everyone happy all the time.

#Level 4: Sublime Beatitudo or ultimate perfect happiness. According to Aristotle, this level of happiness is difficult to describe but refers to finding the right balance between the other levels, and then some. Psychologists believe that the desire for ultimate happiness is deeply rooted in spirituality and people seek to fulfill it through mediums such as religion, philosophy, art, or science. The aim is to find the answers to some of life's biggest questions. Few people reach this point.

Are you happy? Take a minute to really think before answering. What or who makes you happy? Can you relate to Aristotle's levels of happiness? Which level resonates with you the most? Here's what you probably already know: Happiness is something we feel, it is a euphoric emotion, and it happens because of something external. There is a cause, and happiness is the effect. Granted there may be levels but we do see that happiness is also subjective - it is based on and influenced by our personal feelings, tastes, and opinions.

Within my first 5 years of marriage, I learnt that marriage wasn't designed to make me happy but to make me *holy*. Would it surprise you too much to learn that God is not as interested in our happiness is He is in our obedience? I had it all wrong. People, relationships, marriage doesn't exist to make me happy but to make me holy. You should have been there to see the look on my face when I realized that my husband's role was not to make me happy. While it was his heart's desire, it was not his responsibility to make me happy. I sat in disbelief as I was hit with revelation after revelation on my husband's calling, role and responsibility towards me. But get this, I realized it was the same for every other person I was in a relationship with. I was gob smacked. My happiness was not the chief goal in the lives of others. It took me a minute to take it all in. But this is for you too.

Your happiness is not the reason God, people, relationships, marriage, divorce, or anything of significant value exists.

Breathe.

Will you be happy? Sometimes. Will you experience the different levels of happiness in your lifetime? Probably. But happiness is not the point or objective for your existence. A hard truth. But a good one. I promise you it's going to set you free. We have been too conditioned by this world that we can do or be anything, *"as long as it makes us happy"*. This universal lie has had many willfully engaging in sin because of the feeling of happiness, that if allowed to rein long enough, will shut down the voice of conviction. Happiness is good but holiness is better. God in His sovereignty has designed that His deepest work in our hearts and lives be done through relationships, not miracles signs and wonders, although these are important. For some or other reason God decided that relationships would be the atmosphere for God's presence, power and promise *in* your life, yes, from your relationship with God, to self and with others.

It's in relationship that we learn faith, experience grace, and exercise the fruit and gifts of the Holy Spirit. It is in relationship that we learn submission, honour, integrity, and forgiveness; it is in relationship that we are being sanctified. God knew that our greatest brokenness and trauma would come through relationships, but so would His greatest work in and through us.

I discovered this through a series of life altering moments. My husband is the epitome of "husband". He is masculine, cool, calm and collected. Ricardo is temperate, not easily provoked. He is gentle but dangerous; he is not to be messed with. He is both mighty and merciful. I feel safe with him. He has the ability to fiercely protect me. He is competent, skilled, gifted and is secure in who he is. We don't always see eye to eye, but he always takes my hand and makes sure we walk side by side; he is fearless in leading the way. He is a provider and on more than one occasion worked himself to the bone so that I can remain in full time ministry. He honours the call of God on my life. He's my greatest cheerleader and my sparring partner. He is my dearest friend.

And yet I was unhappy.

I realized that he was amazing, but he wasn't perfect. There were things I wanted to change in him; things I thought didn't serve me, things I felt that stood in the way of *my* happiness. In my own opinion, I am easy to love and be in relationship with; most people even enjoy working with and doing ministry with me, but I am *not* easy to *live* with. Had I been married to any other man I would have probably been sworn at, or worse - hurt physically in some or other way. When I listened to some of the things married couples I ministered to were going through, I realized I had nothing to complain about.

What was wrong with him? Well, the question should have been, what was wrong with me? I *thought* my happiness depended on my husband and his ability to make me happy. But remember, God wastes nothing. God used my unhappiness as an object lesson.

I learnt three things, that I will share with you:

I think it's so cute when people post or talk about "relationship goals", and I get what they mean, but if we're honest that rhetoric downplays the power and purpose of relationships and specifically marriage. Marriage is not a goal, it's a gift. This is the first lesson I learnt: Marriage is not something to be achieved or tick off on a checklist; it is not a destination to arrive at, because, what then once we have arrived? It is a gift to be accepted with thanksgiving, to be unwrapped with patience and to be stewarded with wisdom and understanding until the day we must give an account of our stewardship. How we do marriage will count for or against us. Selah.

The second lesson is that marriage, and by extension our spouses, are not the source of our happiness. While we may experience happiness in marriage, our spouses are not responsible for it. And here's why: If your spouse was the source of your happiness, they could easily become the object of your worship. Think about it, the more you desire happiness, the more you would turn and look to them. When a relationship, spouse, or anything else takes the place of God in your life, that's not cute, that's idolatry. As amazing as Ricardo is, when I realized this, God showed me in no uncertain terms that He will not share His place in my life with anyone, not even my husband.

When we build our world around someone, a relationship or spouse, and they hurt or disappoint us, guess what? Our whole world comes tumbling down with them. My husband vowed to love me until death would separate us, but here's the reality, my husband is human and as all humans are, he too, is fallible and susceptible to error, as am I. Worst case scenario is that he breaks his vows for whatever reason - I'll be sad, hurt and disappointed, I'll need prayer and probably therapy too, but I'll be ok - you know why? Because he wasn't my source and I didn't build my world around him. I built it *with* him, but *not* around him. Because God is my source, and it is He who sits on the throne of my heart. I can trust that I can and will continue to build my life. Do I want my husband to break his vows? Definitely not. But should it come my way, without minimizing the trauma I'll experience, knowing God, I'll be alright.

And then finally, I discovered that when happiness gives way to holiness, joy becomes my disposition. When we look to marriage and our spouse as God's ordinance and vessel for holiness we will no longer be swayed by external factors and internal feelings, tastes, and opinions. Happiness is amazing but it is short-lived on all four levels. Joy is more than just a feeling; it's a response that comes from knowing, experiencing, and trusting Jesus regardless.
One thing that has been grossly and gravely overlooked is *why* you marry and *who* you marry. This is important because it plays a vital role in the health of your marriage. There was a time when people viewed marriage as a duty and you didn't marry to *see if it would work*, they got married to *make it work*. Divorce was not an option and

love was something that grew out of watering the seeds of time, presence and commitment. We've come a long way since then, today we enjoy freedoms, opportunities, and privileges but we've seemed to have lost sight of our *why*, and we seem to be messing up on the *who*; because of that we've compromised the quality of our relationships and marriages.

Again, I believe marriage is a God-thing, He created it and unless you do it His way you will always worship the created thing and exchange the truth for a lie; happiness will elude you and flippant divorce will delude you. Base your *why* for marriage on your relationship with God and His Spirit-filled word and make your choice based on the same. Life will still be hard, but you will have a *why* to fight for, and the person you *chose,* will have to be the person you *choose* daily.

When we understand that marriage is a space God uses to mold and shape us into the image of Christ and when we realize that our spouse is not the enemy but a friend, and our safe place for our sanctification - that's when joy comes. I've always quoted Psalm 30:5 to mean literally that joy comes in the morning, but allegorically, it means that when light comes, as in revelation, *that's* when joy comes.

That's when joy came for me.

References

CHAPTER 1
The Holy Bible, New International Version, 2011
Peterson, Eugene H. *The Message: The Bible in Contemporary Language.* NavPress, 2002.

CHAPTER 2
The Holy Bible, New International Version, 2011
https://www.mayoclinic.org/diseases-conditions/broken-heart-syndrome/symptoms-causes/syc-20354617#:~:text=Broken%20heart%20syndrome%20is%20a,after%20the%20heart%20is%20healed.
https://dictionary.cambridge.org/dictionary/english/awaken
https://www.worldometers.info
Kyle Idleman, AHA The God Moment That Changes Everything. First Edition, United States of America, The Gates Group, 2014
Editor, C.J. Mahaney, Worldliness, Resisting The Seduction of A Fallen World. Wheaton, Illinois, Crossway Books 2008, Pg 36-37, 68-89
https://nypost.com/2023/03/01/balenciaga-seeks-crisis-management-expert-after-bdsm-ad-scandal/
https://www.theguardian.com/film/2020/feb/06/corey-feldman-nobody-wants-to-go-after-the-bad-guys
https://www.dazeddigital.com/music/article/54104/1/lil-nas-x-thanks-the-gay-agenda-for-vmas-win
https://www.amazon.com/hz/reviews-render/lighthouse/B07D624MMF?filterByKeyword=revelation+of+the+method&pageNumber=1
https://www.news-medical.net/news/20161209/Psychiatrist-explains-how-the-brain-blocks-memory-to-help-get-through-traumatic-event.aspx
https://www.facebook.com/bertpretorius
The Holy Bible, The Passion Translation, 2017

The Amplified Bible, 2015

CHAPTER 3
https://www.biblestudytools.com/bible-study/topical-studies/why-did-judas-betray-jesus-with-a-kiss.html
https://wikidiff.com/fraud/betray
Jason L. Perry, How Far Can You Go? Straight Talk About Sexual Purity. Third Edition, 2004
https://www.premierchristianity.com/home/joshua-harris-why-i-regret-writing-i-kissed-dating-goodbye/275.article
https://www.christianpost.com/voice/a-response-to-i-survived-i-kissed-dating-goodbye.html
https://www.usatoday.com/story/news/nation/2019/07/29/joshua-harris-i-kissed-dating-goodbye-i-am-not-christian/1857934001/
https://www.mindbodygreen.com/articles/types-of-intimacy-besides-sex
https://www.goodtherapy.org/blog/psychpedia/intimacy
https://www.nairaland.com/4554608/how-female-eagle-chooses-mate
Dr. Henry Cloud, Boundaries For Leaders, Why Some People Get Results and Others Don't. First Edition. Harper Collins Publishers 2013
The Amplified Bible, 2015

CHAPTER 4
https://www.psycom.net/trauma/epigenetics-trauma
https://www.thegospelcoalition.org/article/faqs-know-purity-culture/
https://anchoredsoul.wordpress.com/2012/05/16/purity-is-holiness/
https://www.cbeinternational.org/resource/7-lies-purity-culture-teaches-women/
https://accountable2you.com/blog/purity-important/
The Holy Bible, New International Version, 2011
Jason L. Perry, How Far Can You Go? Straight Talk About Sexual Purity. Third Edition, 2004

https://www.christianforums.com/threads/the-black-dog-and-the-white-dog.7456353/

CHAPTER 5
https://www.youtube.com/channel/UCPBO9gLGy8ujsJ7xjARI7ow
The Holy Bible, New International Version, 2011
https://classroom.synonym.com/dangers-obsessive-crushes-17689.html
https://www.brainyquote.com/quotes/maya_angelou_383371
https://www.urbandictionary.com/define.php?term=Don%27t%20hate%20the%20player%20hate%20the%20game
https://fandomwire.com/bridgerton-5-most-romantic-quotes/#:~:text="All%20Is%20Fair%20In%20Love,The%20Fight."%20–%20Lady%20Whistledown
https://www.insider.com/dating-evolution-through-the-years-2018-4#online-dating-started-to-become-more-mainstream-in-the-1990s-with-the-explosion-of-the-internet-14
https://www.yourdictionary.com/dating
https://hernorm.com/types-of-dating/
https://www.facebook.com/watch/?v=904644817023031
https://www.datingbitch.com/relationships/dating-terms/
https://www.allure.com/story/vabbing-tiktok-trend-explained

CHAPTER 6
The Holy Bible, English Standard Version, 2016
The Holy Bible, New International Version, 2011
The Amplified Bible, 2015
Peterson, Eugene H. *The Message: The Bible in Contemporary Language.* NavPress, 2002.

CHAPTER 7
https://en.wikipedia.org/wiki/Born_This_Way_(song)
https://www.desiringgod.org/articles/born-this-way
https://jackiehillperry.com
The Holy Bible, New International Version, 2011

https://www.psychologytoday.com/za/blog/meet-catch-and-keep/202101/is-living-together-marriage-associated-divorce
https://www.gotquestions.org/one-flesh-marriage.html
https://www.tyndale.com/sites/unfoldingfaithblog/2019/08/15/what-does-the-bible-say-about-sex/
Peterson, Eugene H. *The Message: The Bible in Contemporary Language.* NavPress, 2002.

CHAPTER 8

https://faughnfamily.com/no-human-contact/
https://www.desiringgod.org/messages/battling-the-unbelief-of-lust
https://www.learnreligions.com/types-of-love-in-the-bible-700177
https://www.psychologytoday.com/us/blog/hide-and-seek/201606/these-are-the-7-types-love
The Holy Bible, New International Version, 2011
Life Application Study Bible, New International Version, 2005
https://www.drcarolministries.com/the-difference-between-lust-and-healthy-desire/
Peterson, Eugene H. *The Message: The Bible in Contemporary Language.* NavPress, 2002.
Peter Scazzero, Emotionally Healthy Spirituality, Unleash a Revolution in Your Life In Christ, Publisher Thomas Nelson, Nashville Tennessee USA, 2006
https://www.purelifeministries.org/blog/what-to-learn-from-samson-the-sex-addict
https://www.goodreads.com/quotes/702-it-would-seem-that-our-lord-finds-our-desires-not
The Amplified Bible, 2015
https://www.gotquestions.org/take-control-thoughts.html
https://www.bible.com/reading-plans/4846-killing-kryptonite-with-john-bevere/day/1

CHAPTER 9

*Allison, modern parable inspired by true events

Peter Scazzero, Emotionally Healthy Spirituality, Unleash a Revolution in Your Life In Christ, Publisher Thomas Nelson, Nashville Tennessee USA, 2006

Peterson, Eugene H. *The Message: The Bible in Contemporary Language.* NavPress, 2002.

June Hunt, Counseling Through Your Bible Handbook, Providing Biblical Hope and Practical Help for 50 Everyday Problems, Harvest House Publishers, Oregan, 2008

*Matthew, modern parable inspired by true events

https://health-e.org.za/2021/12/09/rape-childhood-sexual-abuse-continues-to-plague-sa/

James MacDonald, Gripped By The Greatness of God. Moody Publishers, Chicago 2005

The Holy Bible, New International Version, 2011

https://godtv.com/bill-johnson-beauty-out-of-ashes/?fbclid=IwAR0dTR3FzjVMnHBUFw3ag_Ucj0Z4hvqiztzz93VQD0LVhAcE1C4irPujLK0

https://www.christianity.com/wiki/sin/bible-say-about-pornography.html

https://www.christianity.com/wiki/christian-terms/what-is-fornication-why-is-it-a-biblical-sin.html

https://www.gotquestions.org/masturbation-sin.html

https://www.covenanteyes.com/2012/09/12/5-reasons-purity-rings-and-pledges-dont-work/

https://www.reuters.com/article/us-purityrings-idUSN1130986320080912

https://mymodernmet.com/kintsugi-kintsukuroi/

https://www.britannica.com/story/how-did-the-rainbow-flag-become-a-symbol-of-lgbt-pride

https://answersingenesis.org/christianity/values/flag-day-and-biblical-banners/

https://everydayfeminism.com/2017/01/misgendering-trans-people-is-violence/
https://www.baptistpress.com/resource-library/news/legalizing-the-unthinkable/
https://www.forgingbonds.org/blog/detail/the-origin-of-gender-theory-which-fractures-personhood
https://www.sciencedirect.com/topics/psychology/social-contagion
@commonlycensored
https://gloria.tv/share/jxGmV38sQkuR4kZjEdNvhJUtV

CHAPTER 10

https://christianityfaq.com/soul-tie-bible-christian-explanation/
https://www.facebook.com/DoreenVirtueForJesus/photos/a.626436404064341/5149292028445400/?type=3
https://www.medicalnewstoday.com/articles/trauma-bonding#signs
*Denver, modern parable inspired by true events
*Chelsea, modern parable inspired by true events
https://www.hillsbiblechurch.org/theology-the-bible/the-three-tenses-of-salvation/
https://www.gotquestions.org/bondservant.html
The Holy Bible, New King James Version, Copyright 1982
The Holy Bible, New International Version, 2011
https://seattlechristiancounseling.com/articles/what-does-the-bible-say-about-marriage-and-divorce
https://ca.thegospelcoalition.org/columns/ad-fontes/what-the-bible-teaches-about-divorce-and-remarriage/

CHAPTER 11
The Holy Bible, New International Version, 2011

June Hunt, *Counseling Through Your Bible Handbook, Providing Biblical Hope and Practical Help for 50 Everyday Problems*, Harvest House Publishers, Oregan, 2008

https://www.brainyquote.com/quotes/marianne_williamson_635346

Peterson, Eugene H. *The Message: The Bible in Contemporary Language*. NavPress, 2002.

https://www.upsem.edu/alumni/i-wanna-be-whole/

https://www.david-goetsch.com/post/biblical-friendship-is-the-only-real-friendship-proverbs-17-17#:~:text=This%20is%20why%20it%27s%20important,to%20do%20for%20a%20friend.

Peter Scazzero, *Emotionally Healthy Spirituality, Unleash a Revolution in Your Life In Christ*, Publisher Thomas Nelson, Nashville Tennessee USA, 2006

https://aviaryrecoverycenter.com/victim-vs-victim-mentality-addiction/#:~:text="Victim"%20and%20"Victim%20Mentality"&text=Having%20a%20victim%20mentality%20is,you%20have%20a%20victim%20mentality.

The Amplified Bible Classic Edition © 1987 The Lockman Foundation and Zondervan Publishing House

CHAPTER 12

Life Application Study Bible, New International Version, 2005

https://christianscholars.com/shame-guilt-and-the-practice-of-repentance-an-intersection-of-modern-psychology-with-the-wisdom-of-calvin/

https://www.desiringgod.org/messages/battling-the-unbelief-of-misplaced-shame

CHAPTER 13

Peter Scazzero, *Emotionally Healthy Spirituality, Unleash a Revolution in Your Life In Christ*, Publisher Thomas Nelson, Nashville Tennessee USA, 2006

Life Application Study Bible, New International Version, 2005
https://teckphenomenal.wordpress.com/2020/07/05/grasshoppers-do-not-eat-grapes/
Kyle Idleman, AHA The God Moment That Changes Everything. First Edition, United States of America, The Gates Group, 2014

CHAPTER 14

https://www.theguardian.com/global-development/2016/jun/01/46-million-people-living-as-slaves-latest-global-index-reveals-russell-crowe#:~:text=An%20Australian%20human%20rights%20group,people%20are%20living%20as%20slaves.

https://edition.cnn.com/2015/11/10/americas/freedom-project-mexico-trafficking-survivor/index.html

Alex & Brett Harris, Do Hard Things, A Teenage Rebellion Against Low Expectations. First International Trade Paperback Edition. Multnomah Books, Colorado Springs 2008

Peter Scazzero, Emotionally Healthy Spirituality, Unleash a Revolution in Your Life In Christ, Publisher Thomas Nelson, Nashville Tennessee USA, 2006

Peterson, Eugene H. *The Message: The Bible in Contemporary Language.* NavPress, 2002.

Life Application Study Bible, New International Version, 2005

https://files.eric.ed.gov/fulltext/EJ1056376.pdf Expectations

https://www.writerswrite.co.za/the-4-pillars-of-romance/

https://www.writerswrite.co.za/101-romance-tropes-for-writers/

Dr. Henry Cloud, Never Go Back, How to Avoid Ten Pitfalls In Life. South African Edition, Struik Christian Media, 2015

https://www.theworldcounts.com/purpose/four-levels-of-happiness

https://www.wordsoffaithhopelove.com/what-is-joy-in-the-bible/

www.ingramcontent.com/pod-product-compliance
Lightning Source LLC
Chambersburg PA
CBHW032146080426
42735CB00008B/603